First published in Great Britain in 2020 by

Policy Press, an imprint of
Bristol University Press
University of Bristol
1-9 Old Park Hill
Bristol
BS2 8BB
UK
t: +44 (0)117 954 5940
e: bup-info@bristol.ac.uk

Details of international sales and distribution partners are available at
policy.bristoluniversitypress.co.uk

British Library Cataloguing in Publication Data
A catalogue record for this book is available from the British Library

ISBN 978-1-4473-5008-8 hardcover
ISBN 978-1-4473-5012-5 ePub
ISBN 978-1-4473-5014-9 ePdf

The right of David Etherington to be identified as author of this work has been asserted by
him in accordance with the Copyright, Designs and Patents Act 1988.

Cover design: Robin Hawes
Front cover image: GettyImages-641085138

Bristol University Press and Policy Press use environmentally responsible
print partners.

Printed in Great Britain by CPI Group (UK) Ltd, Croydon, CR0 4YY

This book is dedicated to the memory of Blanche and Martin Flannery. They devoted their lives to socialism and the Labour and Trade Union movement. The world is a much poorer place without their unstinting dedication to fighting injustice in all its forms.

Contents

List of tables and box

List of abbreviations

BAME	Black and Minority Ethnic
CA	Collective Agreement
CAB	Citizens Advice Bureaux
DWP	Department of Wok and Pensions
CPAG	Child Poverty Action Group
DPAC	Disabled People Against the Cuts
ESA	Employment and Support Allowance
EU	European Union
GDP	Gross Domestic Product
GM	Greater Manchester
GMB	General and Municipal Boiler Workers Union
GMCA	Greater Manchester Combined Authority
IPPR	Institute for Public Policy Research
IR	Industrial Relations
JRF	Joseph Rowntree Foundation
JSA	Jobseekers Allowance
LP	Labour Party
NAO	National Audit Office
NL	New Labour
PCS	Public and Commercial Services Union
RTI	Real Time Information
SCR	Sheffield City Region
SNAP	Sheffield Needs a Pay Rise
SSAC	Social Security Advisory Committee
TUC	Trade Union Conference
UC	Universal Credit
USDAW	Union of Shop Distributive and Allied Workers
WCA	Work Capability Assessment
WPC	Work and Pensions Committee

Notes on the author

David Etherington is Professor of Local and Regional Economic Development at Staffordshire University. Prior to working in the university sector, David worked in local government (including 10 years at Sheffield City Council) on economic and social regeneration policy. His research interests include Marxist political economy, welfare, work, employment relations, labour and social movements. He has brought this experience and expertise as a practitioner into policy research including work for the Joseph Rowntree Foundation (*Political Devolution Regional Governance and Tackling Deprivation* [2007]), an ESRC/University of Sheffield (Knowledge Exchange Programme IAA) commissioned study *Devolution and Disadvantage in Sheffield City* (2016). He has published widely in international peer reviewed journals including *Environment and Planning A, Journal of European Social Policy, Employee Relations, Cambridge Journal of Regions, Economy and Society*. More recently (March 2020) he has worked with the trade union movement and colleagues at Sheffield Hallam and Manchester Metropolitan Universities on insecure work in connection with the Sheffield Needs a Pay Rise Campaign, *Tackling Labour Market Injustice and organising Workers: The View from a Northern Heartland.*

Acknowledgements

Numerous people have contributed to this book in one way or another. I am extremely grateful to Martin Jones, Allan Cochrane and an anonymous reviewer for commenting on the initial drafts. A special mention to Helen Thompson who did an amazing job copy editing, as well as providing constructive comments. Also, thanks to Laura Vickers-Rendall, Amelia Watts-Jones and Millie Prekop of Policy Press for their assistance and support in writing the book.

Some of the material for the chapters has been derived from previous longstanding collaborative research with Martin Jones and Ruth Beresford. I have also drawn from work undertaken in relation to Sheffield Needs a Pay Rise (SNAP) campaign. I am extremely proud to be involved with this campaign working with Bob Jeffery, Pete Thomas, David Beel, Martin Jones and Martin Mayer (in his role as Secretary of Sheffield TUC). Thanks also to the many individuals and organisations interviewed in the course of the research.

The book also arises from stimulating and thought-provoking debate over the years with a number of friends and comrades. I am particularly indebted to Gitte Hesselman and Leif Mikkelsen for their help with the research on Denmark. Also, a warm thanks to Kate Flannery, Jamie Gough, Gerry Mooney, Paul Hickman, Mick Paddon, Colin Hampton, Lian Groves, Anne Daguerre, Stephen Syrett, Ian Roper, Ian Vickers, Mikkel Mailand, Anna Ilsøe, Jo Ingold, comrades from the Sheffield Stop and Scrap Universal Credit Campaign, and members of the Social Security Consortium (SSC; in particular Josie Tucker and Kelly Smith of Child Poverty Action Group who convene the SSC).

Finally, an appreciation of the love and support from my partner Kate and daughter Niamh which have spurred me on to complete this book.

Acknowledgement

Preface

There are now several books and journal articles published where there is a focus on austerity and its impacts. Richard Seymour's (2014), Mary O'Hara's (2015) and Vicki Cooper and David Whyte's (2017) (just to name a few) are magnificent accounts on the negative impacts of austerity and the growing resistance to it. This book is an updated contribution to this debate except I take a different approach and perspective. At the time of writing (March 2020), two incidents have received significant press coverage. First is the death of Errol Graham who died of starvation in June 2018 when his benefits were cut off. Errol is one of thousands who have died as a result of austerity as the government moves towards downgrading or possibly phasing out benefits as a safety net (Butler, 2020). The second relates to the fact that there have been 440 health and safety incidents reported in the Amazon Company (UK) warehouses since 2015. The GMB union has reported that workers operate under a 'culture of fear'. Tim Roache, the GMB general secretary, accused Amazon of treating workers like robots not human beings and said the official figures gave a 'horrifying insight' into the company's warehouses (Sainato, 2020). In their study of Amazon in Wales, Bricken and Taylor (2018) argue that many workers are coming from the welfare system as the employment services (the Department for Work and Pensions) funnel claimants into low-paid and precarious work – or 'compulsion into precarity'. Driving down wages and benefits are 'two sides to the same coin' in the pursuit of austerity. Increasing conditionality and compulsion in welfare and reducing employment rights and bargaining as I argue in this book, are interrelated.

The implications of this approach are that central to austerity is a 'class strategy' aimed at redistributing income and power away from the working class. The introduction of Universal Credit (UC) and the imposition of conditions for workers to claim benefits blurs the welfare work relationship. For the first time, people in work claiming UC can be subject to conditions and requirements on their claims which can mean that they could be subject to penalties and sanctions. For me, the struggle for a socially just welfare system requires changes to industrial relations that facilitate collective bargaining and trade union representation at work and which, in turn, will ensure that claimants moving into employment have rights and a voice. The book focuses on ways in which the welfare system can provide an adequate social safety net and support people into employment without imposing conditions and sanctions. I attempt to provide a voice and recognition of the role of trade unions as well as welfare and social movements in their struggle and resistance to austerity. In mapping out alternatives I draw on my research on Denmark, which has both a redistributive welfare system and coordinated collective bargaining. As I argue, not only does the austerity narrative and ideology need challenging but we need a different economic model. I present some thoughts and ideas in the concluding chapter on this.

Introduction: the crisis and austerity neoliberalism

But in banking, as in capitalism in general, it's one rule for the elite and another for the rest of us. On the day Deutsche Bank began making thousands of employees redundant, some managing directors at the company's office in the City of London were being fitted for suits that cost at least £1,200. Tailors from Fielding & Nicholson, an upmarket tailor, were pictured walking out of the bank's UK office with suit bags. Ian Fielding-Calcutt, the tailor's founder, and Alex Riley were there to fit suits for senior managers in spite of plans to cut 18,000 jobs worldwide. Deutsche's chief executive, Christian Sewing, has repeatedly said how much he regretted the decision to scrap a fifth of his global workforce. But it did not stop him paying out €50m in golden handshakes to top executives since 2018. (Roberts, 2019)

Estimates of the size of the UK bank bailout range between £289 billion and £550 billion – or nearly £10,000 for every British resident – exceeding the £203 billion of tax that the sector paid in the five years up to 2006–2007 ... by the end of 2009 the total value of bailouts in the US, UK and euro area equalled $14 trillion, or almost a quarter of the world's gross domestic product. (Sayer, 2016: 229)

We know that there's appetite in the Conservative party for a bonfire of workers' rights. (O'Grady, 2018)

Welfare reform employment relations and labour discipline

The 2008 financial crisis and the near collapse of the financial system brought about a response from nearly all developed and developing capitalist countries that is referred to as austerity; this is generally viewed as a strategy for cutting back public expenditure in order to reduce public debts. This was based on thinking by the dominant elites that balancing finances was a crucial factor in bringing about further growth. Sacrifices had to be made for the greater good. We are now living in an age of austerity. While the term austerity is generally used to mean public expenditure cuts, as will be argued in this book, there is more to it. Richard Seymour defines austerity as comprising several elements (Seymour, 2014: 3–4). First, it is focused on reducing government budget deficits through a combination of public spending cuts and usually regressive tax hikes. Austerity is integral to neoliberalism (see Chapter 2 for a more detailed definition), which can be defined as:

> ... an economic policy regime whose objective is to secure monetary and fiscal stability and that is legitimised by an ideology that holds markets are best treated as self-regulating. This has allowed not merely the 'restoration of class power' analysed by Harvey, but also a dramatic redistribution of wealth and income in favour of the rich. (Callinicos, 2012: 67)

Or put in a different way but making a similar point, Mark Blyth observes that austerity 'is not just the price of saving the banks but the price that the banks want someone else to pay' (Blyth, 2016: 7).

Second, the 'disciplining of labour' is a key element of the austerity 'growth project' in terms of restricting its agency and capacities of mobilisation and resistance. This is facilitated by curtailing the bargaining power of labour via industrial relations and employment regulation. In addition, welfare and labour market policies involve the increasing use of conditionality in terms of reducing access to benefits and restricting the capacities of benefit claimants to negotiate and challenge the welfare system (see Umney, 2018). Welfare conditionality holds that access to certain basic, publicly provided, welfare benefits and services should be dependent on an individual first agreeing to meet particular obligations or patterns of behaviour (Welfare Conditionality Project, 2018a).

The disciplining of labour in terms of regulation at work and through welfare are often conceptualised as quite separate processes in both social policy and industrial relations debates. They are, however, closely interlinked. Colin Crouch (1999: 437) states the

> term for 'social policy' in French and Italian discussion refers to both the welfare state and industrial relations ... Historically, both institutionalized industrial relations and the

> provision of various social benefits were a response to the predicament of the growing new industrial working class, protected from the insecurities of the capitalist labour market.

This inter-relationship between employment relations and welfare is a central focus of the book. One of the fruitful aspects of the work of Esping-Andersen (1990) on his comparative welfare regime analysis is the way he draws out the relationship between labour movement power/influence and the regime type. For example, the relatively strong coordinated industrial relations systems of Northern Europe have shaped in turn more redistributive welfare systems which are characteristics of the Nordic countries (see Chapter 7 on Denmark).

Brandl and Traxler (2004) draw out in more detail these relationships:

- Employment effects of collective bargaining have an impact on the welfare state insofar as unemployment benefits are provided by the state.
- Collective/individual wage agreements even more directly affect the public welfare system when the level of and change in social benefits is formally linked to wage movements, which in turn impact on in-work benefits.
- Welfare states influence industrial relations when establishing social protection against the risks resulting from the labour market. For example, unemployment benefits act as a cushion for unemployed persons in order for them to seek work. Where there is no compulsion to take up work they can wait and thus enhance the bargaining power of labour, because there is less incentive to undercut wages and labour standards. However, intensive conditionality can mean that the bargaining power is weakened as welfare conditionality guarantees a ready supply of cheap and compliant labour who can replace workers who are deemed 'too expensive', militant or organised.
- The interrelation of industrial relations and the welfare state becomes most evident when their regulations target the same subject. For instance, provisions for sickness benefits may be endorsed in social policy legislation and/or collective agreements. Negotiation around health and safety, holiday entitlements, maternity rights and other forms of social benefits can 'spill over' into areas of social policy.
- Unions organised in the public sector (employment services, local government and health sector) pursue defensive and offensive strategies to retain employment and services to the benefit of more disadvantaged groups more reliant on the welfare system.

- Union anti-privatisation strategies and campaigns around welfare and public services in terms of retaining service levels and quality, has an important impact on claimant experience of the welfare system.

The most coercive influence of welfare conditionality on employment relations as outlined earlier is the way it reinforces contingent work and undermines wage bargaining. In turn keeping minimum wages low will indirectly influence benefit levels and social security (and vice versa). Weak representation and engagement of trade unions in terms of welfare policy formation can mean that benefit cuts are easier to implement. Conversely, strong trade union presence in the public services can mitigate the impacts of austerity as they struggle and bargain for the retention and improvement of services. The trade union movement has campaigned and created the political space for the implementation of a minimum wage, which benefits those claimants moving from welfare to work.

Since the 1990s, conditions for accessing benefits have become more restrictive; there has also been a tendency to use sanctions (for instance, withdrawing benefits if claimants do not comply with conditions) as a way of disciplining and punishing claimants. Welfare strategies are work-first: they prioritise accessing employment over other policies such as employment support and training. In this way, 'welfare conditionality' becomes an important means of regulating the Reserve Army of Labour (RAL). For Marx (1973), the RAL comprises those people who are unemployed, and a segment who are at the margins of the labour market who tend to move in and out of work. He argued that a key function of the RAL is to keep wages down, increase the competition for work and exert discipline on labour (Jonna and Foster, 2016; Wiggan, 2015). The shift towards work-first policies away from Active Labour Market Policies (ALMPs, or activation), which incorporate vocational training, intensive social support and employment training, has also been driven by austerity (Kalleberg, 2018).

Following Farnsworth and Irving (2018) (see also Dukelow and Kennett, [2018]), there are several dimensions and trends following the 2008 crisis which can illuminate the way welfare reform and employment relations are interlinked.

Financialisation has increased its role in the development of the employment relationship, of which work-first policies play a pivotal role. Many firms have chosen to financialise their operations by investing in derivatives and credit markets for a quick return on investment. Managers prioritise the distribution of dividends for the shareholders at the cost of squeezing production, cutting wages and 'downsizing'. The result is the maximisation of bonuses and profits in the short term at the expense of the wage bill. Top earners have improved their position. For example, on average the wage income share of the top 1% of income earners rose by 20% over the last two decades, while the wage share of the lowest educated slumped (Mercille and Murphy, 2015: 15). Deregulation of labour markets, labour flexibility, capital mobility and global finance are key sources of wage stagnation. Several writers suggest that welfare conditionality and the offensive against employment rights are closely interlinked. Work-first policies adapt people to low-waged employment and, when combined with deregulation of labour rights, succeed in strengthening capital control over the labour process (Grady, 2017: 282).

Work-first policies undermine wage bargaining and reinforce insecure work. This is intended to have the double effect of undercutting wage demands but to serve the low-wage economy with 'compliant' labour (Raffass, 2017). In the UK, Universal Credit (UC, launched in 2013) is the major Conservative government welfare reform launched on the back of 'making work pay'. The stated aim of UC is to 'simplify' the benefit system, as it merges a number of different benefits into one benefit. UC also involves an in-work benefit (work allowance) to replace working tax credits. Access to both in-work and out-of-work elements of UC are subject to demanding work search and progression requirements reflecting the way the welfare reform agenda has involved a stricter conditionality regime as a way of moving people into work (see Chapter 3). In this way the attack on employment rights works in tandem with work-first policies: the two are mutually reinforcing processes.

The financialisation of household debt is due to easy access to credit and mortgages during the housing boom reinforced by the trend towards wage stagnation since the 2008 crisis. Consequently, households are more and more pushed towards private indebtedness and credit consumption. This has been compounded by the cuts in welfare support and the social safety net. Rubery (2015a) refers to this as the shrinkage of the social state in relation to all its four main roles: as a source of income support; as a provider of free or subsidised public services; as a direct employer; and as a defence against marketisation of society. The new 'welfare regime' is downgrading or even phasing out benefits as a safety net. Women, according to Rubery, are disproportionately impacted by these changes. Reproduction services have become financialised, particularly in relation to pensions, care packages, insurance and mortgages, and this has had the impact of fuelling household debt, exacerbated by the cuts in welfare. Given that the public sector is a major source of employment for women, austerity cuts have led to greater instability and uncertainty in terms of employment, career routes and pay (Himmelweit, 2016: 11).

Geography plays an important role in the political economy of welfare and work. Localities (cities and city regions) are important sites for the delivery of welfare-to-work and the reproduction of labour via local welfare services and in turn they shape the contours of labour markets and precarious work. There is also plenty of evidence to show that cities and regions are bearing the brunt of austerity (see Etherington and Jones, 2018; Gray and Barford, 2018). While the rise of insecure and precarious work is an international as well as national phenomenon, there are distinct geographical outcomes and processes at work particularly within deindustrialised cities (see Chapter 5 on Greater Manchester and Chapter 6 on Sheffield Needs a Pay Rise Campaign). Employment restructuring in 'traditional' industries has given rise to a high concentration of new jobs in the service sector, which tend to be low paid and require little vocational training. Polarisation and segmentation of the labour market has resulted, and this has been exploited by industry with support through state infrastructure investment and welfare-to-work policies. The 'de-unionisation' of cities and regions involving lower union densities and collective bargaining coverage has led to gaps in employment protection (or its enforcement), reinforcing and accelerating labour market insecurity and inequalities. From the perspective of labour, the processes for negotiating around employment rights and social protection are highly constrained. However, as discussed in Chapter 4, this needs to be viewed as continually subject to negotiation, struggle and contestation (Cumbers et al, 2010).

Class and agency in welfare and employment relations

The role of agency – how neoliberal politics are offset, modified and resisted by trade unions and other social actors – is of crucial importance in our understanding of the implementation of welfare policies. Central to this is an understanding of class and class relations. I have argued in this Chapter that central to the politics of austerity are the changes to the capital/labour relationship. Within a Marxist approach, capital (the capitalist class who own the means of production) are solely concerned with extracting surplus value and maximising profit; for labour (the working class defined as wage labour) the primary interest is to wages to secure survival and attain a standard of living. This will include 'the social wage' and welfare services essential to maintaining or attaining the reproduction of labour power. It is not difficult to see how these interests can be and are fundamentally in conflict, and how wages and welfare are a terrain of struggle between classes. Inequalities in wealth and income are important measures of the nature of class relations and struggle. In the current period, austerity has underpinned and driven the increasing power of dominant classes as observed by Callinicos, cited earlier (see Umney, 2018).

While there is not a rich vein of work in social policy with respect to the role of agency, there is a body of work in Marxist tradition which has posed the question of struggle and mobilisation in terms of class and collective politics (Ginsburg, 1979; Lavalette and Mooney, 2000). The post-war UK welfare state was forged from a longstanding struggle by the trade unions and Labour Party for more redistributive employment and social policies, including social benefits, education and the National Health Service (NHS). There should be no return to the poverty and blight that prevailed in the 1930s. At the same time, the settlement or 'class compromise' contained some weaknesses, particularly the ideological belief in women's primary responsibility for the home. This assumption regarding gender roles was generally accepted within the Labour Party and some sections of the trade union movement (Blackford, 1993: 220).

This historic legacy of the construction of the UK welfare settlement is important in terms of framing the social divisions and struggles over welfare. As Williams (1994) emphasises, the link between family, work and nation must be understood in relation to a diversity of social divisions – not only gender but also ethnicity, and class (although disability, sexual orientation and age can also be included). Such struggles are influenced 'not only by class relations but also, relatedly, by the relations of other forms of social power – racism, nationalism, male domination and so on – which influence both the demands of the working class and the response of capital and the state' (Williams, 1994: 60). In this way, I assert that the nature of oppressions (and the 'class struggle') must be related to the concrete experiences of social life within capitalism (Lavalette and Mooney, 2000: 8).

Trade unions are important 'actors' or source of agency in the class struggle as they act as a fulcrum for solidarity within the workplace (and reduce competition within the labour market); they also articulate worker resistance and negotiation around the employment relationship (Hyman, 1989: 36). Although trade unions developed through struggles around workplace issues, they have also pursued concerns relating to social reproduction, and social and welfare policy. As Fine states, trade unions will:

> ... often be drawn across the nebulous and shifting boundaries connecting economic and social reproduction. The wage, after all, is only the most immediate source of revenue for sustenance of the working class family, whose capacity to provide able and skilled labour depends upon the range of services that are now commonly thought of as constituting part and parcel of the welfare state, albeit unevenly by country and type of provision (housing, education, health etc). (Fine, 2003: 91)

The debate around trade union survival has been recently focused around representing outsiders as well as 'insiders', their core membership within the workplace (Clegg et al, 2010). The UK trade unions face many challenges in engaging and mobilising 'outsiders'. Traditionally, links between trade unions and social security claimants in the UK have not been strong. Until recently there has been a tacit acceptance of the principles of welfare conditionality and there has not been the same degree of argument about benefit cuts as there has been around wages and the minimum wage. Very few Trade Union Congress (TUC) annual congresses have given welfare reform any priority and, with the exception of the Public and Commercial Services Union (PCS), there was tacit support from the TUC and trade unions to the operating principals of the New Deal work-first programmes under the New Labour government. Only at the later stages of the last New Labour government did the TUC mobilise opposition to the 2009 Welfare Reform Act, which in many ways shaped the post–2010 politics of welfare under the coalition/ Conservative governments (see Chapter 3). In many respects there are signs of some shift in the way trade unions are responding to welfare reform by engaging and campaigning with marginalised and disadvantaged groups, on which Chapter 4 will focus. However, at the same time it is important to recognise the many initiatives that trade unions are involved with which have a direct or indirect impact on 'outsiders' and those who are reliant on welfare services. Trade unions have been at the forefront of defending the attacks on the welfare state and therefore play an important role in relation to the delivery of social reproduction services. An example, the development of the TUC Unionlearn initiative originated in response to the need to address the lack of skills of marginalised workers (Clough, 2017).

The Brexit and COVID-19 crises and the contradictions of austerity

I am writing this book in the middle of one of the deepest political and social crises the UK has witnessed since the Second World War. The December 2019 Conservative government general election victory under Boris Johnson will no doubt pave the way for a 'no deal' Brexit and further austerity. In addition to the Brexit crisis, we are experiencing the global COVID-19 global pandemic, which is accentuating this generalised crisis of the capitalist system. I will, however, as a brief postscript, make my own brief assessment of the implications and significance of these events in Chapter 8.

I view Brexit as a logical extension of the austerity growth model I described earlier in this chapter, but which involves a deepening of the crisis and contradictions of austerity neoliberalism. The COVID-19 crisis has exposed in a fundamental way the contradictions of austerity and the neoliberal growth model even further. Neoliberalism, as I analyse in Chapter 2, emerged as a strategy to restore the profitability of capital post oil crisis of the 1970s, but which has failed spectacularly, evidenced by the 2008 crisis and ongoing structural problems of the economy. Austerity was a key element of this as part of a politics of redistribution in favour of certain class and capital interests. The contradictions take a number of forms. I will highlight two. The first, outlined by Callinicos and citing Georg Lucas (1971), capitalism has a tendency towards a

> deepening rationalisation of specific aspects of society accompanied by the growing irrationality of the whole. In the present case, the banks have acted ruthlessly to pursue their interests as shaped by the existing structure of financialised capitalism. The problem is that this whole structure has at the very least been gravely weakened by the crisis. (Callinicos, 2012: 74)

The Conservative government's COVID-19 policies attempt to insulate financial and 'rentier' interests from the crisis while millions of people are thrown into unemployment, poverty and insecurity. Christine Berry, writing in the *Guardian* (2020), argues that the lending policies of the bail-out will mean that many small and medium businesses, and individuals, will have to pay back their debt while 'virtually no sacrifices have been demanded of banks, landlords or profitable corporations, such as utility companies. The only people in society not being asked to share the burden are "rentiers": those who make money by owning assets they can charge others to use'. Second, fiscal consolidation and the attack on the welfare state and other public services and infrastructure undermine capitalism's requirement for the reproduction of labour and capital accumulation: the deeply rooted logic of state spending and interventions conflicts with neoliberalism's attempts at public spending rationalisation. Conditionality and welfare cuts, combined with long-term spending reductions on health and social care, distort the labour market, leading to increasing segmentation, exacerbating poverty and impoverishment (Gough et al, 2006: 182).

MacLeod and Jones (2018) describe how the long-term impact of neoliberalism and austerity on working class communities and the regions has led to large scale disaffection in the political establishment:

> New Labour had intervened with public money to save Britain's major banks while facilitating the Bank of England to feed 'quantitative easing', in effect boosting the London job market by 18 per cent while further enhancing the lavish spending power of the capital's über-rich ... Further, through punitive cuts in tax credits and housing and disability benefits alongside savage reductions in local government funding ... the austerity state has impacted disproportionately on people in older industrial areas, jaded seaside resorts, and now by-passed towns such that 'by 2016, there were causes enough for a protest vote'. (MacLeod and Jones, 2018: 119)

Taking a similar view to Callinicos, they go on to comment on the divisions within the ruling elites over the direction of travel in relation to the 'growth model' when they suggest that 'the Brexit conjuncture witnessed ideological divisions within an elite that, while generally supportive of further adherence to a neoliberal accumulation regime, had alternative views about how it might be successfully advanced in the UK context' (MacLeod and Jones, 2018: 119).

Peter Taylor-Gooby (2017), in his assessment of the impact of Brexit on the UK welfare state, perceptively points out that through Brexit, elites are positioning the UK economy within an increasingly globalised economy. It is an example of a 'race to the bottom' with the potential for market competition policies being used to reduce even further social protections. Furthermore, employment rights, labour regulation and trade unions are the target of the dominant Brexit class. As Frances O'Grady, General Secretary of the TUC has stated:

'the only employment rights, commitments that come out of the future relationship with the EU are in the Draft Political Declaration. Unfortunately, this section of the agreement is non-binding, it is not worth the paper it is written on' (O'Grady, 2018).

Of course, the divisions among the working class are an important factor. The Brexit campaign, when it became more fixated around race and immigration, was cynically exploiting social and ethnic divisions. However, as emphasised earlier, these divisions are created and inextricably part of neoliberal capitalism. They are also part of Europe as a failed project in terms of delivering social and economic benefits (Gumbrell-McCormick and Hyman, 2018). As Jamie Gough (2017) argues, people's resentment against immigrants and even benefit claimants is a product of austerity, poverty, inequality and oppression, as well as a result of a lack of a coherent alternative socialist strategy. This raises an important point about the nature of critical voices and the range and possibilities of alternatives to austerity neoliberalism. This will be explored in the concluding chapters of the book.

Origins of the book

The book arises from my longstanding comparative research on welfare and labour market policy in the UK and Denmark. What is striking about the Danish model, and indeed other Nordic models, is the role of the trade unions. Narratives on welfare and social policy in the UK tend to ignore the role of trade unions and how industrial relations policies will influence and shape welfare policy. Esping-Andersen (1992) argued that strongly redistributive welfare states are moulded by developed industrial relations and social dialogue. This brings the role of agency or class struggle into the debate. My first publication on Denmark (Etherington, 1998) posed the question of whether the Danish model offered an alternative perspective to the seemingly free-market policies of the New Labour government. This was written at the time of the early days of the welfare-to-work programmes (New Deal for the unemployed): even then my view was that the Blair government had missed an opportunity to develop something more radical with a greater role and emphasis on the role of local government and the trade unions. In fact, the welfare reforms became more work-first and disciplining as they developed, reflecting the dominant neoliberal politics of New Labour.

As argued in Chapter 2, the 2010 coalition government welfare reforms actually display many continuities. At the time of writing, the roll-out of UC is taking place accompanied by unprecedented criticism from sections of the media, trade unions, and social and welfare movements because of its wholescale assault on benefits and social protection. Understanding the nature of response from the trade unions is extremely important. Trade unions are the single largest voluntary organisation in the UK, with over 4 million members; after successive onslaughts by neoliberalism they are still capable of innovation and providing a voice for disadvantaged groups and the working class as a whole in the face of a sustained attack on living standards. They have strengths and weaknesses which this book will explore. Strengths lie in their bargaining activities and capacity to resist austerity and the cuts in the public and welfare services and which are so important for supporting disadvantaged groups. The weaknesses are their low level of presence and activity in large parts of the service sector where poor working conditions and insecure work predominate.

Geography plays an important part of the book's analysis. As a geographer and researcher on labour market policy, I have been interested in the spatial dimension to state restructuring. Between 2005 and 2007, I was involved with a major two-year Joseph Rowntree Foundation (JRF) project, *Devolution and Regional Governance and the Economic Needs of Deprived Localities* (North et al, 2007), which examined the extent to which policies and governance structures in national jurisdictions and regional bodies across the UK linked economic development activity to the needs of deprived areas. A key finding of the research was the extent of deprivation and large proportion of people claiming out-of-work and sickness benefits in deindustrialised areas. The uneven geographies of welfare reform and austerity play a key role in shaping territorial politics within the regions. The chapter on Greater Manchester is based on earlier research on the impact of austerity on devolution and welfare undertaken with Martin Jones in 2017 (Etherington and Jones, 2017). Greater Manchester is chosen as a case study as it represents the flagship devolution initiative where welfare reform is a key element of the devolution process.

The book's focus on insecure work and 'precarious' economies arises from my interest in the way welfare reform impacts on insecure work. This is an important lens under which to tease out the links and relationships between the industrial relations system and welfare policies. From this, the book explores weakness in terms of the lack of employment rights and workplace trade union representation in certain sectors of the economy, and how this has been reinforced by work-first policies, which tend to 'feed' workplaces where exploitation and oppressive working practices exist. My involvement with Sheffield

Needs a Pay Rise Campaign (SNAP) provided an opportunity to explore these links (Etherington et al, 2018). Many workers in low-paid and insecure work places have travelled the welfare–work system, often cycling between the two, and the research – involving interviews with workers, benefit claimants and trade union officials/ activists – provides insights into how trade unions negotiate and resist insecurity and relate (or do not) to the organisations (community, non-government organisations) and other social movements who act on behalf of the disenfranchised. Sheffield, in common with a number of post-industrial cities, has undergone considerable cuts to social protection and services which are essential to the reproduction of labour. The SNAP research provides a useful case study in terms of the relationship between austerity and labour market insecurity.

My longstanding collaboration with Martin Jones (and later with Jo Ingold) has spawned several comparative publications on Denmark and the UK which have contributed to ideas about the inclusive labour market. Given the plethora of excellent critiques on welfare and work, there is a question of what alternative and progressive strategies may look like. I will make some attempt at this towards the end of the book drawing on previous work on Denmark and the UK (see Chapter 7).

Objectives and structure of the book

Summary

The book provides fresh perspectives on the link between welfare policy and employment relations, and their fundamental impact on social inequalities. This analysis is set in a wider context of austerity and the current employment crisis. Work-first policies, specifically UC, undermines employment rights as welfare claimants are pressured under threat of sanctions into low-paid and precarious work. The book analyses the role and strategies of trade unions and civil society organisations in contesting the reform agenda demonstrating the importance of union organisation and bargaining for welfare policies. The geographies of austerity play a central role in the politics of welfare, with the 'left behind' regions bearing the brunt of public expenditure cuts. In the case studies of Greater Manchester, as England's flagship devolution initiative, and trade unions and civil society organising against precarious work in Sheffield, a more detailed insight into the struggles against austerity and labour market inequalities is provided. A central argument of the book is that an industrial relations model based on coordinated collective bargaining and enhanced employment rights will underpin an inclusive welfare agenda. The final two chapters are devoted to exploring alternatives, including lessons that can be drawn from Denmark's more redistributive welfare and industrial relations system, and the importance of challenging the austerity narrative where there is an emphasis on the importance of investing in public services and local government as a basis of building a democratic and accountable labour market.

Outline of chapters

Chapter 2 develops a conceptual framework and theoretical concepts on austerity welfare and the employment relationship in two parts. Drawing on theories of class and power resources, I will construct a framework for drawing out the links between welfare and industrial relations regimes in the context of broader class politics and relations. The second part of the chapter provides a more rigorous theoretical analysis of neoliberalism, austerity and uneven development and the changing nature of the state in the context of the global economic crisis. A key element of state intervention in this respect is the way industrial relations policies underpin changing relationships between capital and labour through the attack on employment rights and representation, and the intensifying conditionality within the welfare system. The chapter situates agency and class struggle by exploring the role of actors (trade unions, social movements) and struggles which are involved in negotiating and contesting neoliberalism. Chapters 1 and 2 should be viewed as providing the conceptual and theoretical context to the book.

Austerity, in the form of attacks on public services and the welfare state has underpinned Thatcher's and New Labour's radical transformation of industrial relations, social security and the benefits system. This is the focus of Chapter 3, which briefly analyses the political and economic basis to neoliberal policies and how these have placed greater emphasis on the attack and reduction of labour rights, with a brief explanation of the impact of the 2008 crisis and ensuing austerity policies. The election of the New Labour (NL) government in 1997 promised a break from the neoliberal policies of Thatcherism. I will explore in this chapter the argument that while there were important policy shifts, the continuities with the Thatcher economics and social policy reflected neoliberal politics pursued by the NL government led by Tony Blair. In other words, this brand of neoliberalism has paved the way to the market fundamentalism and austerity politics of the current 2019 Conservative administration.

The examination of the NL legacy is critical to understanding what I term the embedding of neoliberalism in welfare and employment policy. The chapter starts with an analysis of NL employment and welfare policies and then an overview of the coalition/Conservative government's reforms. As well as tracking key policy changes, the chapter will cover responses and engagements of key actors in relation to welfare and work including trade unions and social movements

Chapter 4 focuses on challenging austerity and, in particular, analyses the nature of resistance to welfare reform and UC, exploring the critical voices and discourses of trade unions and welfare rights organisations. The UC policy of in-work conditionality puts into critical focus the way austerity and cuts to personal support and skills funding have placed considerable barriers for people to progress in work. The TUC, along with individual trade unions and some welfare rights organisations, has been proactive in challenging the way in-work conditionality and progression is being implemented. Women and disabled people are bearing the brunt of the cuts to social protection and benefits as a safety net. The discussion reveals a wide range of strategies deployed by both the trade unions and civil society organisations which are challenging the discriminatory and oppressive practices embedded in the implementation of policies. Of particular importance is the vulnerability of women to financial abuse in the UC payment system and the operation of the Work Capability Assessment (WCA), which is deeply contested by disability rights organisations.

One of the theoretical arguments of the book is that integral to neoliberalism and austerity is the deepening geographical uneven development as illustrated by increasing urban and regional inequality. Furthermore, the trend towards rescaling state policies with a greater role for local institutions in the implementation of welfare and employment policies has been a defining feature of state restructuring since the 1970s. Devolution and the creation of the Northern Powerhouse is a pivotal part of the Conservative agenda for 'regenerating' the regions. Chapter 5 analyses the devolution of welfare policies in Greater Manchester, the government's flagship devolution initiative. Greater Manchester's economy has been impacted by deindustrialisation with major socioeconomic implications. Drawing on devolution research in Greater Manchester the chapter explores the way uneven development and the precarious dimension to economic development in the deindustrialised cities is shaped by wider class strategies particularly around 'Austerity Welfarism' reforms and waves of labour conditionality. It concludes by identifying and analysing the role of key actors (trade unions, local government, community organisations) who are negotiating and challenging the premise of devolution.

Continuing the theme of analysing the way devolved austerity and employment policies are shaping city region economies and social relations, Chapter 6 explores the link between work-first policies, industrial relations and precarious work in Sheffield. Sheffield was identified as the city with the highest proportion of workers paid below the living wage and, from this finding, the local trade union movement established the Sheffield Needs a Pay Rise Campaign. Work-first policies provide a ready supply of compliant labour into insecure and non-unionised employment. This dovetails with policies aimed at attacking trade union organising such as the 2016 *Trade Union Act*, described as the '*final coup de grace*' on an already weakened movement (Tuckman, 2018: 104). This raises the question of how the two processes connect and interact – workfare and employment relations. In other words, how are employment rights and unionisation undermined by a process of funnelling labour into low-paid, unskilled jobs? How do industrial and other actors respond and negotiate the challenges of welfare conditionality on employment relations? The chapter draws from work undertaken as part of the Sheffield Needs a Pay Rise (SNAP) campaign in 2018 (Etherington et al, 2018). The SNAP campaign, initiated by Sheffield Trades Union Council (STUC), is linked to the Britain Needs a Pay Rise campaign organised by the national TUC.

For many years I have sought to explore the political economy of welfare in the UK from a comparative perspective using Denmark as a comparator country (Etherington, 1998; Etherington and Jones, 2004a; Ingold and Etherington, 2013). The value of comparison is that it provides insights and a window into the social processes and class forces which configure a particular welfare settlement (in this case the UK). Comparative research also provides insights into innovations and progressive politics that may offer lessons and another perspective on the UK. This forms the basis of the analysis of the Danish system of welfare and employment relations, which is the focus of Chapter 7. In Denmark, social democracy has arisen from a strong trade union movement and the historic legacy of class politics, where many aspects of the welfare consensus based on universal and relatively generous benefits have been retained. Unemployment insurance (UI) operates under the Ghent system, which has a long history in Denmark, whereby the trade unions have traditionally managed unemployment insurance benefits since the 1930s. These benefits are based on individual contributions through employment;

in the event of unemployment, unemployed people will receive their benefit from the UI office run by the relevant sector trade union. This also includes the provision of state-supported universal childcare (Ingold and Etherington, 2013). There are features of neoliberalism in the restructuring of welfare in Denmark, including the tightening of benefit conditionality, a more workfare approach to targeted groups, and the implementation of austerity and expenditure cuts in the public sector. However, many aspects of universal welfare are retained, including the model of capital/labour relations through social dialogues, coordinated collective agreements and the provision of subsidised childcare.

Chapter 8 concludes by developing the discussion of the Danish model further arguing for an alternative strategy towards an inclusive labour market and welfare agenda (with some of these ideas contained in the Corbyn-led Labour Party 2019 manifesto). As a postscript, I first make a brief 'post-election' assessment arguing how the geographies of austerity and the electoral response from the 'left behind' regions played a crucial role in the results. I follows this with a brief assessment of the impact of the COVID-19 crisis. I briefly set out some ideas regarding another welfare and employment model. For example, a central argument of the book is that an industrial relations model based on coordinated collective bargaining and enhanced employment rights will underpin an inclusive welfare agenda. I demonstrate how this works in relation to the Danish model of job rotation. As 'work' is in the title of the book it is important to consider critically the meaning of work and that it is not the route out of poverty given that large sections of the population are either not able to work and/or categorised as 'economically inactive'. How can work–life balance be achieved in an unforgiving labour market? There is no doubt that strong trade unions and bargaining practices can play a role in developing this balance. Defending and expanding the role of democratic and accountable public services, especially local government, is key to the development of a more egalitarian welfare model.

2

Conceptualising austerity, welfare and employment relations

Introduction

The introductory chapter outlined why it is important to view welfare and industrial/employment relations as inextricably interlinked. This link was highlighted in the work by Esping-Andersen, who identified the association between organised labour and redistributive welfare states. This perspective is influenced by power resource theory, which also has its origins in Marxist political economy on the nature of class struggle and welfare state formation (Ginsburg, 1979). Drawing on this approach, I will analyse how changes to employment relations will impact on welfare and vice versa. As Greer (2016: 170) notes: 'Studying ALMPs (Active Labour Market Policies) critically can enrich work and employment research in a few ways. Market discipline translates into workplace discipline through the well-known mechanism of insecurity, which affects both the precariat and workers in stable employment.' This chapter extends this argument to state that a focus on industrial relations helps us to understand how the erosion of employment rights, which has been a central feature of neoliberalism, will impact on welfare claimants.

The chapter is comprised of three parts. The first part outlines a conceptual framework for understanding the relationship between welfare and employment relations from a state theoretical perspective. It describes how labour movements are a crucial factor in welfare-state building, drawing largely on Esping-Andersen's framework. The second part explores general trends in the restructuring of the state in developed capitalist countries in the context of the global economic crisis. In this part also, I attempt to illustrate the links between welfare and employment relations in relation to an analysis of broad changes in what is termed 'austerity neoliberalism'. The final section analyses the role of agency and class struggle, including the role of trade union and social movements, and the way these negotiate and contest neoliberalism.

The capitalist welfare state

Welfare, social reproduction and the reserve army of labour

Drawing on Marxist theory, the state can be conceptualised as a social relation; the state is a site, product and generator of struggle, and its spatial form is determined by the condensation of political forces that are represented in and through the state apparatus. The state has differential effects on various political and economic strategies in a way that some are more privileged than others but, at the same time, it is the interaction among these strategies that results in such exercise of state (and class) power (Jessop, 2016; Etherington and Jones, 2018).

Following this approach, the welfare state was formed through class and social struggle over the conditions for the reproduction of labour power (that is, education, health, housing, poor relief, social insurance and social services) (Ginsburg, 1979). The development of a more comprehensive welfare and social protection system coincided with the formation of an organised labour and trade union movement. De Brunhoff (1979) considers that these changes in class relations towards the end of the 19th century and the early part of the 20th century in Europe were accompanied by a transition from 'pauperism to social security'. Furthermore, the nationalisation of social assistance generated new relationships between the unemployed, their entitlements to work-related social insurance, and their entitlements to poor relief and social welfare. Social and welfare regulation was designed around the needs of the labour market, and as such reinforced labour segmentation based on work/non-work based entitlements (de Brunhoff, 1979: 23).

Integral to capital accumulation is the creation of a reserve army of labour (RAL), a pool of unemployed and under-employed labour, which functions to increase the competition for work (and in so doing exert discipline on labour) as well as to keep wages down (Marx, 1973 Jonna and Foster, 2016). There have been a number of contributions in relation to the function of the RAL, in particular the relationship between social security and wages (see Grover, 2012; Grover and Stewart, 1999), but Norman Ginsburg's classic book provides some important critical insights into the role of social security under capitalism. He states:

> ... social security is also concerned with those sections of the labour reserve army that are not customarily maintained in immediate readiness for wage work ... this includes

the elderly, the disabled, students, single parents, married women and so on, who are nevertheless brought into wage work, but can be repelled from the labour market more quickly and firmly than the front line if necessary. (Ginsburg, 1979: 48)

Ginsburg argues that residualising welfare and benefits can have a depressing impact on wages and thus erode wage agreements. The level of benefits can act to keep down the price of labour (wages) by establishing a subsistence minimum below the value of labour power as expressed as the average standard of living. Benefits therefore are related to and set below-average wage levels. As living standards of workers via wage reductions decline, so do the level of benefits.

Recently, the concept of reproduction has been given renewed attention in terms of its explanatory insights into the relationship between welfare and gender relations under capitalism. Bhattacharya (2017) considers that Marx was not just concerned about economic relations but interested in the way capitalist society is produced in its totality. From this Social Reproduction Theory (SRT), 'perceives the relation between labour dispensed to produce commodities and labour dispensed to produce people as part of the systemic totality of capitalism' (Bhattacharya, 2017: 2). Another definition is provided by Sue Himmelweit, who defines SRT as analysing the 'activities that result in a society being reproduced; not just the reproduction of the people in it but of the social relations in which they are situated' (Himmelweit, 2016: 1). This encompasses reproduction in the private sphere involving different forms of the family, state and private provision of housing, education, healthcare and care for the elderly. The roots of women's oppression under capitalism lie in the special role women are assigned – including for biological reasons – in the key process of the reproduction of labour power. The working class family according to this approach is the site of the production and reproduction of labour power, not in its internal structure and dynamics but in its structural relations to the reproduction of capital. The welfare state, in the performing of essential social reproduction functions, happens also to be the sector where collective bargaining and unionisation is strong in most developed capitalist countries including the UK.

Historically the design of social security has a strong gender dimension as the benefit system can act to push dependence from the state to the family. Furthermore, women have been excluded from any independent rights of citizenship to social security because of marriage and assumed to be dependent on their male partner's income. The level of means-tested benefit will be related to this, with the implication that the amount women will receive will be residual to what men can claim. This relationship with the benefits system encourages married women as a special category of proletarianised worker (Ginsburg, 1979: 80). Similarly, feminist scholars have focused on 'breadwinner' models to highlight the way welfare in the UK is constructed on the premise that men are the heads of household. This means that laws and policies are based on men bringing home the family wage (that is, full employment means male full employment). The implication of this is that social policies tend to reinforce the reproduction roles of women in terms of the family by restricting women's access to social benefits.

The rules for social security were predicated on the contributory principle through insurance-based benefits, and therefore provide a link between industrial relations and the benefit system. Trade unions' bargaining position was focused on wages and employment retention/ security as a means of increasing entitlements as well as retaining a standard of living. Thus, a whole series of social protection measures via unemployment insurance, earnings-related supplement and redundancy payments were implemented. As Clarke and Langan state:

> ... the systems of income support were made within the continuing underlying assumption that waged work was the primary source of economic support. What did change was the number of people excluded from the labour market – by virtue of age, responsibilities for dependents, disability, or (in the shape of things to come) unemployment. (Clarke and Langan, 1993: 32)

This ensured the separation of the two types of benefit. The fundamental weakness of this model is that in times of rising unemployment labour market inequalities arise as fewer unemployed workers qualify for contributory schemes. Trade unions have tended to concentrate their bargaining around in-work entitlements rather than means-tested benefits. This explains the weak links in terms of negotiation and bargaining between trade unions and the social security system/unemployment benefit system.

Welfare regimes and employment relations

The work of Esping-Andersen (1990) provides a useful framework for understanding the relationship between welfare and industrial relations (that is, the forms and functions of the state) in regulating the employment relationship. He focuses on key functions of welfare in relation to the labour market, pensions, sickness and unemployment benefits and labour market policies. Regimes were defined and distinguished in relation to commodification and decommodification – that is, the degree to which individuals and families can uphold a socially acceptable standard of living independent of the market (Esping-Andersen, 1990: 37). Welfare states can therefore be 'clustered' in relation to both coverage (degree of intervention) and nature of policy mixes such as social rights, and degree of distribution. Three regimes are identified: liberal, social democratic and conservative. The power resources approach of Esping-Andersen's work focuses on the wider relationship between labour movement power and influence, and the regime type.

Esping-Andersen's concept of welfare regimes as systems of power and negotiation between key interests and actors is useful in terms of understanding the social and political dynamics of labour regulation. He focuses on key functions of welfare in relation to active labour market policies, pensions, sickness and unemployment benefits. Esping-Andersen's approach is influenced by 'power resource theory' (PRT), which focuses on the capacity of workers and trade unions to organise collective action through either trade unions or their links with labour movement organisations. The nature and type of schemes are contingent on the 'specific patterns of historical development resulting from the relative power of workers, the presence of political parties to support workers' interests, patterns of family support and relationships which may compensate for lack of government backing, and other institutional and cultural factors' (Kalleberg, 2018: 53).

The UK can be classified as a liberal market regime where industrial relations and labour regulation are based on a system of voluntarism involving three characteristics (Kalleberg, 2018). First, there is an acceptance within public policy towards free collective bargaining between employers and trade unions, but the state would not be involved in regulating it. The industrial relations system (the role of other actors and institutions which influence and regulate the employment relationship) originates from the 1906 Trades Dispute Act, which gave trade unions the right to strike, although there was no obligation on the employer to conduct collective bargaining. Second, there was no tradition of industry wide agreements and generally bargaining was restricted to the workplace. Third, and crucially, there is no obligation on employers to bargain with trade unions and collective agreements are not legally enforceable. The system of social dialogue or partnership is also weak in the UK compared with Nordic and Northern European countries. Trade unions have played a marginal role in terms of formal representation on government forums in the negotiation of welfare and social policies – a reflection of the politics of both the Labour Party and trade union leadership (Crouch, 1999: 438–9). I will discuss this in more detail later.

Lehndorff et al (2018), drawing on PRT, provide a more detailed assessment of the possibilities and potentials of trade union mobilisation. They suggest that trade unions draw on three different (but inter-related) sources of power resources. These are structural – the bargaining capacities of trade unions within the labour market and within the labour process; organisational – to the union's strength in terms of membership, its activities and financial capacities; institutional power, which includes 'institutions of economic governance that shape not only the capacity of unions to organise and represent workers but their position in collective bargaining and corporatist arrangements' (Lehndorff et al, 2018: 10).

While the power resource approach is a useful heuristic device to examine broad trends in trade union mobilisation, there are other perspectives that offer a more nuanced approach. For example, Healy and Bergfeld's (2013) study of women as casualised workers draws on the work of John Kelly (1998), with respect to mobilisation theory, to argue that social mobilisation should be understood in relation to dynamic theories of class and social struggle. Collective action is seen to comprise of several integrated components: interest definition (the way people define their own interests) and societal organisation (the way people organise themselves and the structure of a group). In turn, mobilisation is seen as the process by which people gain control over resources needed for action and opportunity, which involves a complex inter-relationship between the balance of power between groups, costs of repression by ruling groups, and the opportunities available to subordinate groups to pursue their claims. Collective action, as such, can take different forms according to the balance between interests, organisation, mobilisation and opportunity (Kelly, 1998: 25–6). This framework helps to locate the motivations of actions being stimulated by a sense of injustice but also 'activists' notions of workers' rights are often derived from general ideologies which implicate unions in political campaigns that go beyond the workplace' (Healy and Bergfeld, 2013: 29).

Social movements are integral to shaping welfare politics – and also the politics of industrial relations. The link between family, work and nation must be understood in relation to a diversity of social divisions –

not only gender but also ethnicity, and class (although disability, sexual orientation and age can also be included). Taken together 'these three types incorporate much that is significant in welfare policy about the social relations of capitalism, patriarchy and imperialism as well as the key process of production and social reproduction and the ways they are connected to the formation of social divisions in society' (Williams, 1994: 82). According to Williams, it is social diversity that in recent years has led to the emergence of new social and user movements which have contested and bargained in relation to specific welfare policies and arrangements. Struggles over welfare are influenced 'not only by class relations but also, relatedly, by the relations of other forms of social power – racism, nationalism, male domination and so on – which influence both the demands of the working class and the response of capital and the state' (Williams, 1994: 60).

While social movement theory, for instance, has been influential and helps to draw attention to different identities and their specific struggles, much of this work has been constructed as an alternative to traditional class-based labour and trade union perspectives, primarily because there is an a priori assumption that these loci of collectivities and mobilisations are no longer significant. In their book *Class Struggle and Social Welfare* (2000), Lavellette and Mooney argue the strength of the Marxist approach to understanding class and social relations:

> For Marxists, oppressions must be related to the concrete experiences of social life within the capitalist mode of production. This does not mean that women's oppression, racism, gay oppression etc are simple reducible to the functioning needs of the capitalist economy, but they occur and or take their present form in ways in which they are mediated by the wider complex totality of social life. (Lavalette and Mooney, 2000: 8)

This is highlighted in Bradley's (1999) analysis of women in trade unions. In essence, the integration of gender and other identity politics into mainstream political discourse will give recognition to the women's movement in shaping class struggle politics within (and outside) the workplace. But it also provides a link between gender politics and welfare-state building.

The construction of the post-war consensus (or settlement) in the UK (as well as other European states) shaped a specific inter-relationship between the industrial relations and the welfare system:

In other words, the labour market was at the heart of the post-1945 welfare state. People had to be in work to make the contributions that would fund unemployment insurance and pay the taxes to support the National Health Service. But it was unlikely that employment would prove attractive if wages were low and benefits were means-tested – in other words, there would be powerful incentives in the system to adopt a life on benefits. This was where other institutions became important: collective bargaining, wage floors and similar instruments to set decent levels of pay. One can view Beveridge's approach as a suite of mutually reinforcing policies and institutions, with macro-economic policy (demand management, full employment) cutting with the grain of social policy and vice versa. (Coats, 2012: 37)

Within the literature, the analysis of the relationship between social/welfare policy and industrial relations is relatively underdeveloped although this has been explored by Brandl and Traxler (2004), Ebbinghaus (1998), and Crouch (1999). Colin Crouch (1999) draws out this relationship as being formed from historic legacies of welfare-state building within particular national contexts. He describes the relationship when there is an element of a formalised link between industrial relations and the welfare system:

> Given a widespread belief that welfare states, and especially their social insurance components, must be reformed, union participation in the reform process has become fundamental in all systems where unions and employer organizations have a formal role of the kind we are discussing ... no matter how weak they might become in terms of the main indicators of union strength (membership, resources, engagement in collective bargaining), unions with this kind of institutionalized role in an arena high on the policy agenda at the present time cannot be easily marginalized or excluded from national respectability. (Crouch, 1999: 439)

Even though the UK trade unions were marginalised from formal institutionalised arrangements they deployed their societal power resources and links to the Labour Party to pursue their interests.

Table 2.1 is adapted from a study by researchers at the University of Manchester (European Work and Employment Research Centre,

2017), which provides a useful framework to draw out the links between welfare/social protection and employment relations. Their research identifies four key rights gaps: employment rights in relation to workers' entitlements as part of their working conditions; social protection and integration gaps, which relate to the benefit system and the level of social security which acts as a safety net; representation gaps, which relate to the extent to which workers can access a trade union representative or other forms of advocacy. Enforcement gaps refer to the limitations placed on regulatory and industry watchdog bodies such as ACAS (Advisory, Conciliation and Arbitration Service) and the GLA (Gangmasters' Licensing Authority) due to, for example, the impact of budget cuts and low level of resource priorities to fund this function.

I have simplified this in Table 2.1 where employment rights and representation are linked together. While they are not the same, however, often the enforcement and negotiation of rights is an important day-to-day function of trade unions. Because of the weakness of the UK industrial relations model in terms of trade union bargaining strength, various employment rights tend to be set at a low level compared with comparator European countries. The minimum standard of rights such as the National Minimum Wage, holiday and maternity entitlement, unfair dismissal, redundancy payment, employment contract and statutory sick pay can be difficult to enforce without trade union presence within the workplace, and these can be reasons why welfare claimants tend to move between work and welfare. Workplaces where there are established collective agreements are associated with better quality and more stable work. This also applies where there are agreements on training and skills development. Also important is the role of trade unions in terms of health and safety and links to occupational health, which can have a major impact on employment retention for disabled people.

In the UK, the system of social dialogue where the trade unions have an input into welfare policy is virtually non-existent at both national and local level. Trade unions will tend to use established networks and links with the Labour Party to influence policy (see Dromey, 2018). Finally, trade unions play a key role in organising within the context of welfare services, which can lead to quantitative and qualitative improvements for claimants and workers (for example, the Public and Commercial Services Union [PCS] in the Department for Work and Pensions [DWP], which delivers employment services) and Unison/Unite trade unions in local government. I will expand on this later in the chapter.

Table 2.1: Conceptual framework for identifying links between welfare and employment relationship

Employment rights and representation	Implications for welfare claimants
Standard employment rights in the UK are weak compared to other European countries. Limited scope for employers and unions to improve, coordinate and integrate rights. Leads to relatively poor job retentions because of relative ease of dismissal.	Minimum set of standards generally used by employers in low-pay sectors. Workers on short-term contracts or low pay find themselves ineligible for statutory protections such as maternity and sick leave pay because entitlement requires minimum periods of continuous employment with the same employer and/or minimum weekly earnings. Claimants cycling between work and benefits due to work insecurity.
Collective bargaining in relation to union–management consultation and agreements in relation to pay and working conditions have declined.	Migrants, low-paid and under-represented groups tend not to have access to pay and conditions determined by collective agreements. Weak or non-existent formal arrangements of social dialogue at national or local level mean that trade union connections with claimants are based largely on informal links and collaboration with welfare advocacy organisations.
Six in seven workers in the private sector have no formal representation through independent channels of social dialogue.	Can mitigate the impact of welfare reform on claimants.
Role of trade unions and collective agreements in delivery of welfare services.	

Work-first policies	Implications for employment relations
UK social protection system is characterised by relatively low-level contribution-based benefits combined with a high use of means-tested benefits.	Reduction in the value of entitlements, including in-work benefits and housing benefit. Restrictive conditionality to comply with job search, medical reassessments and working hours rules.
Reduction in Universal Credit work allowance, use of sanctions in relation to in-work progression.	Impacts on low-paid workers and reinforcing low pay – workers subject to conditionality in terms of in-work progression.
Austerity impacts on health and social services – childcare cuts in funding and high cost compared to pay.	Women/lone parents vulnerable to labour market exclusion and cycling between low pay and work.
Skills funding cuts and restricted access to training for low-paid workers.	Lack of negotiated workplace agreements means workers vulnerable to minimum access to training.

Source: Adapted from European Work and Employment Research Centre (2017)

Explaining austerity, neoliberalism and uneven development

Neoliberalism and austerity as a class project

Austerity (and the wider range of policies which constitute neoliberalism) can be conceptualised in relation to shifting class relations, the nature of the crisis and the attempts to counteract the fall in rate of profit and restore profitability and accumulation. An important advance in critical political economy is the work by Jamie Peck, Nik Theodore and Neil Brenner, who have analysed how the current period is dominated by neoliberalism defined in terms of policies and interventions that promote market competition, privatisation and deregulation which is multi spatial in character (see later), contested and contradictory (Brenner et al, 2010). In this way neoliberalism is an articulation of as well as a response to crisis and instability but it is dynamic, constantly evolving and changing, which is why they prefer to coin the term neoliberalisation as a process. This approach distinguishes two aspects of state intervention – austerity and fiscal consolidation can be viewed as 'roll back' interventions whereas 'roll-out' prescribes a more proactive interventionist role for the state; for example, the way governments bailed out the banks during the financial crisis (see Peck and Theodore, 2019).

Not all interventions, however, are necessarily driving market relations. The central orientation of neoliberalism in terms of maintaining or reinforcing class relations (similar to the Callinicos quote in Chapter 1) is about interventions

> whose objective is to restore, increase and maintain the power of economic elites relative to ordinary people. It is a class project that has developed as a response to the erosion of the corporate sector's economic power during capitalism's 'golden age' that lasted from the end of World War II until the late 1960s. (Mercille and Murphy, 2015: 8)

While market orientation is definitely a lynchpin of neoliberalism, these set of initiatives need to be seen as integral to specific class strategies that consolidate, underpin and secure corporate wealth and power.

> Government spending cuts and tax hikes, privatisation, reforms to reduce labour protections and wages all translate into a reassertion of power on the part of elites over ordinary

people. Austerity is thus a political, class project designed to roll back the welfare state and redistribute income upwards. Spending cuts are normally favoured over tax hikes because they tend to target programmes on which the poor and vulnerable rely to a greater extent, such as welfare, old-age and child benefits, public health care, and poverty alleviation measures. Taxes, on the other hand, open the possibility of capturing large portions of the income of the wealthy and the corporate sector. (Mercille and Murphy, 2015: 82)

The accumulation of capital involves a tendency of the rate of profit to fall, which can lead to disruptions in accumulation, leading to economic (and social) crises. Marx (1973), however, stressed that counter tendencies were inbuilt into the system which are deployed to stave off the slowdown in the rate of accumulation, although stressing that they postpone rather than resolving the crisis. For Marx, the intensification of competition is one expression of the crisis as 'capital' increases the rate of exploitation (increase in surplus value) by reducing the value of labour power via wage reductions as a means of reducing the costs of production.

> The value of labour power is determined by the social necessary labour time in the production of the commodity-labour power, in other words, equivalent to the value of the commodities necessary for the reproduction of labour power. Hence changes in the means of producing food or housing, for example, directly affect the value of labour power. (Ginsburg, 1979: 22–3)

This value of labour power changes over time as society changes, including what is considered an acceptable standard of living. The average wage or price of labour bears a close relationship with the value of labour power. Ginsburg argues that lowering the value of labour power (and wages) acts as a powerful counter to the falling rate of profit. This can be achieved through the expansion of the RAL by increasing competition in the labour market, which has been the primary aim of work-first policies since the late 1970s.

Uneven geographical development and the regional crisis

One aspect of the approach to analysing neoliberalism by Peck and Theodore is how policies and strategies shape the variegated nature of capitalism and uneven development. Concentrating on the national scale (which even critical social policy tends to do)

> risks overlooking the uneven geographical unfolding and implications of austerity states in and across other geographical scales and relational networks. While much of the locus of authority and power to construct and enact austerity may reside amongst actors in the governing party and state apparatus at the national level, explaining the ways in which actors articulate, mediate and work through the national together with other territorial levels and relational circuits of the state are critically important. (Pike et al, 2017b: 7; see also Peck and Theodore, 2007)

This approach is linked to the tradition of critical human/economic geography which centres spatial uneven development within the political economy of capital accumulation. In the late 1970s, Professor Doreen Massey posed a critical question in a seminal *Regional Studies* journal article, 'In what sense a regional problem?' (Massey, 1979). Massey argued that the regional problem is inextricably tied up with the spatial organisation of production and the economy. This approach helps to explain the key role that cities and city regions play in accumulation and industrialisation but also how global capital and labour restructuring gives rise to spatial differentiation between and within nation states. This provides a useful framework for understanding combined and uneven development and the role of labour in shaping spatial uneven development. Massey (1984) later argued that the economic and social structures of cities and regions can be understood best in relation to an analysis of the spatial organisation of production. Traditional industrial regions originate from their proximity to the raw materials and sources of power that historically gave rise to the growth of steel and coal industrial regions. Massey sees their 'decline' in relation to the combination of global competition and the capacity for 'capital', due to technological and processes of concentration/centralisation, to organise its production and distribution through the geographical or spatial separation of functions.

Here Massey's reference point is Marx's theory of social division of labour in relation to the production and realisation of surplus value. Economic and production functions are not locationally tied in the same way and have become increasingly mobile. Headquarter and administration functions will be located in capital city regions where there is a supply of skilled labour and also specific infrastructures such as transport and tele networks. Other production functions such as Research and Development (R&D) may be located in other places (often in 'capital' cities), and routinised assembly work or distribution tends to be located in the deindustrialised regions where capital can exploit specific resource endowments such as cheaper production costs in terms of site rents and access to (cheaper) labour reserves. From this approach 'any local area (region/country) can only be understood when analysed in relation to the functions in the wider divisions of labour which are performed within it, and in the context of its place within the wider system of relations of production' (Massey, 1988: 252). The process of change and restructuring of a region's spatial structures (as embodiments of class relations and struggle) shape and determine rounds of investment and disinvestment.

In his tribute essay to Doreen Massey, Richard Meegan (2017) draws out the key insights produced in Massey's work:

> 'Spatial divisions of labour' are constructed and reconstructed over time with rounds or waves of investment … [which] incorporate the social relations – of ownership, control, function and status – of production embodied in 'spatial structures of production'. Not only may aggregate investment be distributed unevenly over space but also the various ownership, control and production tasks associated with it. It is a geography of power relationships and, explicitly, of class relations. (Meegan, 2017: 1288)

Massey here attempts to link how social and spatial relations of production are interlinked and as such can provide insights into how urban and regional relations are specifically formed and in turn shape class relations and inequality.

Allan Cochrane (2012) using the UK and South East of England as a case study usefully draws out two important implications of Massey's approach. First, that London and the South East of England as a growth city, city region and region is defined directly in relation to the subordination of peripheral and deindustrialised regions of the Midlands and the North. This 'subordination' is shaped by their respective role in the spatial divisions of labour of production. Thus the London/South East is dominated by and driven economically by headquarter functions, R&D and financial, business and producer services while the peripheral deindustrialised regions which have lost thousands of jobs in their core industries have been restructured largely based on services and branch plant activity. Although deindustrialisation was also a prominent feature of the London economy in the 1950s and 1960s its impact was not as significant as that in the cities of the North and Midlands. For Massey both developments are in relation to each other (an example of combined and uneven development) but are also a consequence of the spatial geographies of class power which leads to the second point. London as a core 'global city' is not just a product of 'globalisation' but as a result of a neoliberal strategy of opening the city to the market and as a location of massive wealth and privilege.

The state, and in particular austerity policies, has played a key role in producing geographical uneven development. Ron Martin argues in an analysis undertaken during the 1980s that the combination of the Thatcher government's monetarist policies and fiscal retrenchment (or austerity) had a disproportionate impact in the regions.

> From mid-1979 to mid-1984, Britain's manufacturing employment base contracted by 1.7 million or 24 percent, a reduction equivalent to more than half of the total decline that has occurred since 1966 ... While there would undoubtedly be a major recession without the Thatcher government, it has been estimated that almost half the jobs lost can be attributed to the 'Thatcher effect'. (Martin, 1986: 240, 280)

Thus, as Beatty and Fothergill (2016) argue, the cause of a high levels of economically inactive claimant rates in the older industrial areas lies with the job loss from an employment base in the manufacturing industries of 8.9 million in 1966 to just 2.9 million in 2016. They also observe that the claimant unemployment rate did not increase dramatically in this period even in the industrial regions where job loss was concentrated. This is due to the trend towards economic inactivity with large numbers − at first mainly men and then increasingly more women − switched to long-term sickness benefits (Incapacity Benefits). This increase in economic 'inactivity' is a form of hidden unemployment mainly because of the evidence that economic inactivity rates are significantly lower in those economies with more buoyant labour markets and higher rates of labour demand. The core of their argument is that the uneven geographical impacts of deindustrialisation combined with welfare cuts have compounded and reinforced regional inequality.

> In brief, our argument is that the destruction of industrial jobs, which was so marked in the 1980s and early 90s

but has continued on and off ever since, fuelled spending on welfare benefits which in turn has compounded the budgetary problems of successive governments. And with the present government set on welfare reform, the places that bore the brunt of job destruction some years ago are now generally facing the biggest reductions in household incomes. There is a continuous thread linking what happened to British industry in the 1980s, via the Treasury's budgetary calculations, to what is today happening on the ground in so many hard-pressed communities. (Beatty and Fothergill, 2016: 3)

It is important to factor in the targeting of cuts to local government, which has had a major impact on the former industrial regions of the UK. Lowndes and Gardner (2016) contend that local government have borne the brunt of what they term 'super-austerity'. Changes to the grant distribution system, whereby local authorities face a 'flat rate' percentage cut to grant funding, results in spending cuts continuing to impact more heavily, in absolute terms, on those authorities who receive a higher proportion of their funding through central grants. The Centre for Cities (2019: 13) observes

> The period of austerity brought about by the financial crisis at the end of the last decade has not been equally shared out across government. ... it has been local government in England that has borne the biggest burden, with its budget being cut by more than half between its peak in 2009/10 and 2015/16.

On average northern cities saw a cut of 20% to their spending. This contrasted to a cut of 9% for cities in the East, South East and South West (excluding London) (Centre for Cities, 2019: 16). The larger cities with higher socioeconomic needs tend to depend more on grant funding. However, the tenth of councils most dependent on grant funding reduced spending on services by 31% between 2009–10 and 2016–17, compared to 13% for the tenth of councils least dependent on grant funding (Institute of Fiscal Studies, 2018: 6).

The nature of the crisis

According to Michael Roberts (2016), the end of the post-war boom was due to a fall in the rate of profit of industry leading to the over-accumulation of capital. One indicator of the pressure on profitability is the intensification of capitalist competition, which has been accompanied by a reduction in real wages, facilitated by the restructuring of the RAL. This was achieved through a combination of importing cheap labour (including immigrants) and attacking employment rights and reducing the bargaining power of labour. The growing divergence between pay and productivity is an indicator in the slowing rate of accumulation and economic growth. Credit has a crucial role in facilitating the accumulation of capital, and relative stable growth of capitalism depends on the balance between credit creation and productive investment. This gets out of balance as accumulation slows down and stalls. The fall in rate of profit stimulates speculation because capitalists will seek alternative sources of profitable investment to investing in production.

Bank-issued debt was the main source of increase in money supply and the growth of the financial sector was based on speculation, with debt playing an increasing role in financial manipulation. The housing market was a key element in this process as people were encouraged to release the equity in their homes (see Mellor, 2016).

> The expansion of global liquidity in all its forms (bank loans, securitized debt and derivatives) has been unprecedented in the past thirty years. The Marxist view is that credit (debt) cam help capitalist production take advantage of prospective profit opportunities, but eventually speculation takes over and financial capital becomes fictitious. It becomes fictitious because it loses connection with value and profitability in capitalist production. This eventually leads to a bursting of the credit bubble intensifying any economic slump. (Roberts, 2016: 97)

The financialisation of economies has a number of elements. During the 1970s the oil crisis had a major impact on the profitability of capital, placing pressures on the rate of productive investment. Policies deployed to fight inflation, including wage and price controls, had deflationary effects. The dominant narrative internationally and in the UK and US was that there was too much state intervention as a cause of the problem and Keynesian economics came under sustained attack. Welfare states and public investment were seen as a drain on the economy and had to be cut back. At the same time as attacking collective public services, government policies (particularly in the UK) privileged financial services as the source of economic growth and recovery.

The deregulation of the financial sector in the UK – a key element of the Thatcher government economic policy – was key to stimulating and exacerbating the crisis. This involved lifting controls on foreign exchange markets as the best return from capital investment was overseas. This was followed by the 'Big Bang' reforms in 1986 which made it easier for financial companies to join the London Stock Exchange as a way of promoting the City of London as a leading financial centre. The government's role in financial deregulation was part of a wider global process, which in turn was responding to the latest developments in financial markets and to secure their competitive position (Norfield, 2016: 67). Developing Economies (DE) became a profitable source of investment for finance capital with a massive expansion of loans to DEs taking place; between 1980 and 2010 this amounted to around $585 billion. The outcome of this was the increasing indebtedness of DE governments and the emergence of debt-led growth with the transfer of values and money flows from DEs to northern developed economies who were supervising this operation. The costs of servicing the debt grew from $89.4 billion in 1980 to $1.74 trillion in 2010 (Marois, 2016: 29).

The financial sector became the main debt-growth sector on a global level. The trigger for the banking crisis was the inability of private capital to service accumulated debt. But there were perverse processes going on, as Roberts observes. When asset and stock prices are rising everybody wants to buy them and this is the beginning of the bubble. This precipitated the crisis, but its cause lay in the long-run squeeze on profitability, lower real wages and public investment, which accelerated an already downward spiral of the economy. In effect, capitalists have 'cut back on the rate of capital accumulation in the "real economy" increasingly trying to find extra profit in financial and property speculation' (Roberts, 2016: 240–41).

The financialisation of the capitalist economy only served to postpone the effects of a long-term structural crisis of the economy. While the neoliberal order gave prominence to free markets, the financial and economic crisis brought about an enhanced role for the state in terms of intervention to stave off the collapse of the banks. This involved the 'socialisation of risks and costs of financial speculation', which in turn increased fiscal deficits and 'transferred the banking sector's toxic assets to the government balance sheet' (Konzelmann, 2014: 723–724).

The ideological moment also plays a prominent role. Neoliberalism has legitimised greed among the financiers, who were quite happy to take increasing risks, not only with their customers' money, but also with that of their own financial institution. Individualism, credit reliance, and consumerism fuelled the various bubbles – financial and housing –while providing ideological cover not only for the 'excesses,' but for the essence of the underlying model. (Laskos and Tsakalotos, 2013: 76–7)

The political and ruling elites immediately generated a number of narratives in the form of an ideological offensive around the cause of the crisis. The work of US economists Reinhart and Kogoffs produced statistical associations between reducing the debt: Gross Domestic Product (GDP) ratio and increased economic growth while the evidence was that, actually, the opposite was occurring (Konzelmann, 2014). Although this work was discredited by other economists (for example, Blyth, 2016), it was latched on as evidence for financial prudence and austerity. The other argument pursued by ruling elites is that there is no alternative (TINA) and that the neoclassical view of how public and private finance work permeated public discourse. An example of this was to treat the economy as analogous to the household which Mary Mellor (2016) terms as 'handbag' economics with the argument that states should balance their books. As Mellor argues, this is based on a contradictory and flawed understanding of the monetary system and the cause of the deficit, which is related to the way the overall economy is managed. This includes policies around private borrowing and debt – hardly a situation of 'balancing the books'. The economy is built around increasing private debt; at the same time, the dominant narrative says that the public sector has to be shrunk because it is a 'burden' on the taxpayer.

An outcome of this is that economic policy has alternated between the unleashing of debt-fuelled consumer binges and excessive asset speculation, followed by the imposition of deep austerity measures when bubbles burst. Having abandoned control of international capital movements and the supply of money, governments have effectively discarded the levers that they previously relied on to regulate the financial sector and to manage deficit financing and debt reduction. However, without these means, economies are prey to hostile speculation in international financial markets and the risks to fiscal budgets of rising interest rates and debt-servicing costs. In this respect, as Greece and other weaker members of the Eurozone have discovered, the votes of speculators in financial markets carry more weight in determining economic and employment policy and outcomes than do those of the electorate. In this context, Konzelmann (2014) concludes that the only clear beneficiaries of austerity are financial speculators, with their proven ability to 'hold governments to ransom'.

There has been a concerted offensive in the form of accelerated cuts to welfare and social expenditure across the European Union. This has largely been driven at the EU level with respect to rules on budget deficits which must not exceed 3% of GDP. Moreover, monetary policy is centralised at the European level and is concerned not with fighting unemployment, but solely with maintaining inflation (or price stability) close to, but below, 2% and this is used to justify wage controls and restricting collective bargaining (Mercille and Murphy, 2015). The evidence of the failure of austerity and retrenchments are compelling, and a number of key indicators according to Fazi (2016) support this view:

- In early 2016 – eight years after the outbreak of the financial crisis – the eurozone's overall real [GDP] was still below the pre-crisis peak (March 2008).
- Overall, the euro area has experienced a stagnant – below two per cent – annualised growth rate since the beginning of 2012 (following a brief post-crisis recovery), averaging 1.6 per cent in early 2016.
- Research into the so-called 'fiscal multiplier' has attributed the euro area's below-average post-crisis economic performance (compared to the rest of the world) to the policies of fiscal consolidation of recent years. Fiscal consolidation in the eurozone over the 2011–13 period reduced GDP by 7.7 per cent. (Fazi, 2016)

An outcome of this is increasing inequality as austerity drives low wages, insecure employment, and rising levels of poverty (Farnsworth and Irving, 2018). In European countries, the Gini coefficient (a measure of inequality) increased on average from 0.28 in the 1980s to 0.30 in 2014. Inequality increased not only in countries with highly unequal incomes – such as the US and the UK – but also in traditionally more egalitarian countries, such as Sweden and Finland. In nearly all developed countries, the labour share of national income – wages, salaries, benefits – has declined during the past three decades. The attack on public services is integral austerity policies across the EU:

> ... the New Public Management philosophy of a small government, privatization and outsourcing of public services, the introduction of market mechanisms and efficiency drives in the public sector and decentralization conquered Europe ... increasingly it is feared that austerity and reforms are affecting the accessibility and quality of crucial public services like healthcare, education and public administration, activities that are crucial to both economic and social development and to the social quality and cohesion of European societies. (Keune, 2018: 2)

This offensive against the public sector particularly in the promotion of privatisation and outsourcing has significant implications for representative democracy and accountability which I will turn to next.

Delivering welfare: undermining democracy and accountability

Ideology plays an important role in the process of implementing austerity. Peter Burnham considers that depoliticisation (central to Marx's theory of ideology and critique of capitalism) is a key mechanism for the political management of an economy. For Burnham, Marx's concept of fetishism relates to the way the social relations of capitalism are considered as 'natural' and 'eternal' – they are seen only as they present themselves on the surface. An example of fetishism is the way the nature of the crisis is presented and that the debt is a problem created by the public sector spending too much money rather than a result of the behaviour of the banks and financial interests and the underlying structural problems of the economy and capital accumulation (Burnham, 2014: 191). For Burnham this underpins depoliticisation – the narrowing of the boundaries of democratic politics, the displacement strategies used by the state to frame engagement, and the emergence of technocratic and delegated forms of governance in the context of neoliberalism. This process reinforces dominant ideologies around what is possible and required, restricting or foreclosing avenues for debate around alternative and critical discourses (Etherington and Jones, 2018; Darling, 2016).

Economic crisis as such potentially threatens class rule and it is the function of state managers who

> seek not to necessarily resolve economic crisis but rather prevent economic crisis from becoming a crisis of political economy and thereby a political crisis of the state. In so

> doing, depoliticisation strategies remain an important, yet inherently contradictory, element in the armoury of state managers both in terms of the preservation of individual governments and, in principle, of the capitalist form of the state itself. (Burnham, 2014: 205)

Depoliticisation processes were at work throughout the 1980s and 1990s, deferring, displacing and transferring the crisis of this economy into more politically manageable state projects to promote, for example, regional and local economic development (Etherington and Jones, 2018). This has been crucial when seeking to manage spatial uneven development and deal with the political problems arising from this. I will explore this in more detail in the discussion of state devolution strategies in Greater Manchester in Chapter 5.

The neoliberal turn, which emerged in its dominant form during the 1970s, has involved the restructuring of modes of representation and democratic accountability involving several aspects.

First, there has been a shift from government to governance, increasing the numbers of actors in policy implementation and service delivery (Swyngedouw, 2005), which includes the transfer of functions and responsibilities to the private sector, involving privatisation and contracting-out of services (Grover, 2009). The state also plays an active role in expanding power of the financial, corporate sector and the wealthy; and in practice this means that the state often plays a key role in enacting policies that redistribute income and power upwards (Mercille and Murphy, 2015: 24). These changes are closely linked to wider transformations of UK's relationship with the global economy where corporate power and capitalist interests have been promoted and integrated into economic and social policies (Farnsworth, 2006: 821).

Second, the shift from government to governance redraws the structures of representation and accountabilities. More opaque systems are generated by new networks and partnerships comprising the state, civil society organisations and private sector, where it is difficult to disentangle the lines of representation and mechanisms of consultation and accountability (Damgaard and Torfing, 2010). Trends towards outsourcing and privatisation have led to increasing financial and private sector influences of policy formation. The outcome of this is the creation of more autocratic, non-transparent systems of governance where entitlement to participate is generally based on positions of power and authority, and consequently leads to further dilution of representative democracy (Etherington and Jones, 2018).

The third element relates to interventions in managing the RAL and the poor in general, which have involved more punitive and revanchist politics – an example is the introduction of a harsher regime of processing welfare claimants and restrictive benefit conditionality as a means of governing individual benefit claimants (Caswell et al, 2010; Grover and Piggott, 2015). The design of services, systems and interventions are intended to bring more target groups into the RAL and paid employment. Services are delivered and targeted at specific population groups (such as lone parents and sick and disabled claimants); 'activation measures can be understood as opening up more of the person to governmental power, requiring them to collaborate in the development of new subjective orientations to the worlds of work and welfare' (Newman, 2007: 366). The streamlining of the delivery of welfare-to-work through 'one-stop shops' (jobcentres) is a way of efficiently categorising and designing systems in order to adapt unemployed people to a changing labour market (Caswell et al, 2010). This categorisation embodies moral and ideological messages in terms of rights, responsibilities and benefit 'dependency' in relation to a 'culture of worklessness,' also drawing distinctions between 'strivers' (people who work) and 'skivers' (those who claim benefits) (Shildrick, 2018). As Wiggan (2012: 391) states: a 'hostile environment is slowly being constructed for all those who find they need to rely on social security, while the principal of solidarity that underpins support for more expansive public expenditure is eroded in favour of a market-orientated system of punitive welfare'.

Finally, welfare has been rescaled, with cities, regions and localities important 'sites' or scales for the implementation of welfare-to-work and labour market policies – the tendency towards decentralisation is seen as an important element of implementation in terms of the proximity of actors and partnerships involved in delivery processes (M. Jones, 2019; Etherington and Jones, 2009). The importance of spatial inequality and the differential development of new spaces of production and welfare means that in practice there are important local, sub-regional and regional variations in the management of local labour markets and the types of initiatives pursued (Cochrane and Etherington, 2007).

Employment relations and work-first policies

Jason Heyes' (2013) survey of labour market policies in the EU finds that the policy focus and tendencies that were prevalent before the crisis have been reinforced. An outcome of this is the rise in precarious and insecure work as employers exploit as well as drive social and employment deregulation. Indeed, the role of activation becomes clearly defined as a policy tool to ensure that precarious jobs are filled by claimants as a way of sustaining the new financialised business model of outsourcing and fragmentation. The removal and downgrading of employment rights and processes that facilitate employee representation in negotiating workplace employment conditions is key to facilitating this process. As Grady states:

> ... capital has demonstrated itself to be dependent on the financialization of the employment relationship in order to continue to extract value for shareholders ... This requires the gradual transformation of the state and the welfare it provides, rather than its abolishment. The implementation of activation, however, allows for low waged work to become naturalized, viewed as inevitable, but also preferable to engaging with workfare. (Grady, 2017: 282)

This adaptation to and feeding of a low-paid labour market via workfare and work–first policies (see Peck and Theodore, 2000) is a key element of a strategy to achieving and sustaining a low–wage economy which is enforced via coercive measures through, for example, benefit sanctions. The shift towards work-first policies away from ALMPs which incorporate vocational training, intensive social support and employment training, has also been driven by austerity (Kalleberg, 2018). This is intended to have the double effect of undercutting wage demands while serving the low-wage economy with compliant labour (Raffass, 2017).

The onset of the 2008 financial crisis stimulated further the process of financialisation of the employment relationship. This involves company strategies in terms of outsourcing, but also becoming involved with financial markets via selling assets and investing profits in financial products and so on (Rubery, 2015a: 640). This said, employer strategies in terms of flexibilisation are predicated on the requirement of international market competition and the need to counteract falling rate of profits. As businesses shift the risks of the market onto workers then the 'exit of qualified/skilled benefit claimants into low-paying, precarious jobs is uniformly considered a sub-optimal result of activation' (Raffass, 2017: 356). Financialisation has also impacted on the way corporations operate in relation to the international financial system with the focus on fictitious capital as a source of profit and surplus. Corporations are bought and sold as a way of levering financial profit and this has implications in terms of the way this process can generate further insecurity for workers.

The reconfiguration of the role of the state in the way social protections and welfare have been rolled back and 'national labour markets are thus increasingly disembedded from effective social regulation' (Hyman, 2018: 571). In the UK, the shift of focus on work and civil society to provide the means of reproduction (wages and benefit income) away from the state is a defining feature of this crisis in terms of the way large sections of the population are now being impoverished. What is significant is that the new welfare settlement is clearly downgrading or even phasing out benefits as a safety net. Services important for the reproduction of labour have become financialised, particularly in relation to pensions, care packages, insurance and mortgages, which has had the result of fuelling household debt, exacerbated by the cuts in welfare (Himmelweit, 2016: 11).

Patterns of resistance and emerging solidarities?

The resistance to austerity and neoliberalism takes on diverse forms which can be summarised as follows (see Kalleberg, 2018: 167–75).

The first is what are sometimes categorised as spontaneous protest movements that occurred throughout Europe, including the Occupy movements in London and New York, and the Losindignados in Spain. These have tended to involve and mobilise young people (the majority also educated/middle class) who have been impacted by austerity. These movements have been generally non-hierarchical and tend to be short term. Most activists have not had generally been involved in politics before and the protests have been short-lived, although effective at the time (Gracio and Giugni, 2016).

The second involves social movements and civil society organisations that are more closely involved in advocacy for working class communities impacted by austerity, including cuts in social protection.

> Whilst acknowledging that social movements and activists have had limited impact in shaping the social policy agenda in the post 2008 period, nonetheless civil society actors, including both movement activists as well as voluntary sector professionals are engaged in campaigning for recognition of unmet needs. (Ishkanian, 2019: 15)

Gumbrell-McCormick and Hyman (2018) in their European survey outline some key trends and issues in relation to union strategies, particularly focused on precarious workers but also the unemployed. The development of activation strategies (ALMPs) within Europe has been the focus of work by Clegg et al (2010) in their comparison of France, Netherlands and Italy, suggesting that trade unions have been forced to develop links with unemployed people as outsiders. This differs according to the degree of strength in terms of membership, resources and the nature of social dialogue. An interesting finding is the role of trade unions in defending existing arrangements and thus attempt to resist policies which erode social protection. In another paper, Hyman and Gumbrell-McCormick (2017) consider that the distinctions between trade unions and social movements tend to be overplayed and the relationships are more fluid primarily because trade unions themselves hold the classic characteristics of a social movement. Furthermore, the 'insider' and 'outsider' distinctions and separation can be found in civil society organisations. The key question is more about how trade unions and civil society/social movements relate within the context of increasing insecurity and retrenchment.

There are studies that suggest that trade unions will exploit and take control of power resources in order to collectivise social risks comprising 'the income and solidarity losses caused by retrenchment of public benefits may be compensated for by gains which result from benefits negotiated collectively through the agreements between unions and employers' (Trampusch, 2006, cited in Johnston et al, 2011: 352). Trade unions will attempt to negotiate on behalf of marginalised groups in terms of compensation for welfare retrenchment. In the Netherlands, unions opposed government reform of disability benefits by means of exploiting sectoral bargaining arenas. In Italy, atypical workers' unregulated status was mitigated by direct union negotiations with employers to contain welfare risks associated with temporary, part-time and marginally regulated work. In Greece, risks of continuous or recurrent unemployment faced by young and workers, because of a lack of training provision, were curtailed by the creation of collective training funds. Johnston et al conclude by suggesting that 'welfare state restructuring does indeed offer unions opportunities to become important players in welfare provision. Even more, these opportunities may be congruent with "coalition-building" strategies (and) unions have not merely been on the defensive; they have proved resilient, taking novel initiatives to prove their continuous usefulness' (2011: 361–2).

Jamie Gough (2014; see also M. Jones, 2019) makes a crucial point when he states that both the attacks on the working class and the contradictions of neoliberalism are clearly expressed – and clearly *visible*

– on the local scale. Cities and localities are important sites of resistance to the downloading or devolving of austerity, particularly in relation to local government and other state institutions. Processes of state restructuring have proceeded hand-in-hand with the decentralisation of collective bargaining and of labour market governance. The labour market impacts of economic and state restructuring place demand and pressures on local institutions, governance structures and trade unions. Devolved economic governance, however, also opens up a new space for trade unions to mobilise their power resources and capacities, to engage in partnerships, and to shape local agreements that mitigate the impacts of restructuring (Crouch, 2014). The sub-national and regional levels often play a crucial part in IR and social dialogue (Bohle et al, 2012: 15, 37). Recent research on austerity in selected European cities (Davies, 2017) highlights how cities and city governance regimes embody alliances and social forces responding to processes of economic restructuring. Regions and localities can be distinguished by specific local labour control regimes characterised by particular patterns of industrial relations; these are derived from historical economic and social forces, trade union mobilisation, social movement networks, state governance arrangements, and forms of social dialogue and partnerships (Gough, 2014).

Conclusions

This chapter has attempted to provide a conceptual framework for analysing the welfare state and how it shapes employment relations arguing that the two are highly interlinked. Integrating class and agency – the role of trade unions and social movements – into the analysis of welfare policies is important; this recognises the central role of trade unions in welfare-state building. Gender and other social relations are of critical importance to understand the links between social movements and the wider class struggle. The approach I have taken is linked to a Marxist perspective which views the state as a social relation and considers the central function of the welfare state is to provide the conditions for the reproduction of labour power and the RAL.

After drawing out the links, the chapter provided an analysis of broader changes and restructuring of welfare in the context of the current crisis. Globalisation, neoliberalism and austerity embody state strategies and policies towards greater labour discipline in two ways: first, the restructuring of welfare and increasing conditionality via work-first programmes in terms of 'managing' the reserve army.

Under conditions of financialisation, activation policies have 'fed' labour to low-paying economic sectors. The other feature of state restructuring is attacking and restricting the role and capacities of trade unions as a way of weakening wage bargaining. Second, the erosion of representative democracy can be seen to be another aspect of restricting and foreclosing on agency. The shift towards centralisation of state power, the privatisation of services and greater role of the market in the delivery of welfare has an impact on 'governing' labour markets because it potentially shuts out the scope for the working class to influence policies.

As agency is important to this book's approach to the study of welfare and employment relations, the chapter concludes with a brief overview of trends in the class struggle and the opposition to austerity. The literature and research highlight the degree to which trade unions display resilience and capacities to innovate. This includes forging links with social movements around issues such as austerity and cuts to public services. Trade unions see their role also in relation to other actors in the welfare and employment relationship. The literature, drawing on and within the industrial relations paradigm, argues that trade unions are collective actors that respond to and resist changes in welfare and labour market policy that they see as detrimental to their interests. Trade union action is motivated through the collectivisation of social risks so that benefits and social protection are integrated within systems of collective bargaining or modes of action which link up with other social groups impacted by austerity. Furthermore, trade unions are constantly fighting the clawbacks on employment rights and exclusion of representation, which is now increasingly important for welfare subjects as they negotiate the welfare/work interface.

3

Embedding neoliberal austerity: from New Labour to the Conservative government

Under Blair, the social exclusion agenda understood that the most excluded need different forms of support than the post-war settlement of welfare state plus universal public services could provide. But its mistake was to paint a picture of 2.5 per cent of the population as fundamentally different to the rest because of disaffection, social dysfunction or lack of opportunity ... The Coalition's 'Social Justice' strategy also focuses on a narrow group facing entrenched social disadvantage and poverty, the causes of which are attributed to family breakdown, substance misuse, crime, debt and welfare dependency, while neglecting wider economic inequalities such as in-work poverty and structural unemployment. The lesson of the past decade or so is that both approaches lead to a settlement for the most disadvantaged that is residualised and unstable. (McNeil, 2016: 22)

Introduction

The construction of the post-war UK welfare state involved significant gains for the working class in Britain and there is no doubt about the influence of Keynesian politics on redistribution as reflected in the expansion of welfare services. Industrial policy and economic planning were seen as key to funding and sustaining the welfare state. This brought about the nationalisation of the railways, coal and steel industries and the attempts to adopt national economic planning strategies geared to industrial modernisation. The purpose of this chapter is to provide a context and reference point to the book by exploring the development and implementation of neoliberalism in the UK with a special focus on welfare reform and employment relations.

The post-war settlement also involved significant developments within the field of industrial relations and trade unions were viewed as an important actor in the formation of the welfare state even by post-war Conservative governments. Trade union membership increased from just over 9 million members in 1948 to just over 12 million in 1979, with the fastest rate of growth occurring during the 1970s (Hyman, 1989: 233). The UK is based on a voluntarist model with a minimal role for state involvement. There were no established laws on the requirements of collective agreements, and these had to be negotiated between employers and trade unions. The post-war welfare settlement involved major redistribution towards the working class and for a period guaranteed rising standards of living and a buoyant labour market. However, the failure of economic planning and the structural weaknesses of the economy gave rise to increasing unemployment, social and spatial inequality and poverty. The cuts to public expenditure imposed by the Callaghan government in the mid-1970s as a condition of a bail-out by the International Monetary Fund (IMF) during a severe economic crisis became a repudiation of Keynesian policies and reinforced existing policy thinking, which favoured a greater role of the market (and private sector interests) and restricting the role of welfare and public sector. It can be argued that this paved the way at the end of the 1970s for the election of the Thatcher government, which placed austerity and public sector cuts in the centre of its strategy. Austerity, according to Konzelmann (2014: 721), was integral to several measures focused on the use of monetary policy and price controls to manage inflation, with employment being left to market forces. Central to this strategy was the attack on employment rights and bargaining as trade unions were seen as an obstacle to labour market flexibility. These policies were combined with major restructuring of the welfare state, benefit cuts and privatisation of public services.

The election of the New Labour (NL) government in 1997 promised a break from the neoliberal policies of Thatcherism. This chapter explores the argument that, while there were important policy shifts, the continuities with the Thatcher economics and social policy reflected neoliberal politics pursued by the NL government led by Tony Blair. In other words, this brand of neoliberalism has paved the way to the market fundamentalism and austerity politics of the current 2019 Conservative administration. The examination of the NL legacy is critical to understanding the 'embedding' of neoliberalism in welfare and employment policy. The chapter essentially provides a broad context to the book, beginning with an analysis of NL employment and welfare policies and then an overview of the coalition/Conservative government's reforms.

After Thatcher: New Labour's continuation of neoliberalism

Economic policy

On coming to power, the Blair NL government pursued a fiscal policy for the first few years which at least bore striking similarities to that of the previous Thatcher government. NL's approach can be summarised as follows:

> Competitive product markets in a globalizing world made it essential that managerial prerogative was paramount; flexible labour markets were essential. Jobs could not be guaranteed or protected. Instead, however, Blair argued that the Labour government was empowering people in the labour market by ensuring that they accumulated human capital. This was part of the philosophy behind the government's educational and training policies. (Cobham et al, 2013: 10–11)

A major decision was the granting of policy independence to the Bank of England and the creation of the Monetary Policy Committee (Burnham, 2014). Labour considered that the financial sector was a key area of economic growth in the economy with the move to liberalise mortgage lending and stimulate the housing market. The government pledged to rebuild the welfare state around work including tackling what they termed welfare dependency, the need to develop people's employability through the right balance of sticks (benefit sanctions in case of non-compliance with programme requirements) and carrots (work incentives), which featured prominently on the legislative agenda in 1997. A windfall tax on utilities financed a suite of welfare-to-work programmes, the so-called New Deals.

Welfare and skills policies

NL launched its welfare-to-work programme, the New Deal for the Unemployed, which represented a comprehensive and sustained programme of initiatives designed to assist people into employment. The retention of the Jobseeker's Allowance (JSA) was a central plank of the New Deal (and subsequent programmes) underpinned by an ideology that focuses on work as a route out of social exclusion. Conditionality was based on a narrative that personal responsibility and attaining employability was key to accessing employment (Levitas, 1998). To complement welfare-to-work programmes as part of a making work pay strategy, NL introduced the minimum wage, and established the Low Pay Commission to regulate the minimum wage.

The policy trend was towards the tightening of conditionality on long-term sickness benefits as the NL government planned to move more disabled people into work. This led to the creation of the Employment and Support Allowance (ESA) to replace Incapacity Benefit. A key plank of the benefit migration from ESA to work-related benefits such as JSA was the Work Capability Assessment (WCA) established in 2009. The WCA is an assessment process that decides whether a benefit claimant's health conditions present barriers to work and, more importantly, focuses on an evaluation of the person's capacity to be able to work. The move to migrate people onto more work-focused benefits was to create a more disciplinary and conditional regime. While benefit sanctions through loss of benefits had been in effect since the introduction of JSA in 1996, the Welfare Reform Act 2009 aimed to make the sanctions system more consistent, automatic and escalating (Daguerre and Etherington, 2014). The WCA was and has continued to be controversial because it is seen as a flawed system of health and work assessment evidenced by the consistently high level of appeals against assessments (Etherington, 2018).

NL introduced tax credits (Working Family Tax Credits, Child Tax Credits) as an in-work subsidy to mitigate the impacts of low pay. The extent to which tax credits have succeeded in making work pay is questionable for a number of reasons. First, the rising numbers of workers in low-paid work can be viewed as a response to economic restructuring and the declining proportion of workers who were affected by collective agreements (Shildrick, 2018). Second, the lack of regulation and enforcement of the minimum wage and employment rights generally underpinned the race to the bottom, which characterises the UK labour market. So, the introduction of regulation on one hand (that is, the minimum wage) has been undermined by the obsession with the deregulation of labour markets on the other. Furthermore, employment rights and representation which could improve pay and conditions were kept to a minimum level, and issues of sustainable work, employment progression, equal pay and the obligations of employers were not high on the welfare-to-work policy agenda (Hirsch and Miller, 2004: 9).

The work-first approach that characterised the New Deal model did not recognise unpaid activities and childcaring as a legitimate activity, illustrated by the increasing conditionality imposed on lone parents. Caring responsibilities are not seen as a valuable activity for the family nor a contribution to society. Many people who are at the fringes of the labour market tend to be either undertaking some form of care work (which can be viewed as a supplement to welfare activities) or voluntary and community activity (Davies, 2012).

Despite the seemingly significant resources devoted to the programme, the New Deal was consistently faced with underfunding, which presented problems for addressing the needs of hard-to-reach groups. In fact, 'many of these issues involve the question of financing. Aspects of the programme have suffered from a lack of resources, especially the gateway, which in the case of the most hard-to-employ individuals appears to have been unable to produce significant improvements in their employability' (Navitel et al, 2002: 928).

Skills policy was also high on the NL policy agenda regarding the need to address the 'low-pay low-skills cycle'. The direction of policy was to try and link welfare-to-work with skills, which underpinned a series of reforms and reviews of employment and skills policy. The Training and Enterprise Councils were replaced by the Labour government with the Learning and Skills Councils (LSC), which funded post-16 non-degree-level education and training, and the Regional Development Agencies (RDAs) as a higher-level spatial dimension to economic development charged with regenerating the regional economies. The RDAs were also involved with the planning of skills policy along with the LSCs at the regional level.

The Vocational Education and Training (VET) system was much criticised as being overly supply-side orientated. In 2005, Lord Leitch headed a major review of skills and training, known as the Leitch Review. The review focused on the need for a more demand-based focus on skills which led to the establishment of the UK Commission for Employment and Skills (UKCES) and Sector Skills Councils (SSCs). These were predominantly employer-led and quasi-corporatist bodies with trade union representation at board level charged with planning skills and vocational training within their respective sectors. The SSCs involved Sector Skills Agreements (SSAs) (see M. Jones, 2019).

There were a number of problems and challenges in meeting the objective of making the UK a global leader in skills provision. The first was the target-driven approach which was embedded in most employment and economic development policy. These targets were centrally imposed and there was little consultation in relation to their formation. Second, skills were deemed to be crucial for people moving from welfare into employment where there would be progression within the workplace. This tended to ignore the reality of the low-paid labour market where in-work progression would be limited, no matter what qualifications were held. Finally, the lack of employer commitment to investment in training was a major barrier that was never going to be resolved even with direct subsidies through the Train to Gain programme (Payne and Keep, 2011).

Governance and institutional changes

The creation of RDA and the LSC, and the promotion of partnerships within cities (Local Strategic Partnerships) were a part of the devolution and decentralisation agenda of NL changes. This key aspect of the new governance arrangements was extending the contracting culture drawing on a private sector model in terms of policy implementation (Jones, 1999). However, the key difference for NL was that localism was important as a way of promoting flexibility where there was no one model of partnership, dependent on existing local governance structures and labour market conditions (see Cochrane and Etherington, 2007).

Local authorities were subject to increasing scrutiny under NL as a performance management culture was imposed via Local Area Agreements, with a greater role for the private sector in the provision of services, continuing policies that were implemented under the previous Conservative governments (Cochrane, 1993). The funding restraints imposed by the Thatcher government were not relaxed to any significant extent, and local authorities were seen as players in a policy landscape increasingly cluttered with different actors, agencies and partnerships. More importantly, local authorities' capacity to address the needs of deprived communities and disadvantaged were constrained by funding shortfalls. All the well-intentioned initiatives that local authorities were to develop or lead on were often underfunded.

> Initiatives and reform often lacked institutional and local roots. In areas such as urban regeneration, health, social services and education, marginal spending secured by the SEU [Social Exclusion Unit] had limited influence on 'mainstream spend'. This was particularly the case in relation to area-based regeneration. A lack of lasting reform was seen in the limited evidence of the re-aligning and re-allocating of mainstream budgets. (McNeil, 2016: 4)

In fact, local authorities were never to claw back in any significant way the resources cut back by the previous Conservative administrations. Furthermore, the structural problems of the economy, especially in the deindustrialised cities and regions, required substantial public investment and intervention (North et al, 2009). This is evidenced by attempts to devolve welfare-to-work programmes. The limitations of supply-side performance of the New Deal were (and still are) exposed in those areas where there is a lack of jobs. These are former industrial areas where there is a high proportion of claimants on long-term sickness benefits (Navitel et al, 2002; Beatty and Fothergill, 2016). The City Strategy Pathfinder (CSP) gave primacy towards the city regions as the spatial scale for devolving welfare reform initiatives. Partnerships and consortia were formed between local employment services, local authorities and the private, voluntary and community sectors, where there was some discretion and additional funding to develop their own priorities and innovate with project development. Underfunding and centralised control limited the scope for real devolution but the lack of sustainable jobs in these areas exposed the real limitations of the supply-side approach (North et al, 2009; Etherington and Jones, 2009).

Industrial relations and welfare policies

The election of NL did not in any way to lead to any policies and legislation that compensated for the anti-trade union policies of the previous Conservative governments. NL's policy pitch was therefore focused on flexible labour markets, which underpinned employer power and capacity to control and shape the work process. NL provided some concessions to the trade unions with legislation to provide some form of minimum employee rights around recognition under the Employment Relations Act 1999.

But, as Brown comments (2011: 4): 'The New Labour branding had been specifically aimed at erasing any memories that the party was influenced by the trade unions'. Union membership fell from just over 13 million members in 1979 to 6.5 million members in 2014 (Tuckman, 2018: 84).

On the election of NL, the Trades Union Congress (TUC) had re-orientated its strategy towards promoting social partnerships and in 1999 established its own TUC partnership initiative. The initiative aimed to engage more with the government and employers (CBI) over key areas of labour market policy. The establishment of the Low Pay Commission and the minimum wage in 1997 was seen by the TUC as an important step in addressing fundamental inequalities in the labour market and the rise in in-work poverty. In terms of organisational and institutional power resources, the trade unions gained members in the public sector where there was job growth, and it is this sector where collective bargaining was strongest. In the private sector the opposite was the case and the impact of NL relaxation of trade union restrictions in both union recognition and collective agreements was minimal in terms of bargaining strength. In 2011, 47% of workers were in workplaces in which trade unions were recognised; 92% in the public sector and 12% in the private sector (Coderre-LaPalme and Greer, 2018: 262). Meanwhile, trade unions' engagement with any form of social dialogue in relation to employment policy was restricted to the Low Pay Commission and UKCES.

It is possible to highlight three areas where trade union policies had a direct or indirect link to NL welfare policies: first, the establishment of the Union Learning Fund (ULF) in 1999 and the creation of Unionlearn as a TUC agency charged with servicing and providing strategic direction (Stuart et al, 2016). Attaining basic skills was a priority for the TUC in order to address the increasing marginalisation and disadvantage that workers experienced in low-paid work, and the focus on promoting workplace learning agreements was seen as an important mechanism for facilitating contact with trade unions. The ULF and Unionlearn, with its focus on low-skilled workers, were attempting to re-orientate towards capacity-building in deprived communities as part of its outreach work. Unionlearn became an important lever in promoting the role of the trade unions on the SSCs (see earlier and Chapter 4). One aspect of Unionlearn was to develop critical discourses around the NL skills agenda, for example with respect to the neoliberal direction of skills policy, in particular putting pressure on the government for more trade union engagement, and partnership in policy consultation and formulation (Clough, 2017). Furthermore, breaking the low-pay low-skills cycle was a key argument by the TUC in terms of engaging people within the activation system and subject to welfare conditionality.

The second area, an example of the deployment of both institutional and organisational power resources, is the delivery of welfare-to-work services, which became a contested area because of trade union opposition to the privatisation and outsourcing that was a central feature of the public services modernisation agenda. A significant development here is the growth of the Public Commercial Services (PCS) trade union, which represents workers in the wider civil service and employment services delivered by the Department for Work and Pensions (DWP), who were constantly subject to job cuts, performance measurement and service restructuring involving outsourcing and contracting-out (McCafferty and Mooney, 2007). For example, private or voluntary sector providers were contracted to deliver on the Employment Zones, and Flexible New Deal (M. Jones,

2019, Chapter 4). As Davies (2008) points out, the role of charities and voluntary sector in the delivery of employment services was becoming a key feature of contracting-out strategies. A significant service change within Jobcentre Plus, opposed by the PCS, was the moving away from face-to-face contact to the use of call centres, which the trade union considered as impacting most on vulnerable groups who needed personalised support. This service change was problematic and seen to be facilitating jobcentre closures and more staff cuts, which were resisted in the form of a number of increasingly bitter rounds of nationally-organised strike action.

> ... disputes are increasingly and demonstrably double edged with an equal focus on the ill effects on workers themselves and those whom welfare services are critical. Importantly, this represents a challenge to the idea of 'wreckers' and is of course and is a world away from their portrayal as self-seeking faceless, bureaucrats with bowler hats and 'skivers' by some politicians. (McCafferty and Mooney, 2007: 227)

This demonstrates that the public services reform agenda as applied to the DWP was about 'efficiency' and cost cutting at the expense not only of decent work within the sector but also a sustainable service for vulnerable groups.

The third area was what we can term as exploiting societal power resources in terms of developing the role of trade unions in campaigning around key policy issues, including building links with communities and those on the fringe of the labour market. The TUC-sponsored unemployed workers' centres are an example, established as a response by the trade union movement to the growing levels of unemployment in the late 1970s. These centres have been a hub for welfare rights and campaigning against unemployment but in recent years, due to decline in funding and active trade union support, a number of centres have been forced to close.

In the 2000s the Living Wage campaign developed through community organising in London in 2001 with the formation of The East London Community Organisation (TELCO), centred in the East End of London, and of London Citizens, which has had a London-wide base as a 'spatially extended social network' (Wills, 2008). In 2004 the Transport and General Workers' Union (now merged into Unite) in collaboration with TELCO recruited a team of multilingual foreign-born workers, modelled on the US Justice for Janitors Campaign, targeting workplaces within the financial district in the East End of London. This brought the trade unions and community organisations together as part of a major campaign that also focused on the Greater London Authority (GLA) as the governance body for London. A consequence of intensive campaigning was the establishment of the Living Wage Unit and subsequently the Living Wage Commission, which promotes the take-up by employers of living wage policies at the national level. This form of organising has stimulated a debate within the TUC around community unionism and the need to engage with those on the margins of the labour market including welfare claimants (Simms et al, 2013).

To some extent trade union involvement with 'grass roots' politics had some tradition via the activities of the local trade union councils (Taylor and Mathers, 2008). Local trade unions councils and Unemployment Centres along with welfare rights organisations were intensifying their opposition to the growing hostile rhetoric to benefit claimants by senior politicians. Pressure was building within the TUC to take a more critical stance on the welfare reform agenda. A case in point was the Welfare Reform Act 2009, which involved the development of a more restrictive and oppressive welfare regime. The statement from the TUC was highly critical of the Green Paper (the Freud Report) and NL's welfare reform agenda:

> The Green Paper was remarkable for the dismay it provoked amongst unions; no welfare reform proposal in the past eleven years has aroused such hostility. For the first time in recent history the TUC's annual Congress debated an emergency motion on social security, which was passed without opposition. TUC policy is therefore to organise opposition to workfare, the abolition of Income Support, benefit cuts for lone parents and disabled people, tougher conditionality for other claimants and the contracting-out and privatisation of services. (TUC, 2008)

To sum up, the NL industrial relations policies ensured that the balance of power was still firmly to the advantage of employers as under the previous Conservative government.

> In nine years of government, New Labour has developed a distinctive form of neoliberalism in which Conservative legislation on trade unions and industrial action has been integrated within a more subtle discourse of social

partnership and collective and individual rights, and carefully defined intervention in the labour market and the employment relationship is designed to promote efficiency. Reality is less subtle. The UK remains in open disregard of international standards on workers' rights to organize and take industrial action. (Smith and Morton, 2006: 414)

Reforming industrial relations to the advantage of trade unions and workers can be viewed either as a missed opportunity in terms of bringing trade unions into the 'mainstream', or as continuing the marginalisation of them as actors in labour markets and politics. The latter path seemed to have been chosen.

The coalition/Conservative government and the turn to further austerity

The attack on the safety net and its unequal impacts

The election of the coalition government in 2010 involved austerity plans that targeted the welfare state for significant cuts. (In this section, I cover policies and outcomes before the COVID-19 crisis. In Chapter 8, I include a brief postscript assessment on Conservative Government policy responses to the COVID-19 crisis with respect to employment rights and the social safety net.) Cuts to welfare benefits have been especially unprecedented:

> In his first budget in June 2010, then–chancellor George Osborne announced spending reductions of £32 billion a year by 2014/15, of which £21bn was to come from so-called 'welfare reform'. Social security was a prime target of austerity, and the government presented existing levels of spending as 'unaffordable' ... By 2020 we therefore expect £27 billion less spending on social security than a decade earlier, an unprecedented reduction in spending. (CPAG, 2017: 8–9)

Local government received a 49% cut between 2010 and 2018 (NAO, 2018: 4). The Centre for Cities in its survey comments:

> The period of austerity brought about by the financial crisis at the end of the last decade has not been equally shared out across government. ... it has been local government in

England that has borne the biggest burden, with its budget being cut by more than half between its peak in 2009/10 and 2015/16. (Centre for Cities, 2019: 13)

Furthermore, local government cuts have marked geographically uneven impacts with those areas where economic and social inequalities are at the greatest disproportionately impacted by the cuts (see Chapter 5).

The coalition and Conservative governments' approach to welfare is strikingly similar to that of NL. The Work Programme (WP) was the coalition government's flagship welfare-to-work programme aimed at assisting people who were long-term unemployed into employment (the WP will be phased out in 2020). The WP operated on a contracting and 'payment by results' model, similar to NL's Flexible New Deal, but was dogged by controversy because of its poor performance and failure to meet intended objectives. Unsurprisingly, as the WP operated on similar principles as NL work-first programmes, it was confronted by similar problems: underfunding and the lack of sustainable employment opportunities in deindustrialised areas (Etherington and Jones, 2016a). The WP has been phased out by the 2015 Conservative government and will be replaced by the new Work and Health Programme aimed at claimants on long-term sickness benefits. The demise of the WP is of no surprise because of its failure to deliver on targets but also because of the Conservative government's clear intention to scale down support services for benefit claimants. (Etherington and Daguerre, 2015; Welfare Conditionality Project, 2018a; 2018b).

A key stated aim of the coalition government in terms of its welfare reform was to 'simplify' the benefit system and create a model that would 'make work pay'. This thinking lies behind the design of Universal Credit (UC), which replaces the main means-tested benefits for those on low incomes in and out of work (Housing Benefit, Jobseeker's Allowance, Income Support, ESA, Tax Credits) with a single benefit paid to the 'head of the household'. UC works by creating one household allowance (called a personal allowance). One of the decisive policy shifts when compared with the NL regime has been to intensify the disciplinary aspects of work-first policies by stepping up the rate of sanctions and to impose a tougher claimant agreement (WPC, 2018a; Welfare Conditionality Project, 2018a).

In 2016, the DWP began rolling out the 'Full Service' – the final digital version of UC, available for all claimant groups – using a 'test and learn' approach. In 2018 the Conservative government undertook a 'managed migration' process so that people on legacy benefits had to apply for UC. The managed migration will involve around 3 million individuals in 2 million households over a four-year period (SSAC, 2018). The Full Service was to have been rolled out to every part of the UK by September 2018, but in autumn 2017, following emerging evidence of problems experienced by people moving onto UC, the government slowed the roll-out plans significantly for January–March 2018 while it introduced measures intended to ease the transition. As will be analysed in the next chapter, the halt in the roll-out stemmed from opposition and resistance from political parties (especially the Labour and Green Parties who are committed to the complete scrapping of UC in their manifestos), trade unions and welfare rights organisations. These included abolishing the seven-day waiting period and increasing the amount of the advance payment made at the start of a claim.

In 2019, Amber Rudd, then minister for Work and Pensions, paused the migration with the aim of piloting the UC in Harrogate in order to test its implementation and iron out its design faults. Trade unions, the Labour Party and welfare rights organisations have called for the complete scrapping of UC and the Work and Pensions Committee have recommended root and branch reforms. It is an understatement to say that UC is controversial, but its future lies with the government.

As highlighted earlier, the delay in the full implementation of UC is due to the way people have been migrated from their former legacy benefits. The Child Poverty Action Group (CPAG) has been forceful in developing the evidence base around the impact of financial changes and benefit delays, arguing that the initial waiting period creates difficulties for claimants (SSAC, 2018: 69). The delays have had a major impact on people with disabilities with the Disabilities Benefit Consortium (DBC) challenging its rationale:

> The rationale for the delay has been lost, in part because it never existed. Hiding behind administrative ease 'we need to know income before we can assess Universal Credit' is an outrageous cost shunt from the Treasury to low income households. The worst thing about this policy it is a one-off cost saving a working capital movement to low paid workers, similar to large corporations paying suppliers late. (Disability Benefits Consortium, 2018)

The DWP's own survey of UC claimants found that the claims process had adverse financial implications (DWP, 2018):

> Around three months into their claim, just over half (53 per cent) of those claiming UC were keeping up with bills and credit commitments, while 44 per cent were falling behind or experiencing real financial difficulties. By the time of the second interview, approximately eight to nine months into their claim, 57 per cent of claimants said they were keeping up with bills and credit commitments, while four in ten (40 per cent) were falling behind or experiencing real financial difficulties. (DWP, 2018: 16)

An indication of the intense disciplining aspect of coalition/Conservative government policy relates to two related policy changes. The first is the introduction of a tough claimant commitment involving the requirements imposed on benefit claimants in terms of job search, interview attendance and so on. The second policy change introduced by the coalition/Conservative government is stepping up the use of benefit sanctions (Etherington and Daguerre, 2015). Their use is unprecedented in their severity, comprising a lack of safeguards and difficulties presented to claimants to appeal. Many sanctions are linked to 'non-compliance' with the claimant agreement – around 40% found the agreement difficult to comply with (Webster, 2018). The rate of sanctions has increased under UC in comparison with JSA. In April 2018, around 7,000 individuals were newly sanctioned under the UC live service, compared to around 2,300 under JSA. This was equivalent to around 5% of all UC live service claimants and around 1% of all JSA claimants (WPC, 2018b: 17). A survey carried out for the Trussell Trust (an organisation which coordinates foodbank provision and campaigns around food poverty) found that there was an average increase of 52% in the 12 months after the roll-out date in the foodbank areas. Comparative analysis of random samples of foodbanks taken from 247 projects either not in full UC areas, or only in full roll-out areas for up to three months, showed an average increase of 13% (Trussell Trust, 2019).

The welfare changes are seen to represent an attack on workers' rights to a wage that guarantees minimum income standards. The TUC has reported that this is the weakest decade for pay growth in 200 years, with real wages declining on average by 0.4% a year, and £10 a week lower than before 2008 (TUC, 2018a). The reduction in the work allowance affects lone parents most, and it is estimated that it amounts to £3 billion less annually than the current tax credit system, resulting in an average loss of £625 a year (TUC, 2018b: 6). The Joseph Rowntree Foundation found that a single full-time income is no longer enough to lift families out of poverty (Joseph Rowntree Foundation, 2020). This is reinforced in Unison's submission to the Low Pay Commission which highlighted the numbers of workers experiencing in-work poverty. Close to one in five employees (19% or 5.1 million) are paid less than two-thirds of the median gross hourly earnings and close to one in four employees (23% or 6.2 million) are paid less than the living wage (Unison, 2018: 21).

While the welfare reform has impacted on low income individuals and families it is important to highlight its unequal impacts (see also Chapter 4). An assessment by the Women's Budget Group (WBG, 2018: 4) reveals that 'women will, by 2021–22, bear around 61% of the total annual 'fiscal consolidation' burden as a result of tax and benefit changes (and 75% of the changes since 2015). Women are hit harder than men at all income levels, and black and Asian women are hit hardest.' Disabled people, especially the most severest disabled, will experience the largest change in terms of loss of income (see Patrick, 2016), and Black and Minority Ethnic Households (BAME) will experience a loss of 5% income, double the amount experienced by white households (EHRC, 2018: 212, 220).

Devolving welfare and skills: institutional changes and geographical uneven development

Institutional change involved localism with a shift in responsibilities for labour market and skills policy to city-region actors through the creation of the Local Enterprise Partnerships (LEPs). The private sector would have a central role in shaping strategic economic development policy. The LEPs replaced the RDAs, with an emphasis on employer engagement; taking control of the skills agenda and market is a central plank of the LEP skills strategy, but with significantly fewer resource than RDAs (see Chapter 5). In late 2014, the flagship Northern Powerhouse initiative was announced, which was promoted as the vehicle to provide city regions with more powers to develop initiatives in their local areas, with a wider policy aim of re-balancing the economy and regenerating city economies, which for many years lagged in terms of growth and prosperity (Beel et al, 2018; see Chapter 5). The underlying principles of devolution growth policies are neoliberal in terms of a greater reliance on the private sector and the market to deliver growth supported by targeted infrastructure investment (Beel et al, 2016; Etherington and Jones, 2016a).

These policies were orientated towards agglomeration growth strategies, but there is an argument that the effect of these policies is to make labour markets more competitive and reinforce their contingent nature (see Chapter 4; Etherington and Jones, 2018). Workfare, because of its compulsion, removes any (supposed) barriers to employers obtaining a ready supply of labour. Groups who enter welfare-to-work and training programmes tend to be vulnerable and disadvantaged (Peck and Theodore, 2000). The work-first principle tends to give prominence to the first job offer and to the assumptions that work will be sustained and that there will be some sort of upward mobility. Additionally, workfare increases competition, or workfare churning, as a result of substitution, as subsidised employment is used to replace 'real' jobs. The direction of the unemployed towards low-paid work creates a crowding effect on the labour market, which puts even more downward pressure on wages in certain sectors. In essence, cities and regions deploy resources and coordinate interventions to enhance employability of excluded groups through education and work-based training, often linked into welfare-to-work programmes (Whitworth and Carter, 2014).

The other element of 'upskilling' strategies is the re-positioning of cities and regions by promoting themselves as knowledge economies or learning regions. This involves competitive marketing and place competition promoting inter-firm collaboration, niche industrial development, science parks and so on, often where further and higher education institutions are key players. As Hudson (2011) has previously pointed out, and an argument that is still highly and indeed increasingly pertinent, these strategies are highly constrained as they tend to be locked into rather than challenge the processes of spatial uneven development that shape labour market inequality and de-skilling.

Successive governments have demonstrably squeezed spending in relation to the regions (M. Jones, 2019). In the area of skills, the government has attempted to shift the focus on demand-side approaches and greater reliance on the private sector for funding. The shift towards decentralisation has placed more responsibility for skills on the local level via devolution strategies and the LEPs. A key reform is the Apprenticeship Levy, which involves 0.5% of a company's overall payroll with an offset of £15,000 (which means that employers will only make a levy payment if they have a payroll over £3 million). The anticipation is that the levy will increase the number of apprenticeship starts. The constraints on skills policies are outlined by Payne:

> The findings also lend support to studies suggesting that current approaches may be struggling to move beyond a

narrow skills-supply, target-led approach, with an agenda
focused on headline growth sectors, coupled with a growth-
first, work-first approach to tackling skills gaps and shortages
which leaves poor-quality employment unaddressed.
(Payne, 2018: 23)

In many respects, the problems which beset NL's skills policies were to
manifest themselves within the those of the coalition and Conservative
governments. In this case, austerity and budget cuts were to play a key
role. Ewart Keep has observed that the nature and intensity of cuts
(post-2013) has been such where the system reached the point when
the 'entire edifice of traditional skills policy started to look unstable
and probably unsustainable, particularly for provision beyond the
compulsory phase of initial schooling' (Keep, 2014: 6). This analysis is
corroborated by the Institute for Public Policy Research (IPPR), which
states that 'by 2020/21 adult skills funding will have been nearly cut
in half in real terms from 2010/11' (Dromey and McNeil, 2017: 17).

Local government has borne the brunt of austerity (see Gray and
Barford, 2018; Lowndes and Gardner, 2016). The geographically
uneven impact of spending cuts is a key feature of austerity, with
northern former industrial cities hit the hardest. On average northern
cities saw a cut of 20% to their spending, contrasting with a cut of
9% for cities in the East, South East and South West (excluding
London) (Centre for Cities, 2019: 16). The larger cities with higher
socioeconomic needs tend to depend more on grant funding.
However, the tenth of councils most dependent on grant funding
reduced spending on services by 31% between 2009–10 and 2016–
17, compared to 13% for the tenth of councils least dependent on
grant funding (Institute of Fiscal Studies, 2018: 6). Local government
is facing a financial crisis and as a recent study demonstrates their
services are crucial to mitigate the impact of cuts on the poorest groups
(Hastings et al, 2017: 2015).

Another area to be considered is funding on local welfare provision.
For 2013–14 and 2014–15 the DWP provided transitional grant
funding to 151 single-tier and county councils in England to deliver
new support in the form of local welfare provision for vulnerable
people, using existing powers. This new support was to be aligned with
other services councils provided, such as housing and social care. For
2015–16, the government included funding for local welfare provision
in councils' revenue support grant; this can be used to finance revenue
spending on any service (NAO, 2016). This funding was to be used
to respond to personal financial crisis, commonly due to economic

hardship such as unemployment, but increasingly as a result of the adverse impact of welfare reforms. The argument that austerity has impacted most on these services is illustrated by the NAO report on local government, which breaks down spending changes by service area.

With reference to local welfare assistance, the government had cut the crisis loans to the extent that spending in 2012–13 was 59% lower than in 2009–10. Both the NAO (2016) and the Centre for Responsible Credit (CfRC, 2017) had reported that a number of local authorities had underspent on their budgets. Devolving the budgets had worsened provision because of overall uncertainty of future funding:

> The decline in local welfare provision therefore serves as an example of what can go wrong when central government devolves responsibility and provides flexibility to local authorities whilst simultaneously holding back resources they need to develop effective provision. (CfRC, 2017: 40)

In effect the roll-out of UC, as described earlier, has generated further pressures on local authorities and local authority-funded services as more and more people fall through the safety net (see later in this chapter and Chapter 3).

Industrial relations and welfare reform: a further race to the bottom?

Drawing on the 'power resources' framework, Coderre-LaPalme and Greer (2018) provide a useful and insightful survey of industrial relations under both NL and the coalition/Conservative governments. They argue that the power resources of trade unions' organisation have been severely affected by the continued decline in trade union densities (proportion of workers who are members of a trade union). Workplaces where trade union organisation has traditionally been strong, such as the core manufacturing base of the UK economy, have disappeared or shrunk in size. However, organisation within the public sector is relatively strong and is where union densities are high, but this is now being severely challenged by the impact of austerity and public sector cuts.

The coalition government's agenda included a further attack on employment rights by halving the period of consultation with recognised trade unions in cases of mass redundancy from 90 days to 45 days, thereby reducing the ability for union reps to avoid job losses; abolition of Agricultural Wages Board; and an unsuccessful attempt to impose fees for Employment Tribunals. However, trade union organisation became a key target of the 2015 Conservative government through the implementation of the 2016 Trade Union Act. The most immediate effect of the Act is the requirement for a minimum of 50% of the membership to vote in any ballot for collective industrial action, and that a minimum of 40% of the entire membership should vote in favour. The government also has denied the right for trade unions to hold ballots electronically. The key aim of this legislation is to attack any mobilisation in the public sector – it is a case that Thatcher decimated union organisation in the private sector and the current government would 'finish the job off'.

The TUC has voiced strong concerns about these proposals, stating that the government definition of 'important public services' is wider than that of 'essential services' as used in international law, and that strikes continue to be an important tool of last resort for public sector unions. They also criticised the government for not allowing electronic voting in strike ballots, which they claim would increase turnout and make it easier for unions to reach these thresholds. These reforms are particularly important in the context of the high level of legal regulation of industrial action. Add to this the fact that the process of attaining recognition within the workplace requires negotiating many hurdles, including having to undertake a ballot process overseen by a Central Arbitration Committee (CAC). As Dromey observes, the impact has been for relatively few non-unionised work places achieving recognition:

> Between 2000, when the current recognition system was introduced, and 2018, there have been 1,041 'part one applications' from unions for recognition, of which 153 achieved recognition without a ballot and 247 proceeded to a ballot, with 156 approved and 91 rejected by the workforce. This represents just 17 incidences of unions achieving recognition through CAC per year. Unions seeking to secure collective agreements at the firm level often struggle to gain access to workers in order to secure sufficient density and to make the case for the agreement, and they often face efforts from employers to frustrate the process. (Dromey, 2018: 28)

Trade union pressure, along with some successful legal challenges to agency and zero-hours contracts and precarious work, led to the Taylor Review, a review of employment practices conducted by Matthew Taylor (Chief Executive, Royal Society of Arts). The review emphasised the importance of quality work – 'fair and decent work with realistic scope for development and fulfilment' – and makes detailed recommendations for the reform of UK employment law in respect of those who are not engaged as traditional employees, both in the 'gig economy' and elsewhere (Taylor et al, 2017). The review has been criticised as being a superficial treatment of the actual depth and complexity of insecure work, and weak on the processes that enable workers to bargain and negotiate better quality employment, and on how trade union rights and rights to representation can be strengthened (see Bales et al, 2017). In fact, the Taylor Review continues the voluntarist tradition of lack of legal enforcement of rights and framework for collective bargaining. Following this, the institutional power resource vested in collective bargaining has been severely weakened, especially in the private sector.

A number of studies, including Crouch, suggest that other factors come into play as 'unions' wider connections with egalitarian political parties and movements are more important than their immediate bargaining' (Crouch, 2018: 59). Thus, wider coalition building at the national level can have an important influence on public perceptions in addition to bringing new actors into bargaining and resistance. In terms of *societal* power, there is evidence that the trade union movement has devoted considerable resources to campaigns against austerity. This has involved organising significantly large demonstrations as well as conducting a number of campaigns around areas that austerity has impacted on, for example, 'Britain Needs a Pay Rise' by the TUC and member unions developed as a response to low pay and the attack on living standards, and other campaigns have highlighted the rise of insecure work (see Chapter 6). The election of Jeremy Corbyn as leader of the Labour Party, not wholly endorsed by the majority of trade unions, has galvanised these campaigns and the anti-austerity movement, strengthening trade union links with the Labour Party (see Chapters 4 and 8).

This forms an important backdrop to more direct engagements with the welfare reform agenda which is explored in more detail in the next chapter. The use of discursive and campaigning resources by the TUC and individual trade unions against the welfare reforms has been relatively effective:

> The TUC's Saving our Safety Net campaign focused on cuts and reforms to benefits and the introduction of the controversial universal credit system. It also wishes to dispute

the increased use by Jobcentres of sanctions, the removal
of a person's benefit payment for weeks or sometime for
years. A survey by the PCS union showed that 23 per cent
of those working in Jobcentres had an explicit target for
sanction referrals and that 81 per cent had an 'expectation'
level. Ministers and the Department for Work and Pensions
denied that such targets existed. (Coderre-LaPalme and
Greer, 2018: 272)

The reform to child tax credit limiting it to two children has had
major implications for workers in the public sector and motivated
trade unions to campaign to abandon the policy (Unison, 2019b).
Furthermore, the TUC and individual trade unions have made
submissions to parliamentary scrutiny bodies such as the Work and
Pensions Select Committee, the Social Security Advisory Committee
and the All-party Parliamentary Committee (APPG) in relation to
welfare reform.

Individual trade unions have been engaging and negotiating the
impact of UC within the workplace. Work-first policies become
clearly defined as a policy tool to ensure that precarious jobs are
filled by claimants as a way of sustaining the new financialised
business model of outsourcing and fragmentation. The removal and
downgrading of employment rights and processes, which facilitate
employee representation in negotiating workplace employment
conditions, is key to facilitating this process. In this way workfare
plays a role in moulding and reinforcing the capital/labour relationship,
which underpins employer control. Thus, claimants' and workers'
rights are more closely linked and inter-related. CPAG, along with
the retail trade union USDAW, found that most members moving on
to Universal Credit were worse off: 'Only one out of 25 respondents
said they were better off on UC and nearly half reported being worse
off. The biggest losses were borne by families with children, with one
couple reporting a loss of £250 a month and a single parent losing
as much as £320' (M. Jones, 2019). Furthermore, it appears that UC
awards are even less clear to USDAW members: in December 2018,
over half of survey respondents said they did not understand their UC
awards, perhaps reflecting the extra complications of working and
claiming UC (M. Jones, 2019).

Developing closer links with the community and welfare claimants
by trade unions has been brought about through the campaigns by
Unite Community against the welfare reforms. In 2011, the Unite
trade union opened to non-workers and formed Unite Community.

This has spawned a number of nationally-based actions over sanctions and more recently in its campaign Scrap Universal Credit. These national campaigns have involved joint actions between trade unions, especially PCS and community organisations such as Disabled Peoples Against the Cuts (DPAC), Boycott Workfare, and local communities and coalitions. This will be explored in more detail in the next chapter.

The TUC, via Unionlearn, is promoting a demand-led skills policy and developing a skills agenda which includes bargaining for skills and the role of the union learning representatives in engaging with low-skilled workers as part of their wider aims and agenda around progression in work. This is seen as a crucial part of the trade union role in promoting sustainable work (see Chapter 4).

Conclusions: new challenges to austerity?

This chapter has attempted to provide a context for the book by charting welfare and industrial/employment relations changes from NL to the current (2015–2020) Conservative government. While there is a decisive shift and a step-change in policies under the Conservative government – the extent of the cuts, the widespread use of benefit sanctions and the more draconian policies with respect to industrial relations and restricting trade unions – there are continuities. The continuities lie in the fact that NL, and large sections of the Labour Party, adhered to the neoliberal politics of Blair until Jeremy Corbyn was elected as leader under an 'anti-austerity' programme in 2015.

The coalition government inherited and, in many ways, implemented many aspects of the 2009 Welfare Reform Act which the TUC, cited earlier in this chapter, had considered draconian. Welfare claimants and the dispossessed have become easy targets in terms of what Tracy Shildrick (2018) has termed poverty propaganda. Taken together, policies of benefit delays, a tough claimant agreement and widespread use of benefit sanctions represent an appalling abuse of human dignity and rights to a decent standard of life. This has been embedded in policy and day-to-day discourse to such an extent that it has created obstacles to the development of progressive alternatives. It is a powerful weapon in enforcing discipline. Under NL, in spite of the changes to benefits which were an improvement on those under the previous Thatcher government, they were set at a low level, reinforcing their residual nature. In this way reliance on benefits under the previous regime risked poverty as it does today under the current regime. Comparing the two government regimes, NL constantly undermined benefits as social security, while the current government is almost at the point of doing away with them altogether.

The other important means by which austerity neoliberalism is being implemented is through industrial relations legislation. The 2016 Trade Union Act is particularly targeted at the trade unions in the public sector, which is bearing the brunt of austerity. As I have discussed, many trade unions have developed strategies to resist austerity through campaigns and day-to-day in the workplace. The defence of welfare and social services have major implications for those who are struggling within the welfare-to-work system. As already highlighted, the trade unions are becoming increasingly engaged in resisting the current welfare reforms and promoting alternatives to UC. However, the current situation raises questions about trade union cultures and organising strategies with respect to marginalised groups and communities.

A final comment and link to the next chapter is the development of a new politics within the Labour Party led by the election of Jeremy Corbyn (see also Chapter 8). The catalyst to the rise of a left anti-austerity movement was the 2015 Welfare Reform Act; sections of the Labour Party seemed to say 'enough is enough' to the equivalent of a 'war of attrition' against the working class, the poor and disenfranchised. The election of Corbyn (at two attempts because of opposition within his own party) involved setting out an 'ambitious' programme of repealing trade union legislation with a framework for employment rights and coordinated collective bargaining, nationalisations of infrastructure industries, Green New Deal, tax and spend reforms, scrapping UC and establishing a more socially just welfare system which were included in the 2017 and 2019 election manifestos. The electoral defeat of the Corbyn-led Labour Party in December 2019 raises a number of questions regarding how austerity policies can be challenged, and the communication and popularisation of alternative politics not just by the Labour Party but by the wider labour and trade union movement. This will be the focus of discussion in the remaining chapters.

Resisting welfare reforms and work-first policies

The blockade of Oxford Circus with wheelchairs tied together with chain on 28 January demonstrated the readiness for civil disobedience – along with the ability to grab headlines. Andy Greene, a member of DPAC's national steering committee, explains that the action came about as the Welfare Reform Bill was going through parliament and was high on the agenda of both DPAC and their partners-in-protest UK Uncut. He says: 'It kick-started consciousness more than anything ... It showed we had the power within the movement to reignite the militant actions that hadn't been seen since the late eighties and early nineties'. (Stephensen, 2012)

It is time for women to get active in their unions, to recognise that the unions belong to them and to use the strength of the union movement to push agendas on women's issues from abortion rights in Northern Ireland to the gender pay gap across the UK. In modern trade unions, the equality structures are already there, intersectionality is recognised, and the political influence is already there. A senior trade unionist in the TUC, Becky Wright, said: 'When I was 19, I was asked if I'd thought about joining a union. I wasn't entirely sure what that meant. They said, "Do you want to learn how to be a campaigner?" And I thought, "Yes I do"'. We are trade unionists because we want change so we should use every tool in the armoury to achieve it. (Mullaly, 2018)

Introduction

The rise of the anti-austerity movement and the 'left turn' in the Labour Party reflected in the election of Jeremy Corbyn as leader was given impetus by the Labour Party's response to the Welfare Reform Bill in 2015, which more or less divided the party. Forty-eight Labour

MPs defied the party whip and voted against the Bill although the rest either voted with the government or abstained, on the advice of Harriet Harman (Wintour, 2015). This represented a significant sea change in the politics of welfare in the Labour Party. Only two years earlier, Rachel Reeves, the shadow work and pensions secretary under Ed Miliband (former party leader), claimed that benefits would be tougher under Labour 'long-term unemployed would not be able to "linger on benefits" for long periods but would have to take up a guaranteed job offer or lose their state support' (Helm, 2013). The election of Sir Kier Starmer in April 2020 with Rachel Reeves in the Shadow Cabinet possibly represents a shift to the Right or Centre Ground within the Party. Most of the current Shadow Cabinet were involved in publicly opposing Corbyn before and during the last election so there are questions about how he will deal with the growing tensions around this, the current COVID-19 crisis, recession and the grass roots in the Party who are still adhering to an anti-austerity agenda (see also Chapter 8).

The purpose of this chapter is to analyse in more detail how the reforms are being challenged and negotiated by trade unions and welfare rights organisations. In spite of the heavy electoral defeat of the Corbyn led Labour Party in 2019, all the leadership contenders committed to the scrapping of Universal Credit (UC) and most positioned themselves on a broad 'anti-austerity' platform. The question is how this anti-austerity pledge relates to the day-to-day struggles of trade unions and social movements. As described in Chapter 2, trade unions and social movements are responding to the crisis by adopting new strategies (and exploiting power resources) as a way of resisting neoliberalism. The chapter analyses the resistance and opposition to the implementation of welfare reforms and UC policies. For example, UC in-work conditionality puts into critical focus the way austerity and cuts to personal support and skills funding have placed considerable barriers for low-paid workers to progress in work. The welfare reforms have disproportionately impacted on women, disabled people, and BAME groups. This chapter attempts to capture the critical voices and the strategies from the women's and disability movement. The chapter concludes with a discussion and assessment of how these struggles impact on policy and the relative strengths and weaknesses of strategies deployed.

Assessment periods and workers claiming UC: Child Poverty Action Group work with USDAW

Child Poverty Action Group (CPAG) has been working with USDAW, a major trade union which represents retail workers (a predominantly low-paying sector). This collaboration has been around advising shop stewards and representatives in responding to UC. For example, a union survey found that most members moving on to UC were worse off. 'Only one out of 25 respondents said they were better off on UC and nearly half reported being worse off. The biggest losses were borne by families with children, with one couple reporting a loss of £250 a month and a single parent losing as much as £320' (K-M. Jones, 2019). It appears that UC awards are even less clear to USDAW members. In December 2018, over half of survey respondents said they did not understand their UC awards, perhaps reflecting the extra complications of working and claiming UC (K-M. Jones, 2019).

This is related to the operation of Real Time Information. Assessment periods run for a calendar month, starting from the date on which UC was awarded (so they are different for each claimant). Each month, claimants' circumstances and income are assessed to determine their entitlement to UC, with payment made a week later in arrears. This system is intended to 'mirror the world of work', although in reality more than half of people moving on to UC from work were in fact coming from jobs where they were paid weekly or fortnightly. In other words, the payment situation is designed on an employment model that does not exist in many workplaces – particularly in those where UC claims will be more common such as where zero hours, part time and generally insecure work predominate.

CPAG (2018b) has highlighted some key problems which will adversely impact on workers:

- For these people, a monthly UC payment which adjusts to monthly earnings makes little sense, as they inevitably have some months with more paydays in than others, leading to variability in their UC income when there has been no change in their earnings.
- The majority of couple families have two earners, meaning that each partner receives an income in their own name. These payments may be received on different days of the month or on different payment schedules, further complicating the picture of how much pay UC records.
- Even for people on monthly pay it is not the case that payments are necessarily made on the same date every month. Some are paid on the last working day of the month or the last Friday of the month. Some are paid early at Christmas and most are paid early when the regular payday falls on a weekend or bank holiday. If, due to an unfortunate collision of paydays and UC assessment period dates, this means being paid twice in some assessment periods and not at all in others.

The design of the system can mean some workers lose out as people find themselves with hugely variable UC awards even when their underlying earnings have not changed – they simply appear higher in some months than others due to the design of the UC system. CPAG, along with a host of other organisations, argues for a

> fundamental rethink of the strict system of monthly assessment of earnings would be sensible. For some claimants, weekly assessment would be more suitable, while for others (e.g. the self-employed with lumpy earnings and costs across a year), longer assessment periods might be more suitable. The current system is not fit either for people on non-monthly pay cycles or for those self-employed people whose costs and earnings are not evenly spread throughout the year, such as farmers. (CPAG, 2018a: 17)

Trade unions responding to in-work conditionality

Barriers to in-work progression: the employment support and skills gap

The welfare reform agenda has involved compelling UC claimants to progress in work in terms of earnings and hours: this will eventually involve approximately 1 million people. Conditionality requirements depend on earnings and whether wages are over the earnings threshold, usually 35 hours at the minimum wage. This has potentially major implications for people in low-paid and insecure work and is a major shift in welfare policy in terms focus to conditionality for low-paid workers.

In-work conditionality, as noted by Gingerbread, the organisation which advocates for lone parents, is focused more on disciplining people rather than providing the required employment support to enable progression in work (Rabindrakumar, 2018; Clery et al, 2020).

Citizens Advice observed that the Department for Work and Pensions (DWP) evidence on the viability of the policy is questionable:

> ... the DWP have conducted an initial study into the effects of in-work conditionality regimes in UC. This found that people who were subject to some form of in work conditionality increased the number of hours they spent working after one year. However, the independent review found no statistically significant difference in earnings between those in the 'minimal support group' (for whom all work search actions were voluntary) and those in the

'moderate' and 'frequent' support group (who had mandatory work search requirements). (Citizens Advice, 2018: 5)

A survey of trade union members by USDAW found that

> Complying with the UC claim conditions can be an ordeal as well. Respondents to the USDAW survey were all employed. Nonetheless, nearly two thirds reported being subject to conditionality – meaning that they had to follow certain instructions to avoid incurring a sanction (a reduction in their entitlement that can last for a period between 7 days and 3 years). One respondent reported being told to find work when they were off sick. Another, who worked full-time but only had a 16 hour a week contract (topping up their earnings with overtime), was told that they had to attend Jobcentre appointments and keep looking for a job with more contracted hours, in addition to working their full-time job. (K-M. Jones, 2019)

The CPAG has undertaken collaborative work with USDAW highlighting the oppressive nature of in-work conditionality for workers (see K-M. Jones, 2019).

The Social Security Advisory Committee (SSAC, 2017) review of in-work progression found that there are several challenges to overcome to achieve this. Childcare commitments and shortfalls in and the expense of provision play a major role in preventing people (parents of young children and lone parents) from being able to access the labour market. The SSAC also pointed out that employers often do not offer the flexibility to facilitate work–life balance for families with young children; it is usually women who are disadvantaged. Furthermore, employers were also antagonistic to a conditionality regime which placed the onus on workers to ask for more hours:

> One large employer in the retail sector told us that they would be concerned if the Department was adopting a high frequency/high intensity regime. They also felt that it would be unheard of if, as a general rule, their employees were pressurized into asking for more hours as their job design was driven by the nature of the business… (SSAC, 2017: 31)

Research on welfare conditionality led by the University of York found that the policy is a means of disciplining workers as UC claimants were subject to demanding and in most cases unrealistic and demanding job search requirements and 'surveillance' (Welfare Conditionality Project, 2018a). In the submission to the SSAC review of benefit migration, the TUC (2019) highlighted that one of the key barriers to in-work progression is the lack of skills support for workers.

> The available evidence also shows that UC claimants will be less likely to benefit from training opportunities in the workplace because low-waged workers face the most barriers on this front. The result is a system where large numbers of low-skilled workers have little opportunity to build up their skills and escape low pay. (TUC, 2019: 9)

The apprenticeships policy has been seen as a vehicle for aiding workplace skills attainment for disadvantaged groups but, according to Unison (2018), low pay rates for apprenticeship participants threatens its sustainability. Pay is not the only issue. Gingerbread's survey of lone parents in terms of opportunities/barriers to accessing apprenticeships found that the system does not work for lone parents (Dewar and Clery, 2019a). A number of issues were raised in the report. First, it noted a lack of hours flexibility in terms of marrying caring and work. For example, there were few apprenticeships (one in ten) offered with fewer than 30 hours' work a week. Pay was another factor: pay rates are often so low that it is not viable for lone parents. The corollary of this is that the costs of apprenticeships also affect their viability for lone parents. The report cites a survey of the Young Women's Trust which 'found that 43% of young people reported that the costs of doing an apprenticeship, such as travel to work, buying clothes or the cost of childcare, were higher than their earnings, rising to 60% among those who are parents' (Dewar and Clery, 2019b: 9).

In its submission to the government in relation to in-work conditionality, the TUC exposes the weaknesses of the skills policies and funding which will support in-work progression (TUC, 2019). The TUC argues that the Unionlearn model (established under New Labour, see Chapter 3) is seen as relevant to supporting in-work progression. All major trade unions use the Union Learning Fund to promote workplace skills and bargaining.

Unionlearn and bargaining for skills

Unionlearn staff represent the TUC on various skills bodies, including the Strategic Transport Apprenticeship Taskforce; the Institute for Apprenticeship's stakeholder panel; Movement to Work; the Department for Education's (DfE) Apprenticeship stakeholder board; the DfE's Apprenticeship equality and diversity advisory group; the Skills for Londoners Business Partnership; and CEDEFOP (EU skills research body) (TUC and Unionlearn, 2019).

The TUC argues that the Unionlearn Rep (ULR) model is relevant to addressing the issues of low pay and skills including promoting social dialogue, forging learning partnerships within targeted firms and workplaces at the regional level. The Collective Learning Fund, for example, provides funds to promote work-based learning and learning agreements with targeted workplaces. Unionlearn has promoted community learning centres in areas of deprivation and ULRs, who are sponsored by individual unions as well as Unionlearn, provide one-to-one services for workers experiencing disadvantage, assisting them to access education and learning.

An equally important priority has been to build the capacity of all union reps to provide direct support to apprentices and other youth trainees in the workplace. Unionlearn is formulating and promoting TUC policies on apprenticeships, including standards relating to their delivery through the apprenticeship charter. This has brought about agreements within city regions such as one between West Midlands TUC and West Midlands Combined Authority.[1] This work has involved the production of a range of guidance and briefings for unions in the context of the new funding and regulatory arrangements that have come into place since the introduction of the apprenticeship levy in 2017. In addition, there has been a strong focus on addressing equality and diversity issues so that unions can play a lead role in widening participation in apprenticeships and pre-apprenticeship programmes to specific groups facing significant barriers (TUC and Unionlearn, 2019).

Unionlearn also contributed to the policy debate on apprenticeships by submitting evidence to the government's review of the levy, calling for a number of flexibilities to boost the numbers of high-quality apprenticeships accessible to all. At the beginning of 2019, the TUC and Unionlearn organised a roundtable of senior employers and union officials, under the auspices of the Public Services Forum, to discuss the challenges and opportunities for public sector apprenticeships. This includes a national retraining scheme that is being developed by the government in partnership with the TUC and CBI. However, in order to address the extensive barriers to training and development facing British workers, the TUC is calling for an expanded national retraining scheme that would be linked to a number of associated developments, including a new lifelong learning account open to all adults; a right to a mid-life skills/career review; and a reform of the right to request time to train so that it is changed to a new strengthened entitlement to paid time off for education and training (TUC, 2019).

Public and Commercial Services Union campaign against cuts to Jobcentre Plus services

Similar to other policies there are questions about whether in-work progression is achievable or whether it represents another weapon to control and oppress workers and claimants. The capacity to monitor and provide the means of progressing low-paid workers is affected by the job cuts in the civil service overall, and specifically in the DWP. In the timescale for migration across to UC there will be a significant number of new UC claims, and 'by the end of UC rollout, work coach caseloads are expected to increase significantly – from 85 claimants per work coach to 373 in 2024. For service centre staff, caseloads will increase from 154 claimants per case manager to 919' (TUC, 2018a: 5).

The emergence of the Public and Commercial Services Union (PCS) as a proactive trade union under New Labour, as described in Chapter 3, has been an important aspect of trade union engagement with the welfare reform agenda. The coalition and Conservative governments since 2010 have implemented cutbacks to employment services, including jobcentre closures. Throughout 2019, PCS held a series of one-day strikes as part of its campaign against the increased pressures on staffing. This campaign has followed previous concerns over the reorganisation of the employment services within the DWP.

> Our members working in Universal Credit Service Centres constantly report problems with backlogs of work and the number of telephone calls that result from this. The issues are similar for both UC Live and UC Full Service, with no discernible difference for Full Service. Although DWP's anticipation is that customers accessing Full Service will use alternative methods of communication in order to interact with DWP about their claims, there has been no significant reduction in the number of people using telephony as their main means of contact. The DWP has been forced to concede that UC applicants are required to arrange an initial appointment over the phone. (PCS, 2017a: 3)

The closure of jobcentres is directly linked to the DWP looking to reduce the size of its estate by around 20%, and to increase co-location of Jobcentre Plus offices with other local services such as local authority benefit teams and mental health services. This 20% reduction is part of a wider plan to sell £4.5 billion worth of government land and property by 2020–21 (House of Commons Library, 2017). The government has digitised the service with the stated aims that 90% of new claims will be made online.

> The roll out of Universal Credit and our reforms of Jobcentre Plus have increased the number of interactions claimants now have with us online. As a result, we only need 80% of the space we currently occupy to continue to deliver our services and make sure that people will always be able to access the support they need to get back to work. Moreover, we are recruiting and expect to have 2,500 more Work Coaches in post by March 2018 compared to today. (House of Commons Library, 2017: 3)

The PCS campaign included strike action (in 2019) in response to the closures. The union arguments against closures are (see PCS, 2017b):

- Staff will face job losses, and in some cases, unreasonable travel journeys to and from work. Those with caring responsibilities, childcare commitments and access requirements will be particularly disadvantaged. Staff losses are coming at a time when UC is being rolled out, hampered by delays, IT failures and backlogs. DWP could redeploy staff to UC where resources are needed.
- The government has not consulted claimants who use these jobcentres on the closure plans. Many are in areas of high unemployment and social deprivation. Disability claimants, staff/users with caring responsibilities and vulnerable users must be given due regard in terms of the equality impact assessment and the disadvantage that they will face if offices close or are relocated. Having to travel because of these proposals also means some users are unfairly out of pocket and run the risk of being sanctioned for lateness.
- The ministerial criteria for the proximity of a jobcentre to claimants is that they must be two to three miles' distance or 20 minutes by public transport from the old to the new site. One striking criticism is that some of the journeys have been assessed as appropriate using Google Maps. This has meant bus routes have been considered

which no longer exist. Consideration of factors such as traffic and accessibility for users with disabilities and vulnerable users has been inadequate.

• The closure of 'back office' locations represents a significant qualitative change in the service as many of the staff have considerable experience of dealing with legacy benefits. Redundancy and redeployment involve an overall reduction in the service and as UC roll-out involves an increase in volume of claimants, many with complex needs, and this will add to increasing workloads for existing staff.

Gender discourses and campaigns around Universal Credit and welfare cuts

Universal Credit and financial abuse

For some time, the Women's Budget Group (WBG), along with lone-parent organisations (see Rabindrakumar, 2017), has highlighted how austerity disproportionately impacts on women and the roll-out of UC has presented significant challenges for women (WBG, 2018). The 'male breadwinner' model is designed into UC as benefits are paid only into one bank account rather than having the facility to split between two partners' accounts. This can impact on financial independence: it hands control to the person who controls the account and, for instance, increases the vulnerability of women in an abusive relationship if their partner has control of the receipt of the benefit. This vulnerability is exposed by the fact that if one partner does not sign the claimant commitment then the whole application is invalidated (see Miller and Bennett, 2017: 177). Women's groups campaigning around domestic violence have highlighted financial abuse as one aspect of domestic violence occurring within the context of controlling and coercive behaviour: 'It may also mean a higher risk of financial abuse, and greater difficulty for women to have access to money to meet their own and their children's needs and to leave abusive relationships' (WBG, 2017: 2).

A TUC-commissioned study carried out by Women's Aid on the impact of UC on financial abuse (Howard and Skipp, 2019) highlighted that a high proportion of women in UC claimant households had experienced financial abuse.

> Survey respondents made similar comments about what a split payment could mean in practice. Most concerns were

that the abuse could worsen when their partner found out, and that it could lead to more arguments about money; or that the partner would simply take the money back anyway or ask DWP to reverse their decision. Even asking for a split payment could put survivors at risk. (Howard and Skipp, 2019: 47)

Two-child tax credit limits

Parents applying for UC will only get help for the first two children. It is estimated that including the impact of other changes since 2010, families with three or more children will be more than £5,000 a year worse off, on average, by 2021–22 (End Child Poverty and the Church of England, 2018). The two-child tax credit limit has been the focus of a major campaign by all the welfare organisations, including Unison, who have promoted a petition to parliament arguing against the two-child tax credit because of its impact in terms of increasing vulnerability to poverty (see also Unison, 2019b).

Lone parents

Since the New Labour government, lone parents have been subject to increased benefit conditionality. Key advocacy and representative organisations for lone parents have voiced concern about the impact of austerity and a harsher claimant regime. Currently, single parents make up approximately one in six of all claiming households, with 112,000 single-parent families on UC. This is a major claimant population and it is mainly women who are heads of lone-parent households. Single parents were the household type worst affected by the 2010–15 coalition government's programme of welfare reform.

Under the new system post-2017, full job-seeking activities will now also apply to single parents (and the main carers in couples) with children aged three and four – before they reach school age. One of the key issues raised by rights organisations is that the welfare system while imposing stricter conditionality on lone parents does not facilitate work and family commitments. The pressure to take any job available can mean more insecure, rather than sustainable, work and limited gains in living standards as a result. Single parents are more likely than the average employee to be trapped in low-paid work.

Targeted support for lone-parent families has fallen away in recent years, with an increased use of the blunt tool of benefit cuts to encourage employment. Rather than encouraging single parents to work, this approach leaves many single parents facing financial penalties from which they cannot escape. Single parents have the highest poverty rate among working-age households. Given the ongoing financial strain faced by many single-parent families, there are questions as to the practicality and legitimacy of withholding or suspending benefit payments. Research suggests these policies increase families' vulnerability and risk of debt rather than moving them to a more secure financial footing (see Gingerbread, 2018).

Childcare

The tapering of UC at 63% for net income (above the level of the work allowance where relevant) reduces the incentive for second earners to enter paid employment, or to work more hours in relation to the tax credit system. In many couples the first earner will have used up the work allowance in relation to their own wages already. Lone parents and second earners on the minimum wage (who are generally women) are particularly disadvantaged by working over 30 hours a week as it translates into lower disposable income compared with working fewer hours, since the childcare allowance and the pay received will not be enough to cover the tapering of UC, the tax that has to be paid on the income, and childcare costs.

The changes to childcare financial arrangements will severely impact on women and families with young children. For the cover of childcare costs, the movement to UC represents a significant reduction in financial support. The Children's Society (2017) estimates that the movement from benefits combined with tax credit to UC represents a significant cut in subsidy. Added to this is the way conditionality has been tightened for parents of children: parents of three- and four-year-olds are expected to be available for and actively seeking work, and parents of two-year-olds are required to attend work-focused interviews, with a work preparation requirement, while parents of one-year-olds are required to attend work-focused interviews (WBG, 2017: 4). Furthermore, the move to child tax credit for a maximum of two children has a significant impact on family incomes. In all these above cases, it will be women who will be negatively affected as they tend to manage budgets and have responsibility for childcare.

Equality and Human Rights Assessments

An example of partnership working between trade unions and civil society organisation is the commissioning by the TUC of Coventry

Women's Voices (CWV) in 2011 for the development of an anti-cuts toolkit, based on the campaigns organised locally by Coventry Women Voices which led to the production of a report, *Unravelling Equality* (see TUC, 2011a). The toolkit is an Equality and Human Rights Assessment (HREIA) which uses the provisions in the 2010 Equality Act requiring public bodies to undertake a Public Sector Equality Impact Assessment (EIA) of policies. The design of the EIA enables campaign groups to carry out their own HREIA as a way of challenging what can be perceived as decisions that undermine equality principles. It is a mobilising tool which can bring together and unify different campaign and pressure groups as a way of challenging austerity.

Since its publication, *Unravelling Equality* has had a huge impact. CWV members have used the findings of the report, and the media interest it generated, in order to lobby locally and nationally on behalf of themselves and the communities they serve. CWV has been asked for the first time to speak at meetings of all councillors, the Coventry Partnership and the Coventry Trades Council. Several CWV member organisations have used the evidence provided by the report to support applications for funding from public bodies and trust funders. The report has generated much local and national media coverage and has been used by MPs to highlight the work and the impact of the cuts (including a parliamentary seminar in partnership with the Fawcett Society).

Unite Community holiday hunger and grass roots campaigns

Unite Community, in conjunction with DPAC, foodbanks and other community organisations organised a national day of action against UC on 1 August 2019, timed to coincide with the start of the school holidays. The day involved a wide range of campaigning activities in towns and cities throughout the UK. While the campaign embraces all disadvantaged groups experiencing hardship from claiming UC, it has a particular resonance for women and parents of children. The actions involve collecting food for foodbanks and providing information about how UC works. The Unite survey found that more than four-fifths (79%) of parents in a survey of over 1,000 UC claimants said they found it hard to make ends meet during the school holidays. Many had been put into debt, forced to rely on foodbanks or the help of friends and family (Unite Community, 2019).

The growth of 'grass roots' struggles around welfare reform in London has been given impetus by the London Unemployed Strategies (LUS), which has been active in providing welfare rights on similar lines to the claimant unions of the 1970s. The LUS, working closely with Unite Community, provides leaflets and advice about representation, claiming and challenging decisions. An example of the way the LUS has developed is the formation of Waltham Forest Stand Up for Your Rights (WFSUFYR) which has progressed in less than two years to becoming an autonomous body with a combination of alternating open group and steering group sessions, meetings with the jobcentre management via the steering group's DWP liaison officer, and now its own funding from Trust for London.

Another example is the work of Derbyshire Unemployed Workers Centres (DUWC). DUWC is an advice organisation set up with the support of Chesterfield Trades Union Council in 1983. It is supported by Chesterfield Borough Council, North East Derbyshire District Council and Bolsover District Council as well as many town and parish councils. The organisation receives over 10,000 enquiries per year and represents hundreds of people at benefits appeal tribunals. In 2018 the DUWC undertook its own survey of a survey of 100 UC claimants in Chesterfield in June/July 2018 regarding their experience of the claims process. This is part of the campaign to make more people aware of UC, attract claimants to the activities of Unite Community in the area and to inform DUWC policies regarding welfare rights. One of the key findings of the survey, which comprised a submission to the SSAC, was the high proportion of individuals and households moving into debt because of the combination of delays in benefits payments, problems associated with the digitisation of claims and the deployment of sanctions (Etherington and Hampton, 2018).

Disabled people and the struggle for equal rights

Disabled people facing benefit cuts

The migration process from the old Incapacity Benefit regime to Employment Support Allowance (ESA) and then on to UC represents a significant loss of benefit income for people with disabilities and underscores how austerity is so key to the design of the welfare reforms. The Work and Pensions Committee summed up the evidence on the managed migration process (of over 1 million ESA claimants) move onto UC:

> Amongst them will be some of the most vulnerable claimants the Department supports: people who have been on benefits for long time, have little in the way of a safety

net, and have severe disabilities and health conditions. The Department says that it will safeguard claimants moving from ESA to Universal Credit. But it has provided next to no detail on how it will deliver those safeguards and ensure no one's benefits are stopped before they have made a successful claim for Universal Credit. (WPC, 2018a: 13)

The Work and Pensions Committee states that changes

to disability benefit top ups – the 'disability premia' – under Universal Credit are amongst the most complex differences between Universal Credit and the system it replaces. And they are also one of the areas where disabled people could find themselves with lower levels of benefit under Universal Credit than under legacy. (WPC, 2018a: 20)

Work Capability Assessment (WCA)

Since its introduction in 2009 by the NL government, the WCA has been a controversial and highly-contested policy. There is considerable dissatisfaction with the WCA, which is reflected in the number of appeals against WCA decisions. According to Disability Rights UK in its submission to the Work and Pensions Select Committee (a parliamentary watchdog, or scrutiny committee), 160,000 successful appeals were made for new ESA claims between October 2008 and September 2013 although the true figure is considerably higher – some 567,000 successful appeals (Disability Rights UK, 2014: 1–2).

The mandatory reconsideration process is designed to increase the proportion of disputes resolved without an appeal. If the claimant disagrees with a decision, they have to write to ask for a reconsideration of the decision before being allowed to lodge an appeal. Prior to 2012, any appeals were always referred back to the decision maker, but this was done informally, without the need for the claimant to formally ask for a reconsideration of the decision. Currently there are no time limits for the decision maker to issue reconsideration, but the claimant has one month to ask for a mandatory reconsideration. In fact, the main rationale for the reform is to reduce the volume of successful appeals around ESA.

The government commissioned five independent reviews of the WCA, and criticism has also come from some unlikely quarters. The Employment Related Services Association (ERSA), which represents Work Programme providers, suggested that a 'significant' number of people who were referred to the Work Programme have had an inaccurate assessment. 'One member estimated that 25 per cent of referrals were inaccurate; although many of these would not go on to appeal the WCA decision.' (ERSA, 2014: 3) Neither the WCA nor the government's evidence reviews recognise the impact of employer discrimination or reluctance to make even basic adjustments to work in order to accommodate people with health barriers.

Disability employment and pay gap

Disability Rights UK highlights the inherent injustices that are built into the employment and welfare system – one rule for one group and a different set of rules applied to employers. For example:

> … disabled people are over 60 times more likely than employers to face sanctions for noncompliance with requirements. In 2015–16, disabled people were sanctioned 69,570 times for missing appointments or infringing work-related conditions of benefit payment, with resulting reductions in benefit. Employers in the same year were in effect 'sanctioned' only around 1,100 times when disability discrimination cases were either settled or won by a disabled person at Employment Tribunal. (Sayce, 2018: 9)

The TUC, along with other organisations such as Disabled People Against the Cuts (DPAC) and Disability Rights UK, have campaigned the employment and pay gaps (TUC, 2018c; Sayce, 2018). For example, 49.2% of disabled people between the age of 16 and 64 are in employment. In the same quarter (Q2, 2017) the employment rate for people without disabilities was 80.6%, giving a disability employment gap of 31.4 percentage points (TUC, 2018c: 3). The pay gap is compounded by the fact that disabled people earn less per hour on average than a non-disabled person. Furthermore, there is a higher proportion of disabled people working in part-time jobs and they are over-represented within certain occupational groups: in administrative and secretarial occupations; in elementary occupations; in caring, leisure and other service occupations; and in sales and customer service occupations (TUC, 2018c: 7).

Campaign against Work Capability Assessment

The disability rights movement has been vociferous in its campaigns against the conditionality rules for disabled people as well as the benefit cuts, and as John Pring points out 'the birth of the disabled peoples' anti-cuts movement can be traced back to the austerity protests held outside the Conservative Party conference in Birmingham in 2010. Disabled activists wore t-shirts warning that 'cuts kill' (Pring, 2017: 54–5). This led to the formation of DPAC, which has focused on campaigning around the impact of austerity on disabled people. DPAC has been joined by trade unions, including Unite Community, in its campaigns. Launching its campaign against cuts affecting people with disabilities, the TUC called on other trade unions to give priority to the impact of the cuts and welfare reforms:

> Unions need to understand the multiple impacts of the cuts on this community and to ensure both that these attacks on disabled people are challenged by unions, and that trade union campaigns reach out to, and link, with campaigns led by disabled people. (TUC, 2011b: 2)

A focus of the campaigning has been around the Work Capability Assessment putting together evidence of the experiences of disabled people in relation to the WCA process. This has been stepped up to highlight the number of deaths that could be attributed to the WCA process. Since 2010 DPAC and other rights organisations have worked in collaboration with Unite Community (and in London, this also includes LUS) on a series of days of action around demands to scrap UC.[2]

DPAC and Inclusion London (2017) made representation to the UN Committee on the Rights of Persons with Disabilities (CRPD) inquiry into the impact of the UK government's policies on the rights of disabled people. The UN report, widely reported by the press, states that welfare reforms violate human rights of disabled people, and that the WCA plays an important role (DPAC and Inclusion London, 2017). The Work and Pensions Select Committee stated that the 'flaws in the existing ESA system are so grave that simply "rebranding" the WCA by taking on a new provider will not solve the problems: a fundamental redesign of the ESA end-to-end process is required, including its outcomes, and the descriptors used in the WCA' (WPC, 2014: 8).

The DPAC and Inclusion London (2017) report makes the recommendation that the WCA, which is based on the discredited bio-psycho-social model of disability must be replaced with an assessment based on a social model of disability. This is an important focus as it shifts the attention away from medical definitions of disability on to the wider structural causes of disadvantage.

TUC disability campaign strategy

The response by the trade unions and welfare coalitions has been to focus on both the impact of welfare changes and employment relations. In 2011 the TUC launched its Disabled People Fighting the Cuts strategy, followed by its Disability Employment Strategy, with respect to people with mental illness, in 2015 (TUC, 2011b, 2015a); this was followed up with its promotion of reasonable adjustments campaign (TUC, 2015b), and then a report highlighting the extent of the disability employment gap (TUC, 2018c). These are summarised in Box 4.1.

Box 4.1: TUC campaigning for disabled people – Some key demands

Unions in the workplace
This involves defending disabled members: making use of legal rights such as using the Public Sector Equality Duty (PSED). Demands should be made on the government to restore genuine commitment to the PSED.

Unions in the community
Trade unions should be involved with organising inclusive campaigns involving disabled people around the slogan 'nothing about us without us' which entails mobilising disabled people within and outside the workplace developing the following actions:

- The TUC supports a key principle of the disability movement, 'nothing about us without us', in preference to those claiming to speak on their behalf.
- Where the union has a local disabled members' structure, ensuring their involvement may encourage their participation across the union. Where the union does not have such structures, actively promoting inclusive anti-cuts activity may spark disabled members' involvement.
- When organising local activities, the TUC recommends actively seeking support from disabled people by facilitating their participation.
- Many disabled people may not be able to take part in traditional protest activities, because of the barriers preventing them getting there. In response, disabled people have begun to devise alternative ways of registering their voices, using electronic communication to make their views known. Unions need to consider how to harness the possibilities of modern communications technology to include people who cannot be physically present.

Highlighting and campaigning against the disability employment gap
TUC proposes statutory requirement for employers to report on their disability pay gaps and employment rates, which must be accompanied by targeted action plans identifying the steps employers will take to address any identified gaps.

Promoting reasonable adjustments
Negotiating in the workplace adjustments agreed between worker and manager to support them at work because of a health condition. Agreements are used as a tool by union reps to negotiate adjustments and can be transferred to other work situations without a new agreement. This is referred to as passported policy.

Work capability assessments and employment support
The government should create a new, fairer assessment to replace the WCA altogether and ensure it becomes better integrated with employment support programmes. A specialist employment support scheme that is responsive to the unique needs of people seeking work who have a range of mental health impairments should be created.

Source: TUC (2011b, pp 8–9), TUC (2015a, pp 44–47), TUC and GMB (2019, pp 8–10)

Trade unions promoting reasonable adjustments in the workplace

Unsurprisingly, the trade unions have focused on workplace issues and the campaign around reasonable adjustments is significant in this respect. All employers have a duty under the 2010 Equality Act to make adjustments in the workplace to remove, prevent or reduce disadvantage. The public sector has additional duties to assess how its policies impact on disabled people and other groups. A survey of trade union reps found that over half of the reps had case work concerned with negotiating on behalf of disabled people and one in ten disabled workers had to leave their employment compared with one in twenty non-disabled people. The reasonable adjustment disability passport is an agreement between the trade union/the employee and management around adjustments that are required to remove barriers to equality in the workplace (see TUC and GMB, 2019).

The GMB trade union put a motion to the TUC congress in 2018 for the passport to be implemented and used by trade unions and employers. The design of the passport was undertaken by the TUC Disabled Workers Committee and the GMB. The passport applies to workers who change jobs or where there is new management, and it avoids making a new agreement. The passport is constantly subject to review and adjustment.

Discussion and conclusions: resisting labour discipline and building new solidarities?

A consequence of the Conservative and previous coalition reforms is a shift towards a residual model of welfare where primacy is given to family, voluntary (especially the foodbanks) and market-based services and benefits that are actually well below subsistence level. The cumulative impact of the reforms corresponds to a recasting of the British welfare state, with an erosion in terms of substantive social rights, both through statutes, regulations and policy implementation. As Philip Alston, the UN Rapporteur investigating poverty in the UK, states

> Universal Credit and the other far-reaching changes to the role of government in supporting people in distress are almost always 'sold' as being part of an unavoidable program of fiscal 'austerity', needed to save the country from bankruptcy. In fact, however, the reforms have almost certainly cost the country far more than their proponents will admit. (Alston, 2018: 5)

However, I consider that this process is not just about denying social rights, it is also about restricting the agency of welfare claimants. Thus, as Umney et al (2017: 343) claim, work-first policies are 'disciplinary since they aim to increase the threat of unemployment ... putting downward pressure on wages ..., thus rendering workers insecure'. This has been a long-term trend since the 1970s as a consequence of work-first policies and the maintenance of benefits at a low level. Conditionality and discipline were the core of thinking around welfare under NL.

> James Purnell declared in February 2008 that 'for the small number of people who refuse to take up the opportunities available, we will be looking at how we can develop a strict sanctions regime, including either cuts in benefits or an option of permanent work for benefits ... if you can work you should work, and that will be a condition of getting benefits'. (Daguerre and Etherington, 2014: 29)

Even under opposition, until recently, this attitude has dominated Labour Party thinking as illustrated by the comments by Rachel Reeves earlier, and also some party MPs during the debate around the Welfare Reform Bill in 2015.

Brexit has shaped the social and political landscape in such a way that has led to the intensification of social divisions including hate crime based on race, gender and disability – culminating in the Windrush scandal with the government's illegal deportation of immigrants from the West Indies. In Tracy Shildick's analysis of 'poverty propaganda', the demonisation of benefit claimants and the stereotyping of claimants in the media (for example, the television series *Benefit Street*) can be linked to this:

> What all these discourse produce is a problem-focused analysis, whereby social problems such as unemployment become problems that can be explained by the behaviour of those experiencing the problem and the structural causes of poverty can be conveniently removed from view. These issues are then reworked in popular and political discourses, perpetuating the view that that those experiencing poverty are undeserving of support and culpable of their own situations. Periodic announcements from powerful senior political figures frequently refer to the welfare state as purely meaning out-of-work benefits and depict the system as 'broken' or 'failing' and responsible for producing generations of 'work shy' families. (Shildrick, 2018: 24)

This has relevance in our theoretical understanding of the nature of the current welfare struggles that have been described in this chapter. Traditionally there has been a lack of engagement by the trade unions with unemployed and welfare reform, which can be viewed as reflecting their focus on insiders and their traditional membership. This may be partly to do with survival strategies as a result of concerted attacks by successive Conservative governments, weakness in the nature of social dialogue and the marginalisation of trade unions within the wider political process (weakening their institutional power resources) which remained under NL. Traditional values dictating what trade unions should prioritise have also contributed to the previous low-level commitment by the trade unions to supporting claimants and to campaign to reform benefits. It can also be argued that this is a result of elements of conservativism within trade union hierarchies and leaderships (see Holgate, 2018).

Nonetheless, the analysis in this chapter shows that the trade unions are a growing force and actors within the politics of welfare. Kevin Rowan and Carl Roper from the TUC commented that unions can learn from community organisations, 'but all too often the representatives of community orientated campaign groups and organisations display an ignorance of what unions are and have achieved whenever they speak of us and even to us' (Rowan and Roper, 2013: 4). Examples shown earlier of struggles against UC highlight the way this is being contested and negotiated by a variety of social forces ranging from trade unions and state workers to welfare rights organisations. In many respects the account suggests how the roll-out of UC is failing to 'close off' the state to political contestation. Kennett and Dukelow (2018: 457) comment 'while shifts towards the radical right might be seen as one outcome of discontent with the current situation, the crisis has also generated new grassroots mobilisations on the left against neoliberalism, evident in anti-austerity protests'. As highlighted in Chapter 2, drawing on John Kelly's work on class and social mobilisation, a sense of injustice felt by various groups has motivated organisations to voice and articulate their opposition to regressive welfare policies.

The case examples illustrate the common agendas between trade unions and welfare/community movements. There is a close relationship between workplace bargaining and the defence of social protection as shown in the work of the TUC and member trade unions on sickness and disability issues. There is much discussion on the male-dominated and paternalistic cultures that dominate trade unions, but a number of feminist scholars have highlighted how trade unions are themselves a terrain of struggle for gender equality and women's involvement in the workplace. At the same time, this work does reveal the importance of the way trade unions are key in the struggle and campaigns around the impact of austerity and workplace insecurity on women such as through the TUC Equality Impact Audits (Healy and Bergfeld, 2013). Welfare organisations have also promoted links with trade unions; for example, CPAG, as part of its early warning system, is developing work with USDAW in responding to the impact of UC within workplaces. DPAC has had a major role in influencing the Unite policy to scrap UC. Unite Community has built up a campaign against UC involving days of action mobilising welfare claimants, welfare rights organisations and trade unions with aim of scrapping Universal Credit.[3] In October/ November 2018 and in 2019 the trade union undertook its own national online survey finding that over three-quarters of respondents were in debt or pushed into debt due to UC.[4]

5

'Devolving' welfare policies in Greater Manchester's precarious economy

> Broadly, the approach to public service provision continues to be one of outsourcing the delivery of services to private contractors, sometimes with the use of payment-by-results mechanisms, such as in the working well employment support scheme. In employment support, this is a requirement of the devolution deals, and there is therefore little space for change. Research into outsourcing has demonstrated that this risks both waste and inefficiency, and increases the influence of corporate interests over politics. (NEF, 2017: 15)

Introduction

The inception of a Mayoral Combined Authority, following a number of stages of deal-making, has seen Greater Manchester's 'Devo-Manc' in the vanguard of recent English devolution debates (Greater Manchester comprises the local authorities of Manchester, Bolton, Bury, Salford, Trafford, Stockport, Wigan, Oldham, Rochdale and Tameside). The devolution agreements relate to economic growth and the management/coordination of health, social care and welfare (Hincks et al, 2017). This chapter will focus on the restructuring of the economy and employment relations, and how this is linked with the way welfare and local government policies are being configured by austerity within the city region. The true problems and crisis of Universal Credit (UC) and how they impact on employment relations are only fully grasped by understanding the process of roll-out in regions, localities and devolved settings.

Some scholars have focused on how austerity involves the 'downloading' of expenditure cuts on to cities, giving rise to fiscal crises and retrenchment reinforcing labour market insecurity (see Hastings et al, 2017; Pike et al, 2018). This critical engagement and focus are extended in this chapter to include an investigation of how social and institutional actors exercise agency within cities in terms of contestation and negotiation (Meegan et al, 2014). Attention is drawn to the role of trade unions, which still have a voice within the growth agendas, particularly in terms of the increasingly precarious nature of the economy. The focus of the chapter is also on the way local authorities operate as regulatory intermediaries (and sites of social reproduction), adapting, responding and reacting to austerity crisis. In this respect, local authorities will devise various strategies to protect the poor and disadvantaged groups who tend to depend on local authority services (see Donald et al, 2014; Fuller, 2018).

The next section provides an analysis of the implementation of welfare reform in the context of devolution in Greater Manchester (GM) and how this reinforces social inequalities and poverty. One of the key contradictions of austerity is how it undermines neoliberal objectives for a free market supply of labour. This is illustrated in the increasingly unstable nature of the labour market because of the rise in precarious work. The chapter then focuses on the role of actors, exploring the way they negotiate and contest austerity politics.

The Greater Manchester city region deal, austerity and uneven development

As highlighted in Chapters 2 and 3, during the 1980s the Thatcher government's neoliberalism had two major impacts. The first was that the politics of redistribution was replaced by the politics of the market where private interests were accorded prominence in terms of access to and as beneficiaries of urban policy. The second, related, impact was the shift in representational structures that increasingly marginalised the role of local government and the electoral democratic process, challenging traditional models of accountability in public services. The underlying principles of this model of devolution and localism under the post-2010 landscape are for a greater reliance on local governance and the private sector and the market to deliver growth supported by targeted infrastructure investment. Based on the application of agglomeration theories, and 'trickle down' economics, there is an assumption that growth and employment from such investment will benefit everybody (see M. Jones, 2019). Much of the devolution debate, though, has been focused on North American-inspired agglomeration models of economic 'growth', with pressing questions now being asked about what the nature of local and regional development is, and who is it for. In relation to this, devolved authorities have greater scope to design their own labour market policies and welfare-to-work strategies. These interventions are now emerging at a time when the government is undertaking major restructuring of welfare.

The devolution settlement, under the leadership of the GM Labour mayor, Andy Burnham, includes major infrastructure, planning, housing, health and social, welfare and employment investment initiatives. In the area of employment and social inclusion, the Greater Manchester Combined Authority (GMCA) has piloted a health and employment programme, Working Well, and is intending to draw the lessons from this by rolling out a work and health programme as the devolved welfare-to-work programme. Developed in 2017, the Working Well programme was designed to support people in addressing their barriers to work and moving into employment. It comprised a pilot phase, a subsequent expansion and then a third phase (in 2018). The pilot was co-designed between the GMCA, central government and the DWP to test whether a locally developed and delivered model of welfare-to-work could deliver better outcomes for Greater Manchester residents with multiple barriers to work in comparison to nationally-commissioned programmes such as the Work Programme.

The Working Well expansion programme was commissioned across the GM area. Referrals to the programme opened in April 2016, and were extended to the end of 2017 to allow up to 20,000 people to be offered support by the programme and ensure that there was no gap between the Working Well programme and the introduction of the Work and Health Programme, which started in early 2018. The Work and Health Programme is commissioned nationally by the DWP in regional contract package areas, as with the Work Programme. However, as part of the devolution agreement, GM is a distinct contract package area and the programme has been jointly designed based on the learning from the Working Well programmes. It will run from March 2018 to 2024 and will allow around 22,500 disadvantaged people to be supported to address their barriers to work. The main point of this work and health experiment seems to be about delivering a different model of support absent from the UC regime, although there can be referrals from UC to the Work and Health Programme (see Manchester City Council, 2018; also later in this chapter). But the key point to emphasise is that while operating on different principles to the Work Programme, now being phased out, it is also extremely small-scale in comparison.

NHS England and the national Work and Health Unit are looking to test new and improved ways of supporting disabled people and those with long-term health conditions into appropriate work, seeking to work with a small number of areas to trial new services, undertaking robust evaluations that will inform future service provisions. This will involve investing £40 million over four years. Another organisational change of significance is that, since June 2016, the two Jobcentre Plus districts have been brought together under a single management structure to match the GMCA footprint and better support spatial alignment between Jobcentre Plus direct delivery and DWP-commissioned programmes with GMCA structures and services.

The financial context of devolution is crucial to understand in terms of the impact of austerity on the GM region., The National Audit Office (NAO) reports that, in England, over the five-year period 2010–11 to 2014–15 the government will have spent £6.2 billion on local growth programmes, including that spent via Regional Development Agencies (RDAs) and their legacy, and on new funds and structures. By comparison, the RDAs spent £11.2 billion over the preceding five-year period (2005–06 to 2009–10). It is not possible to calculate the spending on welfare and other labour market policies in devolved English city regions except to state that the UK also devotes significantly lower resources as a proportion of GDP on active labour market policies compared with most other countries in the EU (Etherington and Jones, 2017). More specifically, during the period where localism and then devolution were being promoted, funding programmes seen as essential to support economic growth and labour market attachment were being cut:

- The adult skills budget has been subject to repeated cuts since 2010. Between 2010 and 2014, funding fell by approximately 35% and by 2020–21 adult skills funding will have been almost halved in real terms when compared to 2010–11.
- Spending on specialist support under the new Work and Health Programme has a projected budget of £130 million representing a cut of more than 80% from the Work Programme and Work Choice alone (Etherington and Jones, 2017).

Devolution 'growth' strategies place an emphasis on the importance of the role of the private sector in terms of policy delivery (contracting out, outsourcing and so on) and where the contribution of the public sector to achieving economic growth is marginalised. The Greater Manchester Public Sector Reform process (GMPSR), for instance, is about renewing public services based on responding to reducing the levels spending (GMCA, 2013). There may be improvements and innovations arising from this process, but the GMPSR is a strategy of managing the cuts imposed by the centre. Similarly, the area-based reviews (ABRs) relating to the further education sector, which devolved authorities have to manage, involve a rationalisation based on major cuts in further education funding. Government guidance on the review process, included in a parliamentary briefing on post-16 area-based reviews, states that the ABRs need to be undertaken with consideration to funding limitations and wider policies to tackle the deficit (House of Commons Library, 2018).

With respect to health, devolution is also more about delegation rather than actual real local control with the *commensurate* resources to meet needs of GM (IPPR, 2016). The financial deals associated with devolution bear no relation to the deeply embedded structural problems of the deindustrialised cities, nor does it take account of the funding lost by the transitions from RDAs to Local Enterprise Partnerships (NAO, 2013).

From welfare to increasing low pay and labour market insecurity

It is important, then, to situate the discussion on welfare reform, its impact and unfolding contradictions and tensions in the context of more unstable and insecure city region labour markets and employment relations. Following the arguments of Beatty and Fothergill (2016), it was in the early 1980s that the economic shocks to regional economies were traumatic in terms of job losses and unemployment. GM had a large manufacturing base and in 1959, the manufacturing industry employed over half of the GM workforce; today, it accounts for less than one in five jobs. The de-industrialisation of the latter 20th century hit the regional economy hard, as it did in much of the UK's industrial north. Some parts of the city were particularly affected: East Manchester, a former centre for heavy engineering and chemicals, experienced 24,000 job losses between 1974 and 1984 alone. This growth has been driven by the service sector, in particular, financial and professional services which account for one in six of all jobs, approximately 20% of gross value added (GVA) and almost half of GVA growth in the decade leading up to the onset of the recession. The manufacturing industry contracted by 37.6% over the period (1974–84), reflecting the wider structural shift in the economy from manufacturing centre to service economy. Manufacturing activities remain an important employer, though, providing 10.3% of jobs (Hunt, 2012).

The GM economy and city region need to be seen directly in relation to the subordination of peripheral and deindustrialised regions of the Midlands and the North. This 'subordination' is shaped by their respective role in the spatial divisions of labour of production as explained in Chapter 2 (Massey, 1984). Thus London and the South East are dominated by and driven economically by headquarter functions, R&D and financial, business and producer services while the peripheral deindustrialised regions which have lost thousands of jobs in their core industries have been restructured largely based on services and branch plant activity. The GVA and growth trajectories of London significantly outstrip the rest of the UK, particularly the northern regions and large parts of Wales and Scotland (M. Jones, 2019).

> Against this background ... [there] will always be a large GVA gap against London because the capital city has political and economic opportunities for claiming revenue and sustaining employment that are denied to a second city ... Greater Manchester's failure to pull away from other core cities is sobering and the persistent inequalities between the central city and the northern boroughs, and within Manchester City itself, are deeply troubling. Worse still, as we will argue, these relativities persist not because nothing has changed but because the political classes have sponsored a rebuilding which is embedding these inequalities. (Folkman et al, 2016)

Fast-forward to the 2008 recession: this had a major impact on economic growth in GM, which had not recovered from the 1980s. Economic development has largely been centred on a restructured and more flexible labour market with employment growth based on insecure work and low pay. The dominant trend in GM, as highlighted by the Resolution Foundation (D'Arcy et al, 2019), is a distinct squeeze in wages and living standards for a significant proportion of the population.

Pike et al (2017b) provide some empirical analysis of some of the embedded precarious and unstable nature of the regional economies. In their study for the Joseph Rowntree Foundation, they tackle the question of how many more and better jobs need to be created to address the demand deficiency in the major industrial cities. They categorise the labour market in terms of the 'more jobs gap' and 'better jobs gap'. The more jobs gap comprises those people who are unemployed, inactive people who want to work, and underemployed workers who would like more hours, such as people working part time. The better jobs gap incorporates those on low-paid work, and those jobs classed as insecure, such as temporary contracts when workers have a preference for a permanent employment contract. Table 5.1 provides an analysis of the breakdown, which is a stark admission to the scale of economic disadvantage and to the long-term impacts of de-industrialisation that underline the failure and inadequacy of supply side policies.

Critically, de-industrialisation entailed the restructuring of capital–labour and class relations; the majority of jobs lost were in unionised workplaces and where replacement jobs tended to be low-paid, insecure, where trade union influence in terms of representation and bargaining was weak. This process of restructuring has a major influence in driving precarious work and economies. As Rubery (2015a) emphasises, before this period the UK comparatively had weak employee rights and bargaining, but the combination of trade union resistance and social norms practised by most employers towards the treatment of workers shaped labour market practices. Following the Thatcher government employment reforms of the 1980s, these 'norms' were broken along with the bargaining power of trade unions (and the rationalisation of employment stimulated by the economic crisis and public sector cuts) giving rise to more unstable working and career patterns (Rubery, 2015a: 637).

The rise in low pay, in-work poverty, precarious and insecure work has hollowed out the deindustrialised economies of England's North and Midlands (more on this in the next chapter). This is especially the case of GM, where people in the welfare system are pushed into sectors and workplaces with low levels of trade unionisation and where insecure work (temporary employment, zero hours contracts) predominate. This can be illustrated with an overview of employment and income trends in Manchester (see Table 5.1). The number of people in GM who earned less than the low-pay threshold (defined as two-thirds of national median income, or £7.74 an hour in 2014) has increased to 233,500 in 2014 (Greater Manchester New Economy, 2016). Furthermore, the chances of progressing out of low pay are limited. According to one key source:

> Most people who were low paid at the start of our period of study were low paid at the end. Our findings are in line with others that suggest that in many low wage labour markets, there is very limited scope for progression to better paid work. There appear to be substantial numbers cycling in and out of low paid work as they change jobs. Yet a relatively small minority show a clear sense of moving up out of low pay. (Greater Manchester New Economy, 2016: 68)

Table 5.1: Employment gaps in Greater Manchester

	Better jobs gap (%)	(000')	Earning < living wage (%)	More jobs gap (%)	(000')	Unemployed (%)	Under-employed (%)	Inactive wanting work (%)
Manchester	20	292	19	25	357	7	12	7
Sheffield	19	185	18	25	248	7	13	7
Cardiff	18	140	17	27	204	7	13	8
Liverpool	18	140	17	25	192	8	11	8
Newcastle	21	154	19	24	182	7	11	8
Bristol	15	92	14	21	126	6	12	5
London	14	677	13	23	1,127	6	12	6

Source: Adapted from Pike et al (2017a: 7)

Insecure and low-paid work can be linked to the process of 'de-unionisation' in the region, with people within the welfare system being vulnerable to exploitation. Trade union density (proportion of workers who are members of a trade union) is 26% in GM, slightly higher than the England average of 23%. Collective bargaining coverage at 30% is also slightly higher than England average of 27.9% (EWRC, 2017: 12). These figures show that most workers in GM are either not members of or do not have access to trade unions. Furthermore, and an important factor in the bargaining equation, these are workplaces where trade unions have difficulties in accessing in terms of recognition (EWRC, 2017; see Chapter 6).

> For trade unions and civil society organisations, the proliferation of insecure jobs has caused a diminishing in the social and economic status of individuals. The more that employers depend on insecure employment forms and contractual forms of work that reduce entitlement to employment rights and social protection the greater the risk that segments of the more vulnerable workforce (whether due to age, disability, or limited education for example) are rendered 'invisible' and both the worker and their work become marginalised in the city … For their part, unions are playing a clear role in promoting core rights to which all workers should be entitled to such as sick pay, holiday pay and the chance to contribute to a pension scheme. (EWRC, 2017: 8)

GM is an important site for the implementation of work-first policies, and because of the role of conditionality and compulsion, the policies remove any (supposed) barriers to employers obtaining a ready supply of labour. Groups who enter welfare-to-work and training programmes tend to be vulnerable and disadvantaged (Peck and Theodore, 2000). Edward Yates's study of the labour market in respect to young people in GM provides an interesting and insightful view on these dynamics of low-pay and welfare policies (Yates, 2017). He argues that young people are a source of cheap labour and various policy instruments such as training and welfare only reinforce their exclusion and marginalisation. With respect to training, there has been a trend towards a shift from training without jobs towards education without jobs as the increasing number of graduates are competing for low-paid jobs (see IPPR, 2017). Apprenticeship programmes, the majority of which offered in GM tend to be run by low-paying employers who offer below minimum wage rates, are of poor quality and undercut wages. The other factor that shapes the labour market transitions of young people is the discriminatory practices of the welfare system where young people are denied access to benefits, transferring the costs of social reproduction from the state on to young people and households:

> But since 2010 the dominant form which labour market interventions towards young people have taken are coercive and disciplinary. Young people have experienced removal of state welfare such as housing benefit and have been targeted by punitive active labour market policies such as the 'Work Programme' and 'Youth Obligation'; these schemes force young people to engage in compulsory training or work placements or have their already diminished welfare payments completely removed entirely. (Yates, 2017: 475)

Yates acknowledges that this trend has been shaped by the absence of trade unions and enforcement of employment rights (only a small percentage of young people are members of trade unions) in workplaces in which the majority of young people regularly move between work and welfare. In GM, the lack of resources to support people of all age groups to retain their jobs with continued in-work support (as discussed in Chapter 4) is seen as a reason for many disadvantaged groups returning to the benefit system. The impact of cuts to benefits and social support, including vocational training, underpins and shapes this trend towards poverty and exclusion. I will discuss this impact in more detail in the next section.

Implementing welfare reform and the reduction in social protection

Welfare cuts and social disadvantage in Greater Manchester

In the early period of Incapacity Benefit migration to ESA (2010–12) a relatively high proportion of claimants were being found 'fit to work' even though many of these decisions have been challenged as being incorrect (Greater Manchester Law Centre, 2017). One of the consequences of incorrect assessments is the relatively high proportion of sickness benefit claimants vulnerable to benefit sanctions. However, the migration to UC from legacy benefits (see Chapter 3) has been observed by the authorities to have major negative implications for people's incomes and wellbeing (see SSAC, 2018). According to the GMCA (2018: 10) the migration numbers are significant in terms of the roll-out in GM – involving 198,500 out-of-work benefits (ESA, JSA), Tax Credits (211,000) and housing benefit claimants (207,600). The GMCA has emphasised the complex nature of the migration process and challenges in estimating the impacts. Furthermore, the GMCA has not been able to quantify the impacts except that there is a proportionally greater increase in the use of Trussell Trust foodbanks in the city region (19%) compared with the North West Region (13%). Also, the GMCA has through reference to national assessments identified the various 'threats' from UC in terms reduction in incomes and vulnerability to financial hardship (GMCA, 2018: 5).

To sum up, benefit cuts hits the GM area disproportionately as there are large numbers of out-of-work benefit claimants and those who are in low-paid work claiming tax credits (Beatty and Fothergill, 2017: 8). As Table 5.1 shows, the benefit freeze has significant financial consequences for families and individuals in the GMCA. Similarly, the GMCA and New Economy (2015) have highlighted the way the welfare reforms will have differential negative impacts in the GM local authorities related to the incidence and concentrations of deprivation. Manchester City Council has summarised these impacts:

> The personal impacts of welfare reform cannot be quantified but there will be detrimental impacts on individuals and families affected by reforms. These will include impacts on mental and physical health, particularly for those who are already in receipt of benefits such as DLA or ESA and are at risk of losing their entitlement; and those being forced to move house and leave established communities and family and social networks. There may also be negative impacts as a result of wider reforms, which could cause an increase in food poverty and fuel poverty. (Manchester City Council, 2016: 18)

The cuts to welfare spending including tax credits taken together will push more families and individuals into deeper poverty. In another assessment, Manchester City Council states:

> The combined and cumulative impact of these welfare reforms alongside the introduction of UC is difficult to monitor due to its complexity and the fact that individuals will have very different experiences based on their

circumstances. However, evidence suggests that vulnerable residents in particular, who have barriers to employment could be at risk of greater poverty and housing instability. (Manchester City Council, 2017: 7)

The cuts to welfare spending including tax credits will push more families and individuals into deeper poverty. In another assessment Manchester City Council states:

> The combined and cumulative impact of these welfare reforms alongside the introduction of UC is difficult to monitor due to its complexity and the fact that individuals will have very different experiences based on their circumstances. However, evidence suggests that vulnerable residents in particular, who have barriers to employment could be at risk of greater poverty and housing instability. (Manchester City Council, 2017: 7)

The council, in its response to the migration process to UC, mirrors the criticisms made by the GMCA:

> Evidence shows some households in England are being pushed into more precarious circumstances as result of the cumulative impact of welfare reform, and this is felt most severely among vulnerable households. Forty % were experiencing difficulties keeping up with bills eight months into their claim and over a third were experiencing housing payment arrears. Consequences of waiting for their first payment pushed many into debt, rent arrears and serious hardship, including going without food and utilities. However, few were offered alternative payment arrangements. Non-judgemental individually tailored advice and support by DWP staff was appreciated where this occurred, but this was not always apparent. (Manchester City Council, 2019: 10–11)

As the new system involves cuts in social support this is leading to the undermining of benefits or social security as a safety net. Table 5.2 draws on data collated by Beatty and Fothergill (2016) on the financial implications of welfare changes. The table focuses on estimated changes to key benefits, including ESA, UC, Benefit Cap Extension and Benefit Freeze, which together amount to significant cuts in

Table 5.2: Estimated total income loss via post-2015 benefit changes in Greater Manchester

	Employment Support Allowance (£)	Universal Credit cuts (£)	Benefit freeze (£)	Total loss pre- and post-2015 reforms per working age adult (£ per year until 2020)
Manchester	20	102	134	870
Salford	26	98	127	870
Trafford	51	71	81	590
Stockport	67	83	95	660
Tameside	72	107	129	880
Bolton	81	115	133	870
Wigan	94	94	109	770
Bury	52	98	113	770
Oldham	76	128	144	970
Rochdale	76	118	134	980

Source: Beatty and Fothergill (2016)

income for claimants. The final column refers to the accumulated loss in income from the post-2015 reforms and the implications of financial changes for working-age adults.

Graham Whitham's study of local welfare support illustrates how austerity has impacted on the capacity to respond to increasing impoverishment and destitution when he points out that the funds for local crisis support have taken a significant cut:

> Spending on crisis support in 2017/18 was £3.8 million. This is over £15 million lower than spending under Crisis Loan and Community Care Grant provision in 2010/11. The number of successful applications for support through local schemes in Greater Manchester was just over 10k in 2017/18 compared to 123k Community Care Grants and Crisis Loan awards made in 2010/11. (Whitham, 2018: 13)

Furthermore, the Health and Work Programme which is aimed at assisting those who are 'furthest away' from the labour market, will be smaller and more focused than the Work Programme and Work Choice (formerly the major welfare-to-work programmes that are, in 2019, being wound up). Both programmes comprised a combined expenditure of £540.8 million in 2015–16 (£416.4 million Work Programme; £124.4 million Work Choice). This compares with the £130 million allocated for specialist employment support. Thus, the new welfare-to-work system places more emphasis on the jobcentres and work coaches for signposting unemployed people into work with less funding available for personalised support and to assist people with long-term health conditions (Etherington and Jones, 2017). This said, the success of this programme has been questioned by Disability Rights UK, which, drawing on DWP released figures, claims that (on a national basis) nine out of ten disabled people do not access sustainable jobs, underlining the limitations of work-first policies that are focused on improving people's 'employability' (see Disability Rights UK, 2019). In GM, the job outcomes are expected to be 'modest' (Manchester City Council, 2018).

Universal Credit displacing austerity on to local authorities

UC has major impacts across the board on a variety of services delivered by local authorities. The Joseph Rowntree Foundation has made a detailed assessment of the impact and cost of cuts on local government, which in its case studies highlights the crucial role local authorities play in the growth agenda, as well providing essential support to disadvantaged groups (Hastings et al, 2017). Gray and Barford (2018) argue that there are profound geographical impacts of local authority cuts, with those in the more deindustrialised and disadvantaged regions where local authorities are more reliant on central government experiencing more disproportionate cuts. For example, as a result of cumulative reductions of funding from central government, Manchester City Council, the largest economy and source of employment within the city region, had to deliver a massive £339 million of savings between 2011–12 and 2016–17, with a further £14 million saving required in 2017–18 (Manchester City Council, 2018: 26). Despite these cuts and retrenchment, local authorities are, in terms of 'their duty of care', having to manage the impact of the UC migration process. Table 5.3 outlines some of the analysis of the roll-out of UC in Manchester, which reveals the extent to which local authorities are required to absorb the cuts and delays in benefit payments.

The city council sums up the impact of UC on the city council services thus:

> Research identified the risk of welfare reforms pushing additional unmet costs on to local authorities and partners including voluntary and community sector (VCS) organisations, as they manage both the administrative and

Table 5.3: Summary of impact of Universal Credit on Manchester City Council

Policy and service delivery	Actual and potential impact and local authority response
Delays in benefit payment, benefit cap	The city council's Welfare Provision Scheme (WPS) provides support for vulnerable residents. As at the end of December 2017, WPS had seen an increase in spend of almost £50,000 when compared to the same point in 2017 and an increase in applications by more than 500.
Alternative payments system	At present only DWP and registered housing providers can apply for an Alternative Payment Arrangements (APA) on behalf of a claimant. It is possible that some vulnerable clients will fall through the system, such as private sector tenants who do not disclose problems to their jobcentre work coach.
Housing and rent management	The loss of a private rented tenancy has recently become the prime reason for people being owed a statutory homelessness duty in Manchester. Figures for the first three quarters of 2018–19, since the Homelessness Reduction Act came into force, show that a total of 5,846 households presented as homeless, a 24% increase compared with the same period in the previous year. In the same period, 2,991 statutory homeless applications were taken, a 34% increase when compared with the same three quarters in the previous financial year. In recent years, there has been a significant increase in the number of households approaching the council for a homeless service because they have lost their private rented sector tenancy.
Digitisation of claims and role of advice services	The DWP originally entered into a delivery partnership agreement with the city council to deliver Personal Budgeting Support (PBS) and online supported access. Manchester City Council used this funding to commission the PBS from Shelter and the Assisted Digital Service (ADS) from a partnership of Citizens Advice Manchester and Cheetham Hill advice centre. Since the first roll-out of full service began in 2018 the Universal Assisted Digital Service has been able to help support over 2,000 people in Manchester to make their initial claim. However, a further 2,100 people have had to seek additional help from Citizens Advice Manchester and its citywide advice partners with over 6,000 issues related to UC.

Source: Manchester City Council (2019: 3, 7–19)

wider policy consequences of welfare reform creating significant workload pressures. Councils are uniquely placed to support families to adjust to changes brought about by wider welfare reforms. (Manchester City Council, 2019: 11)

This raises an important question in terms of the actual impact of the full roll-out in the context of austerity. At the time of writing, this has been stalled by the government but there will be thousands of workers who will be transferred from Working Tax Credit to UC, which in turn will have major implications for in-work poverty and its impact on local welfare services.

The contested politics of devolution, austerity and welfare

I have attempted to capture the multiple actors and their agendas in terms of negotiating and contesting welfare and employment policies in Table 5.4. As highlighted by the research as part of the Just Work programme carried out by the University of Manchester (Johnson et al, 2017), it is important to understand the economic context in order to situate social organisation and mobilisation. Deindustrialisation has involved the loss of unionised work and led to the fragmentation of both the labour market and business structure which creates significant challenges for trade unions to organise and coordinate collective action. That said, there exist active trade councils within the boroughs and a trade union structure within GM. The metropolitan geography and relatively strong interconnectedness from previous rounds of city region building has provided a platform for social action to be networked across the city region (Beel et al, 2017).

There is an emerging agenda which recognises that quality of work and employment rights need to be built into policy agendas. The University of Manchester Inclusive Growth Analysis Unit (IGAU) has played an active role in shaping a discussion on 'responsible businesses' (Rafferty and Jelley, 2018) along with the GMCA, which has developed its own employment charter, broadly similar to that created by the North West TUC (University of Manchester IGAU, 2018; North West TUC, 2018). The increasing awareness and discourse around representational gaps and lack of employment rights within the city region economy has therefore brought to the fore campaigns around living wages and anti-poverty strategies.

One of the features of devolution under neoliberalism is the tendency to marginalise trade unions and voluntary sector engagement with the devolution political process (see Smith Institute, 2017). In many respects, this may explain why there are tensions between the trade unions and the devolved authorities around the devolution process. This can be illustrated in Unison's response to the Greater Manchester Health and Social Care Plan, which goes to the heart of trade unions' lack of engagement with the devolution process and the way devolution embodies the implementation of privatisation:

Table 5.4: Actors and strategies in opposing labour market policies in Greater Manchester

Key policy interventions	Tensions and conflicts	Agency (key actors) and sites of negotiation and struggle
Devolution deals	• Growth versus distribution • Funding gaps for devolution • Undemocratic modes of representation	• Trade unions, civil society, local authorities – negotiating 'social dialogue' formalised in Greater Manchester, informal in other devolved arrangements • Greater Manchester devolution and democracy • Inclusive growth politics via IGAU
Employment rights	• Low level of unionisation • High levels of insecure work	• North West TUC • GM trade unions • GMCA Good Employment Charter
Welfare reform/ Universal Credit	• Increasing impact of austerity • Labour market marginalisation • Working poor, cuts in funding • PBR model, negative impact • Conditionality and sanctions • Delays in benefit, tough claimant regime	• Local authority employment and anti-poverty strategies and role of anti-poverty coalitions, disability rights • Organisations, advice services, trade union/NGO campaigns against welfare reform • Links between NGOs and trade unions in Greater Manchester • Negotiating with central government (submissions to Work and Pensions Select Committee)
Social, health and community support services	• Impact of austerity on both local authorities and disadvantaged groups • Local authority conflicts with public sector trade unions	• Local authorities, frontline services and Work Programme providers, NHS • Providers, advice services – advocacy for benefit claimants, trade unions • Opposition to cuts in services and jobs
Apprenticeships and skills, area reviews	• Cuts to skills funding, including adult skills budget, area-based reviews, phase out of European funded skills programmes, extent of employer buy-in in face of recession, quality of provision and engagement of limited access to advanced skills by disadvantaged groups to skills	• Skills providers especially further education colleges, (playing an advocacy role for disadvantaged groups) • Work trade unions negotiating funding gaps in work representation around apprenticeship quality

Source: Department of Communities and Local Government (DCLG) (nd)

Our concerns include:

- the lack of employee and trade union involvement in the production of the Plan.
- the lack of focus on improving the quality of employment as a means of improving health outcomes and the absence of any plan to implement the living wage at a Greater Manchester scale.
- the implications on our members delivering public services of new delivery models, we believe that health service delivery and employment in Greater Manchester should be very much part of the National Health Service. (Unison, 2016)

Furthermore, the TUC (2014) argues that LEPs often do not recognise or understand the role that unions can play as agents for change. While it is recognised that LEPs should be held accountable for their development, there are no mechanisms currently in place for this to happen (see Pike et al, 2018). The devolution of employment policy tends to be taking place without any structural changes or adjustments that will allow the voice of disadvantaged groups to be heard within the city region policy process, especially as there is no trade union representation on the GM LEP. As GM has involved the devolution of major public services such as health and social care, it is of little surprise that some form of social dialogue has been established with the trade unions via the Greater Manchester Strategic Workforce Engagement Board and a Workforce Engagement Protocol. The election of a high profile Labour mayor (Andy Burnham) in 2017 'was seen by the trade unions and voluntary sector organisations as an opportunity to contribute to a progressive agenda around poverty and inequality' (Johnson et al, 2017: 7).

The role of actors and collective action has been extended to include the analysis of representational structures such as local government as 'anchor institutions' in terms of engagement with unemployed and disadvantaged groups (see Hastings et al, 2017; Etherington and Jones, 2018). As Johnson et al (2017: 13) emphasise, as 'wider systems of welfare have retreated over the past 30 years or so, paradoxically local government has assumed a greater burden of responsibility for regulating the market in various ways'. In this way they represent sites where trade union densities and organisation are still relatively strong and often act as anchor institutions in terms of providing a focal point for negotiating and in some cases challenging the impact of welfare reform. For example, Oldham Borough Council established its own Fairness Commission to track and monitor the impact of welfare reform. Salford Borough Council established its own inquiry into the impact of benefit sanctions (Etherington and Jones, 2017). Of course, this is a contradictory process as they are also at the same time implementing public expenditure cuts. Negotiating neoliberalism, in what Newman terms 'landscapes of antagonism', thus needs to be contextualised within a 'contradictory field of political forces', where:

> ... the vibrancy of local democracy can serve as a challenge to hegemonic projects ... Landscapes of antagonism are formed (and reformed) through the discursive constitution of new subjects and the orchestration of new lines of antagonism, resistance and alignment ... [and] local governments are both actors in such landscapes of antagonism, with their own interests and political projects, and the mediators of wider struggles in which they seek to privilege some and mitigate others. (Newman, 2014: 3298–9)

GM possesses a history of coordinated action across the different local authorities, which has aided city-region wide network building within civil society (Hincks et al, 2017). There is evidence of this by the critical engagement with the welfare reform agenda such as Manchester City Council's submission to the Work and Pensions Select Committee, Oldham Fairness Commission and Tameside Poverty pledge.

There are, however, tensions around these arrangements, as devolution involves devolving and managing austerity (Beel et al, 2018; Etherington and Jones, 2017); devolution authorities efficiently administer centrally-determined cuts. This means while there is greater (and formal) engagement of trade unions in GM, this is tenuous given their opposition to the overall thrust of the devolved economic and social strategies (Nelson, 2017: 8).

Another pressing question and tension relate to the lack of control the devolved local authorities have over the implementation of welfare reform, UC and skills policies. An example of this is the operation of advice organisations such as the Greater Manchester Law Centre, GM Centre for Voluntary Organisation (GMCVO) and TUC that provide some form of basis to negotiate and challenge regressive welfare policies. The Greater Manchester Law Centre has lobbied with respect to the impact of welfare reforms on disabled people (Greater Manchester Law Centre, 2017) and the Greater Manchester Coalition of Disabled People has responded to devolution making demands on the mayor to shape a more progressive agenda when they declare:

> whilst the Greater Manchester mayor does not have direct responsibility for delivering all of the services that we require to protect and promote our independence; the mayor will have an important ambassadorial role and opportunity to promote best practice. This manifesto for disabled people has been produced to assist the mayor in becoming our ally and champion in our fight for equality. (GMCDP, 2018)

The forging of cross-city mobilisation is also illustrated by the campaign against Welfare Reform and UC (as part of a national campaign) comprising a wide range of organisations across GM. The campaign, also supported by the mayor, has focused on resisting evictions due to non-payment of rent as a result of benefit cuts and delays built into the UC system (Greater Manchester Law Centre, 2018).

Conclusions: recomposing city regions

At one level, this 'mythic Manchester' (Haughton et al, 2016) reveals a city region at breaking point, with cracks appearing in many services. However, the devolution project also involves the devolution of austerity, which is being internalised and 'managed' by local authorities, Combined Authority and Local Enterprise Partnerships. City region authorities and local authorities tend to have a role of 'sweeping up' the problems of UC and absorb its impacts (Etherington and Jones, 2017). Massive cuts in welfare benefits and local government funding, leading to a depth and intensity of social problems never experienced before, are pushing a series of critical capacity issues across the public and voluntary sectors. Getting behind this and exposing its 'class composition dynamics' (Shukaitis, 2013), I have argued that insecurity is a key facet of neoliberalism, work and the geography of contemporary capitalism.

To understand and make sense of austerity city regionalism itself, I have sought an understanding of the ways in which prevailing dominant class interests has driven through austerity. This has been via a class struggle reworking of the capital–labour relation, exhibited through the local politics of welfare-to-work – the 'new politics of austerity' as MacLeavy (2011) has previously noted. The growth model and trajectory of GM is pitted with multiple tensions as local and city region institutions come to terms with the failure to redistribute the gains of 'growth'. The implementation of welfare reform and the UC benefit migration will only accentuate social and labour market inequalities because this is taking place within the context of major cuts in local authority and welfare spending.

Chapter 2 outlined that one of the key elements of the austerity-neoliberal growth 'model' is the way it undermines democracy and systems of accountabilities. Devolution in the UK and in GM has an inbuilt democratic deficit in terms of the way local actors are highly constrained by central directives. As Dan Finn (2015) has noted, the UK has one of the most centralised welfare-to-work systems within the OECD countries, and this is reflected in the nature of the implementation of welfare reform. UC becomes a vehicle for downloading austerity and a source of contestation rather than negotiation and influence by local actors and institutions. The other element is the scope for influencing devolution policies by trade unions and civil society organisations. The institutional and governance changes have not in any way integrated social dialogue between those organisations representing trade unions and disadvantaged communities. This has major implications for the establishment of employment rights, fairness at work and bridge building between policy-making stakeholders and disadvantaged groups and communities.

Challenging welfare conditionality and insecure work

... workfare seeks to maximize rates of employment by eroding benefits packages and activating transitions into work, ... and it explicitly socializes welfare recipients for unstable, contingent jobs, reconciling (in a downward direction) the needs and aspirations of welfare recipients in accordance with the realities of low wage in local labour markets. Second, the generation of administrative pressures to enter the first available job self-evidently erodes the capacity of labour to wait for more favourable employment opportunities, while intensifying competition for entry-level positions. Third, it effectively market-tests access to residual welfare services, rationing these services according to the criterion of employability. (Peck, 2002: 332, 347)

'The airwaves should be full of outrage ... It's labour you can turn on and off like a tap', says Loach, 'It follows on from Daniel Blake because while researching the film we were struck in the foodbank that a number of the people were working, and when we were in the benefits office, most (claimants) were working. The idea of the working poor loomed large in our conversation.' (Ken Loach, interviewed by Aditya Chakrabortty, 2019)

Introduction

Chapter 3 described how Universal Credit (UC) and the social security system help to impose discipline on reserve labour by ensuring that there are strict rules for eligibility including the requirement to accept work offers. Contemporary moves towards 'workfare' can be seen as a further development in the process of managing the reserve army of labour. Instead of – or in addition to – the relatively passive approach implied in the notion of social security, workfare seems to promise a more active management of the labour market. It builds on the disciplinary aspects of social security adapting labour to fit more closely with the specific needs of particular industrial sectors or local employers (Grover, 2012). The previous chapter on Greater Manchester demonstrated how the welfare reform agenda has had major impacts on the Greater Manchester economy, leading to a more precarious and insecure labour market. Since the 2008 financial crisis there has been an increase in labour market inequalities with a rise in low-paid and precarious work which is integrally connected to austerity/neoliberalism as a strategy of disciplining labour (Umney, 2018). The key focuses of this chapter are the way the welfare/work relationship and interface drive precarious workplaces, how workers experience insecurity, and the strategies used by trade unions and communities to resist it.

This chapter is based on research supporting the Sheffield Needs a Pay Rise (SNAP) campaign which was carried out in 2018. SNAP was initiated by Sheffield Trades Union Council (STUC) and came about as a response to a Resolution Foundation report (Clarke, 2017) which concluded that Sheffield contained the highest proportion of workers paid below the living wage compared to other UK cities. Nationally, wages have stagnated and are £10 a week lower than before 2008; in Sheffield wage levels are lower than 2004 (Clarke, 2017). As in Greater Manchester, as described in Chapter 5, for the past 30 years deindustrialisation and employment restructuring have been based on the creation of low-paid and insecure jobs (low pay is defined by the Resolution Foundation is two-thirds of median hourly pay; Corlett, 2016). The research explored the hypothesis that austerity-driven cuts and welfare reforms are fuelling low pay and insecure work. SNAP carried out an evidence review to inform debates and raise awareness and discussion about low pay and precarious work in Sheffield from the perspective of workers, trade unions and civil society organisations, drawing on a number of mixed-methods sources. Stage 1 involved policy scoping (qualitative and quantitative sources) and a literature review. In stage 2, narrative policy analysis and discourse analysis were carried out alongside stakeholder mapping, to capture both the insecure/precarious work and welfare policies flowing in and through Sheffield.

Semi-structured interviews with 24 key actors (trade unions officials, workers, community activists, policymakers, practitioners, and stakeholders in general) were undertaken. SNAP's research approach involved targeting workers and claimants who were involved with the campaign and were part of the wider Sheffield TUC network. An important part of the research strategy was to capture the voices in and at the margins of welfare and the labour market and this involved contacting relevant voluntary sector stakeholders involved with the

Sheffield Equality Hubs (disability and gender) and the advice services, such as Citizens Advice. Interviews were carried out with trade union officials and activists to obtain data on trade union strategies, and with local policy makers in order to analyse the interventions of social and welfare services in Sheffield. Face-to-face interviews were carried out, recorded and transcribed between February and September 2018 and analysed with respect to the key research themes relating to experiences of work and welfare. In addition, a focus group was convened comprising eight young people connected to a Big Lottery Group Project on young people and employment in the Sheffield City Region (SCR).

Insecurity and the Sheffield economy

The SCR economy, typical of the 'peripheral' deindustrialised economies, is characterised by a high proportion of workers on lower rates of pay compared with the rest of the UK. There are deep-rooted labour market inequalities in the city region economy, comprising 'poor jobs' growth and a largely unskilled workforce. It is estimated that the number of those in low-paid and insecure employment amount to 185,000 (Etherington et al, 2018). In the SCR, nearly 127,000 people of working age possess no formal qualifications and a further 150,000 have qualifications below Level 2 (basic qualifications). Under-employment is a prevalent feature of labour market inequality in SCR as many new jobs created are self-employed, temporary, part-time or often zero-hours contracts. There are significant barriers for disabled people and those claiming long-term sickness benefits trying to access either employment or vocational training. In the SCR, there are 85,640 people claiming Employment Support Allowance/Incapacity Benefits (7.4%) and 16,090 receiving disability benefits (1.4%) − above the national average (6.3% and 1.1% respectively). Women are particularly disadvantaged in the labour market in terms of employment opportunities and pay. The majority of part-time employment is taken by women, with a higher proportion of women earning below the living wage compared with men. Young people are experiencing high unemployment − approximately 35,700 16 to 24-year-olds in the SCR are unemployed; this is 22.3% of the total. The number of 16 to 18-year-olds not in education, employment or training (NEET) is over 3,700 (Etherington and Jones, 2016b).

In terms of the 'jobs gap', the number of jobs in the SCR that need to be created to bring the employment rate to the national average amounts to around 248,000 (Pike et al, 2017b). This analysis is corroborated by a report by the Sheffield City Local Enterprise Partnership (LEP) on the SCR economy which acknowledges the scale of the jobs gap:

> The SCR currently has a shortfall of around 65,000 private service sector jobs, when compared with the employment density in other LEP areas ... This position has worsened since 2009 ... Based on the forecast growth in other parts of the country the SCR would need to create 120,000 jobs to have closed the gap with the national average in 2023. This would require GDP growth of almost 5% and nowhere in the UK grows at this rate. (Sheffield City Region Local Enterprise Partnership, 2014: 8)

While there are likely to be significant impacts from the introduction of the National Living Wage, the government's minimum wage rate is separate to the Living Wage rate as calculated by the Living Wage Foundation (LWF). Unlike the LWF's rates, it is not calculated according to the cost of living and is therefore lower than what would be needed to afford a decent standard of living. Furthermore, the Resolution Foundation cautions that there are still significant challenges in relation to those at the bottom end of the low-paid labour market. Almost one in five employees in the SCR, around 130,000 people, will be on the wage floor by 2020; this will mean that progression within work will be a big concern for a growing share of the population (Clarke, 2017).

Cuts to social protection services and barriers to employment

While conditionality enforces compulsion to take up work, many aspects of the welfare system and recent reforms can prevent this. Earlier research undertaken by Beatty and Fothergill (2014) on the impact of welfare reforms on Sheffield show the way the reforms are reinforcing labour market and social inequalities. Between 2010–11 and 2017–18 Sheffield City Council experienced a reduction of £430 million in funding from central government (Sheffield City Council, 2019a). An assessment of the impact of austerity by Sheffield City Council (2019b) emphasises the cumulative impact in terms of reduction in services and the deprived areas and communities impacted the greatest. A whole range of services that assist people to access and retain employment (childcare, health, youth services, employment initiatives) are being reduced or cut altogether.

At the time of writing, UC was being rolled out in Sheffield, albeit in a limited way because of the government's temporary halt (Chapter 4). The city council, along with the local DWP, in 2018 established a Universal Credit Partnership, with representatives from Sheffield City Council, DWP, Citizens' Advice Sheffield and other voluntary, community and faith organisations, to respond to the roll-out of UC and deal with the increasing number of claims (Sheffield NHS Commissioning Group, 2019).

The partnership was formed in order to mitigate the negative impacts of UC on claimants. Earlier in 2018, Citizens Advice Sheffield (CAS) had produced a report on its early impressions of the roll-out in Sheffield stating that (there) 'are so many practical, technical and structural problems with UC ... that it is very difficult to know where to focus campaign efforts' (CAS, 2018a: 2). There is an increasing demand for advice services and there will be knock-on impacts on social and health services. There has also been a reported increase in the demand for foodbanks, which have formed as another arm of social protection. In this way the welfare system perpetuates insecurity and locks people out of employment completely because of the constant struggle to survive.

> The impact of delays in living costs means nothing to eat and reliance of help from foodbanks. It also impacts on the ability to pay for fuel for heating, cooking and heating with had a particularly detrimental impact on the poorest who use pre-payment meters meaning for some an inability to heat up the tinned food received from the foodbank. (CAS, 2018a)

Disability Sheffield, an advocacy organisation promoting independent living for disabled people, has highlighted the fact that on many fronts, things are becoming more difficult – cuts caused by austerity are one major cause but there is a reported rise in hate crime and negative attitudes towards disabled people. Just under 104,000 people in Sheffield said their health condition or disability resulted in them experiencing some degree of difficulties with their day-to-day activities. This represents almost one-fifth (19%) of the population of the city classified as being disabled under the Equality Act (2010) definition (Disability Sheffield, 2015). The reliance on unpaid care was raised by a respondent. In a survey of registered carers commissioned by Sheffield Occupational Health Advisory Service (SOHAS), the majority of the respondents were over 40 years, over half identifying themselves with a long-term disability, with 41% stating that their caring commitments hindered their ability to work (Sheffield Carers Centre, 2019).

The key issue is that incorrect assessments have major implications for benefit entitlement and therefore vulnerability to in and out of work poverty. This will have knock-on consequences on disabled people's experience of work. According to Disability Sheffield:

> [SOHAS] research demonstrates that there is an ambivalent attitude from employers to employing and retaining disabled people. Around 40% of employees employed by organisations who signed up to the Disability Confident scheme have been referred by their GP to SOHAS because their employers have not been helpful in supporting them to manage their long-term health condition and disability.[1]

In Sheffield, a lack of sufficient and affordable childcare is one of a number of barriers to work:

> 'But basically what people are saying is, there's not enough childcare, some women are still having to make up the cost, so they're juggling an additional cost, the provider of childcare sector has been affected because childcare providers cannot, (we're talking about day care here), can't keep going, the lack of flexibility of childcare because the women that are, and there are quite a lot of women who seem to go from job to job.' (Interview with lone parent advocacy worker)

There is evidence that families are getting into debt because of having to pay in advance for childcare, particularly as most nurseries require advance payments to cover an extended period. Although the 30 hours' free childcare provision introduced by the government in 2017 provides some support, the level of funding is insufficient to cover provider costs (WPC, 2018a: 20). The Family and Childcare Trust (WPC, 2018c: 4) reports that less than half of English local authorities have enough childcare for children using the 30-hour extended entitlement. Previous research in the SCR (Etherington and Jones, 2016b) found that the lack of affordable provision of childcare as a barrier to employment especially for women from working class backgrounds.

of things when you've got such a scattered [workforce].'
(Interview with Unite union official)

This was then further compounded due to a lack of recognition of
trade unions. As members in precarious working conditions do not
or feel unable to join, they are not then being represented within the
unions themselves:

> 'So if you are a regional organiser and you're dealing with
> half a dozen companies – big companies – and then you
> might have two or three of these smaller cleaning companies
> and security companies, who are you going to concentrate
> on? You know who you're going to concentrate on because
> you've got fully trained reps there.' (Interview with RMT
> union official)

Other difficulties arose due to language barriers. A number of
respondents suggested that with some international workers, who
would potentially know very little of their employment rights and
were hence vulnerable to exploitation, gaining trust alongside raising
their awareness of what a trade union is could be difficult:

> 'It's left a situation that we've eventually got round to
> addressing but it's a very, very difficult area because what you
> have is you have a high turnover, English isn't necessarily the
> first language, as I said, and there's no trade union culture in
> a lot of these places.' (Interview with RMT union official)

Finally, there is the 'low-hanging' fruit argument, where trade unions
will recruit where it is easier to gain access and organise:

> 'I don't do organising work in unorganised sectors,
> unorganised workplaces, unless, I'm getting demand for
> that from those. I would rather recruit more people in
> the places where we are than use up a lot of energy for
> no gain because it's really, really difficult.' (Interview with
> Unite official)

Innovations strategies

Building solidarities with welfare claimants has been a focus of
campaigns around welfare reform and UC by some trade unions in

Sheffield. For example, the closure of the Eastern Avenue jobcentre in Sheffield serves as a useful case study to demonstrate the role of the Public and Commercial Services (PCS) union in terms of taking action to oppose the reduction of employment services to claimants. Union members voted to strike for a total of 26 days until the centre was closed in November 2017. The union's case against closure as submitted to the DWP (PCS, 2017b) was based on several reasons. First, the jobcentre was in a deprived area with wards containing higher than average numbers of people claiming out-of-work benefits. Second, the area had already suffered from austerity and the closure of an important social service would exacerbate the problems of deprivation. Finally, the alternative locations offered to claimants were deemed inadequate. There would be overcrowding in one jobcentre and the other, located in the centre of Sheffield, would involve increased travel time and transport costs for claimants. The trade union claimed that the changes breached ministerial guidelines as the closure involves claimants travelling an extra 20 minutes or three miles to a newly allocated jobcentre. Finally, the closure is seen as detrimental to staff and as the union argues that this has negative consequences for delivering an effective and efficient service to claimants.

Although the campaign was not successful in preventing the closure of the jobcentre, it brought together trade unions and community activists around issues relating to welfare reform. This has been built on by Unite Community along with Sheffield Trade Union Council (and other labour movement organisations) in relation to the campaign to scrap UIC. The national campaign, spearheaded by Disabled People Against the Cuts (DPAC) and Unite Community, has raised the profile of trade unions in relation to questions around welfare reform. An important element of the campaign is the work undertaken by Unite Community in Sheffield, which has developed strategies to engage with workers/claimants as a means of promoting unionisation and displaying solidarity with those who feel isolated in the workplace. One of the key roles played by the UC campaign is undertaking outreach initiatives in the more deprived parts of Sheffield to connect with claimants and workers by providing support, information and signposting to advice services.

The Sheffield Needs a Pay Rise Campaign (SNAP) illustrates the movement towards innovating and attempting organising strategies among workers in precarious employment. There has been a concerted campaign by the trade union representing fast-food workers in Sheffield, the Bakers Food and Allied Workers Union (BFAWU), to organise and recruit workers. A campaign targeting McDonald's fast-food outlets was aimed at securing a higher minimum wage of £10 an hour and the right to union representation. Organising efforts have focused on a number of outlets throughout the country and led to the first ever strikes in the history of McDonald's, at stores in Cambridge and Crayford in September 2017. The organising strategy is premised on the idea of getting the workers' initial attention by communicating facts on issues such as, for example, corporate pay, and asking the worker to make an initial, but small commitment to take action (such as speaking to another worker). The actions that BFAWU members have taken have already led to major victories, such as a pay rise for all directly employed McDonald's staff in January 2018. Yet being among the smallest unions of the TUC, BFAWU has had to look to the wider labour movement on national basis to help in the raising of funds to employ further full-time organisers (BFAWU interview).

Sheffield TUC has been inspired by the successes of innovative organising strategies being deployed by unions such as Unite, BFAWU and the General Municipal and Boilermakers (GMB), and seeks to share best practice and replicate such work among union branches in the city. The STUC has crowdfunded the employment of an organiser in the fast-food sector as a way of developing the campaign for employment rights and union recognition. This has led to the development of more outreach work such as the Summer Patrol organised by the Yorkshire and Humberside TUC. This initiative developed from a similar one organised by Norwegian trade unions. The project sent groups of young trade unionists from Yorkshire and Norway into workplaces across Sheffield, Doncaster and Barnsley in order to connect with young workers in a different way, giving them a positive introduction to trade unions. As one regional official commented:

> 'We need to get back into workplaces and talk to people about their issues (particularly on declining high streets where staff are feeling the squeeze). We used the data capturing website Typeform to conduct our interviews, which saved us loads of time which would have been spent inputting data at the end of the day. We also trialled the peer to peer texting software GetThru to send texts to all the people we met on Patrol to follow up with them on any issues. GetThru allowed us to keep in touch with people who showed an interest and invite them to a follow-up meeting to build a campaign to improve working life

in South Yorkshire. But face-to-face conversations are what makes the difference.' (Interview with Yorkshire and Humberside Regional TUC Official)

Similar actions have been undertaken by the GMB trade union in relation to drivers delivering for Amazon in Sheffield:

> 'We've been outside the gates, we've handed them leaflets, we've got Facebook pages set up to say to people, "You need to get in the union. This is what we can do for you." And those that are, we're then taking on the challenge for the legal route. How I see it is it works like this: we need to challenge legislation nationally to change law, but we also then need to organise on the ground to hold them employers to account, because even when legislation's change, employers aren't just going to stop doing it.' (Interview with GMB regional official)

One of the largest employers in Sheffield, the social care sector, has presented a major challenge for trade unions because of the prevalence of low-pay, zero-hours contracts and shift work. Nonetheless, trade unions are making progress in the city, with membership at one social care provider increasing from 10 to over 50 in the last year and being close to achieving the statutory recognition threshold. One organiser we spoke to stressed the importance of personal contact with members, at the very minimum through a phone call, though acknowledged how resource intensive this is:

> 'We've got their details, many of them have given us their telephone numbers, you can email them and write to them, but you'll probably never hear back. If you ring them, then they'll speak to you and often they'll speak to you for half an hour, 'cause they've never had anyone call them before and ask them how it's going.' (Interview with Unison official)

Given the poor working conditions, low pay and oppressive working practices, representative trade unions in the care sector (Unison and GMB) have formulated care charters providing a set of demands to campaign around pay and working conditions. Sheffield City Council has signed up to Unison's care charter guaranteeing basic terms and conditions as well as the living wage.

Discussion and conclusions

This chapter has explored the link between the welfare system seen in its broadest sense and insecure work in Sheffield. Jill Rubery et al (2018) succinctly summarise the relationship when they state:

> … activation strategies influence the potential pool of labour available for precarious work through combinations of sanctions and financial support. The consequence is a blurring of the unemployed/employed divide and a normalisation of the take up of fragmented, low paid and short-term jobs. (Rubery et al, 2018: 521)

Following Strauss (2017), the SNAP study has found that the boundaries between work and welfare have always been blurred as shown by the way the interaction between the two has given rise to the incidence of cycling between the jobcentre and workplace – a process that has characterised labour market policy since the 1980s when conditionality on benefits was tightened. This is partly a reflection of the way employer strategies, combined with workfare, are shaping a more contingent and precarious work. A number of studies provide evidence that this process of work–welfare cycling as an indicator of welfare and work inequality has been embedded in the welfare-to-work programmes. Ray et al (2010) use survey data from an evaluation of a government Employment Retention and Advancement (ERA) programme. The study focused on participants in the New Deal for lone parents and New Deal for over 25 years as implemented under the previous New Labour government. One of the key findings of this study is insecure work as a factor in structuring movements in and out of work. These types of jobs were the main reason for exiting work because of their temporary nature or earnings were unsustainable. Women, in particular lone parents, were disadvantaged in terms of the barriers to reconciling work and caring commitments. The study also found that those in 'stable' jobs were vulnerable to low pay and financial insecurity. Opportunities for progression were limited because of the lack of access to training or that the training completed did not necessarily guarantee progression and promotion. Again, women are disadvantaged in this respect because as primary child-carers it was difficult to manage caring commitments to the working hours offered as part of promotion.

> The research has added to the growing body of findings about the 'poor quality' of jobs at the bottom end of the

labour market. Particularly in terms of their lack of security and means for progression. The survey analysis showed that almost a third of the low-qualified workers in the sample lost their jobs and spent some time out of employment within the two year time frame. This was much more likely among those who were entering work from benefits (the New Deal for Lone Parents [NDLP] and New Deal 25+ [ND25+]). (Ray et al, 2010: 38)

UC will only reinforce and intensify this process. The design of UC guarantees subsidies to low-paid work including 'mini jobs' and zero-hours work. Work conditionality rules mean that UC claimants will be required to accept zero-hours work and then, in order to meet the requirements in the claimant agreement of working a set number of hours a week or enhancing take home pay, claimants will be under pressure to look for other mini jobs.

Cuts to childcare, health and benefits, and 'social reproduction' services are factors which hinder workers moving and progressing in terms of pay and career. Sheffield City Council, which plays a key role in supporting disadvantaged groups, is having to come to terms with many years of austerity-driven cuts. One of the key components of insecurity is therefore the inadequacy of the welfare and social protection system in supporting people in and out of work. The role of actors and collective action can be extended to include the analysis of representational structures such as local government in terms of engagement with unemployed and disadvantaged groups (see Hastings et al, 2017; Newman, 2014; Etherington and Jones, 2018). The council (along with the employment services) is forced to make substantial cuts and savings itself which impact on the services that are most relied on by disadvantaged groups.

Related to this, the operation of the benefits system locks people out of the immediate labour market – particularly lone parents and people with long-term health conditions. This is not only because work does not pay but because employers have little regard for making workplaces amenable for the needs of marginalised groups. So, for a large proportion of the working-age population, work is not an option. In this way benefit conditionality can reinforce women's role as unpaid carers within a dependent male breadwinner family model (Williams, 1994). In this context unpaid care and voluntary work essential to social reproduction is undervalued and hardly recognised as a priority for trade unions, which reflects the weak links between the trade unions and voluntary sector.

Richard Hyman and Rebecca Gumbrell-McCormick, in an important contribution, situate the blurring of the boundaries between insiders and outsiders within the context of labour market restructuring:

> Not only does labour market insecurity not create a homogenous 'precariat,' it does not result in a simple polarisation between insiders and outsiders, and affects in different ways social groups with contrasting capacities for collective mobilisation ... but in recent years most have accepted that insecurity will not go away, and have recognised the need to represent the interests of these often disparate groups of workers. Otherwise they risk the continued erosion of their membership base and their capacity to regulate the world of work. (Hyman and Gumbrell-McCormick, 2017: 545, 547)

In the face of globalisation, economic restructuring and the massive loss of trade union jobs, it can be argued that trade unions operate around principles of 'swords of justice' in terms of engaging both with workers and communities impacted by economic and social inequalities (TUC, 2010). To some extent, the formation of Unite Community and the 'community turn' by the larger trade unions has led to greater engagement with welfare claimants and the welfare system in general. But this is highly uneven, both within and between trade unions and geographically.

The formation of Unite Community was a product of the trade union movement responding to the increasing incidence of marginalisation among the working class (see Chapter 4). Furthermore, this has opened spaces and opportunity structures to forge strategies for engaging with outsiders – unemployed and welfare claimants (Holgate, 2018). In Sheffield, there has been a distinctive shift of focus towards engaging and joining up with marginalised and disadvantaged groups, as evidenced by the UC and SNAP campaigns. But there are distinct limitations and barriers. The research carried out for SNAP grappled with issues about how trade unions connect (or not) with communities and civil society organisations who advocate for marginalised and disenfranchised groups. In many respects, trade unions and their activities can be far removed from social networks which support disadvantaged groups in the labour market. Also, for most, work is very much of a short-term and unpredictable character and joining a trade union does not appear on people's horizons.

Holgate, in her discussion on the role of Unite Community, argues that there is an essential tension within the organisation model:

> Unite is actually facing in two directions at the same time. While the UC [Unite Community] strategy is developing a new approach to union activity (recognising that organising in the community requires a reanalysing of where power and leverage might be located), the main body of the union – the industrial membership – continues as it has done in the past to focus on the workplace and has a completely separate organising strategy. In terms of the way the union functions, this means the two sections of the union are acting independently with little interaction. (Holgate, 2018: 18)

In many ways this applies to all the trade unions who have difficulties in jettisoning their traditional approaches to organisation. Furthermore, trade unions operate based on 'low-hanging fruit' principles in terms of recruiting people to trade unions; that is, where it is relatively straightforward to recruit and organise. While in Sheffield all the major trade unions have adapted to some extent to the challenges thrown up by the labour market crisis (for example, Sheffield TUC funding a part-time organiser) but there is a considerable way to go before tackling and organising precarious workers and communities are mainstreamed among the main trade unions.

These critical reflections of the processes and mobilisations of trade unions in the face of insecurity need to be situated in a more complete picture of the direction of travel of trade unions. The Labour Party, along with the TUC, is committed to delivering a more regulated labour market including coordinated collective bargaining and despite the election result the struggle for employment and bargaining rights will remain high on the agenda (see Chapter 7 on Denmark). The SNAP campaign represents a step-change in the thinking and mentality of the local and regional trade union movement around the way it can influence national politics and the struggles of the labour movement.

7

Towards a more inclusive labour market: lessons from Denmark

Overall, the regulative setting provides rights and protection to the majority of the workforce, so that employment covered by a collective agreement in general cannot be considered precarious employment in Denmark. At the same time, the Danish welfare system provides different forms of comparatively high social security standards for the majority of the workforce. Because this regulation apply to most types of employment, persons working in what is often referred to as non-standard forms of work such as part-time work and fixed-term employment enjoy the same rights and have the same level of protection as those working in the standard, open ended contract – at least at the formal level. Because of the degree of regulation and protection for these forms of non-standard work, they are not at a general level considered precarious in a Danish context. (Rasmussen et al, 2016: 21)

In spite of the changes in the favour of capital, the Danish development has also been one of the continuities. The national institutions regulating labour market and working life are still strong and encompassing. The class compromise founded in 1899, although reformed and changed in many respects over the years, is still in force. Strong corporatist features are still present, although increasingly encroached by market forces. Danish industrial relations are still distinctly different from liberalist as well as legalistic models. (Lind and Knudsen, 2018: 599)

Introduction

This book is positioned within theoretical perspectives that focus on welfare states as systems of power and negotiation between key social forces acting in and through the state apparatus. In this context, we suggest that successive welfare reforms – from New Labour's welfare-to-work programmes to the development of a more punitive welfare strategy under the coalition and current Conservative government – are generating considerable debate on the re-regulation of labour markets and alternatives to work-first policies. There is an emerging consensus, as demonstrated in this book, that the work-first approach is deeply problematic. While there are calls from the policy and political community to scrap or stall Universal Credit (UC), the question of what will replace it needs to be explored in more detail. An important contribution to this is made by the Welfare Conditionality Project (2018a), which argues for the removal of the disciplinary aspects to the implementation of UC such as conditionality (including in-work conditionality) and sanctions, the need to make work pay, and the focus on more support such as quality training and other related services. Implicit in the analysis is the need for claimants to have a voice and welfare rights which should be integral to the claims process. Currently, claimants are negotiating and challenging a hostile system as reflected by the significant numbers of appeals to decisions and the virtual breakdown of the managed migration process from legacy benefits to UC in 2018/19 (see Chapter 4).

The current politics of austerity, the crisis in the labour market and the rise in inequality have led to a greater focus on industrial relations and the role of trade unions. For example, the Institute for Public Policy Research (IPPR) Commission on Economic Justice highlights the link between the decline in trade union membership and collective bargaining coverage and rising inequality:

> This has been exacerbated by the decline of trade unions in the UK economy. There is extensive evidence that the presence of trade unions in workplaces helps improve not just pay, but a variety of aspects of job quality, from training and working time to job security. It is therefore likely that the decline of union membership and collective bargaining in the UK over recent decades has contributed to the worsening conditions experienced by many workers. (IPPR, 2018: 111–12)

The key arguments and evidence that link trade unions and collective bargaining which can bring about a reduction in economic inequality have been put forward by the Institute of Employment Rights (Ewing et al, 2018; see also Hayes and Novitz, 2014). Trade unions play an important role in protecting low-paid workers, suggesting that the increase in the incidence of low pay has been a result of the decline in trade union representation in workplaces. Trade unions are key to defending and enforcing employment rights and in this way can be a buttress against workplace exploitation. In Denmark there is a low incidence of zero-hours contracts and most workers in insecure work have access to basic employment rights and conditions which are determined by collective agreements.

Trade unions and collective bargaining are associated with wage growth and the decline in wage share is (partly) a cause of the fall in union density and the reduction in bargaining coverage. One feature of this is the nature of the voluntarist system and the fragmented structure of wage bargaining in the UK, which is generally confined to individual firms, and where there is an absence of government coordination. This is in contrast with Denmark, where there are strong interest associations involved with decision making in the labour market and welfare policy.

Socal dialogue has an important role to play. An EU-wide study found that 'there is a growing body of evidence that points to the power of social dialogue, in its many diverse channels and constellations of actors in its contributing to raising and extending employment standards' (Grimshaw et al, 2016: 294). In Denmark, it has been instrumental in shaping labour market policy where the industrial relations system supports active labour market policies, including relatively generous benefits. The UK, the marginalisation of trade unions and other social actors in relation to decision making and representation on welfare reform and UC implementation has only reinforced the exposure and vulnerability of claimants to abuse in the system.

The Labour Party has proposed a return to coordinated collective bargaining, drawing on proposals formulated by the Institute of Employment Rights (2018) with similar proposals put forward by the IPPR (see later). The main proposals involve (see also Chapter 8):

- a legal framework for collective action and organisation;
- the amendment of trade union legislation to allow all workers who choose to join a trade union to be represented in collective bargaining;
- a legal framework for sectoral bargaining;
- the defence of human rights which protect the functioning of trade unions;
- giving trade unions access to workers and workplaces in order to provide advice and representation; and
- enabling workers to have access to information about trade unions at their workplace in order to have a choice of joining a trade union.

So far, I am arguing that much can be learned from the Danish model of welfare and industrial relations. This chapter explores the evidence base for how the Danish model works in practice and what lessons can be drawn. The next section analyses how social dialogue and industrial relations play a pivotal role reducing economic and social inequalities and in shaping a more inclusive welfare system. This is followed by a more detailed analysis of the Danish model, which contains many elements of the system proposed by UK trade unions and the Labour Party.

The Danish model of welfare and employment

Denmark and flexicurity

Danish social democracy and the Nordic model were born of mass struggle at the end of the 19th century, which established the trade union movement's rights to association, representation in policy decision making through the creation of tri-partite bodies and a series of welfare reforms embracing social insurance, health and universal benefits (Etherington and Jones, 2004a). Within the framework of welfare regime analysis pioneered by Esping-Andersen (1990; see Chapter 2), the Danish welfare state can be characterised as social democratic, because of its strong orientation towards income redistribution and the role of the public sector in the provision of welfare and social services. Esping-Andersen's concept of welfare regimes as systems of power and negotiation between key interests and actors is useful in terms of understanding the social and political dynamics of labour regulation. In this respect, and in contrast to the 'liberal' regimes found in the US and the UK, the social democratic welfare regime consists of strong labour movements and trade unions, reflected in their relatively high employment to union membership ratios.

The power configuration of this welfare regime is, therefore, frequently constructed around corporatist networks and institutional arrangements in which trade unions are key bargaining partners in the formulation and implementation of economic and social policy making. In this way, Esping-Andersen (1992) drew a strong link between labour movement power and welfare state development. Through this approach, welfare regimes can also be explored as 'labour market regimes', whereby institutions and policies in a social democratic context are geared towards labour market integration. Crucially, labour regulation comprises employment rights and protection, wage regulation and the minimum wage, and active labour market policies. Furthermore, other aspects of welfare policies that enhance integration, such as childcare provision and regulations on maternity rights, are also of importance within a social democratic model.

Furthermore, the active role of the women's movement within the trade union and labour movements was crucial in defending redistribution, the universal components of social policies and the design of policies such as maternity rights and comprehensive childcare (Borchorst and Siim, 2007). The state taking on caring roles generally performed by the family (women) has been crucial in facilitating women's access to the labour market. This strong basis for social solidarity within the welfare model has also informed policies for disabled people and the integration of occupational health within municipal social and health interventions (Etherington and Ingold, 2012).

Since the mid-1990s, Denmark has been championed as the 'ideal' model of flexicurity, an idea that has been promoted by the EU. The Danish labour market involves a combination of high labour market flexibility (low employment protection), high levels of unemployment benefits and a high level of active labour market policy and education. Around 84% of the total workforce are covered by collective agreements, and Denmark is one of the highest spenders on active labour market policies including comparatively generous unemployment benefits (Bredgaard and Kongshøj Madsen, 2018).

Collective bargaining

Several institutional factors have contributed to maintain relatively high levels of union membership and density (70% to 80%) in the Nordic countries, even after the culmination of post-war unionisation in Europe in the 1970s. First, the presence and wide-ranging functions of unions in the workplace have facilitated acceptance and support of unions as a 'matter of fact' in Nordic working lives (Lind and Knudsen, 2018). Collective agreements (CAs) cover wages and all issues around working conditions, with a co-determination system and co-determination committees at the occupational as well as local levels. Social partners establish general wage scales and terms and conditions at the overall level (state, region or municipalities), which are then integrated into individual agreements for different occupations. Additionally, the key role of social partner bodies in labour market and welfare policies has been an important historical feature of welfare state-building in Denmark through a highly decentralised local government system with responsibilities for a wide range of welfare, social, health services, as well as managing social assistance for non–insured unemployed. An important part of the collective agreement system is the role of employer associations, which compared with the UK are relatively highly organised. The main employer association, the Danish Employers Association (Dansk Arbejdsgiver, DA), has to approve the outcomes of the CAs. An interesting question is: why has the DA not, despite having rules that says it is in favour of deregulation, attempted to call off the old class compromise dating back to 1899, for instance by pulling out of bargaining at the national level? A fair answer could be: 'The employer side's acceptance of union organisation is linked to functionality. The labour market functions better when wage earners are organized' (Lind and Knudsen, 2018).

That said, the employers have shaped the industrial relations (IR) system to their advantage and a major change that was introduced during the 1990s is the decentralisation of CAs. This means that more and more components of wage bargaining are negotiated at the plant level. Decentralisation has resulted in a change of power in favour of the employer side, in particular since local wage bargaining is not subject to industrial action. The bipartite character of the bargaining model is still intact. Unions continue to play an important role, in national as well as local bargaining, and have in most cases upheld the principle that outright cuts in pay are unacceptable (Lind and Knudsen, 2018).

Unemployment Insurance Funds

Belgium and all the Nordic countries except Norway have unemployment benefit systems administered by trade unions (generally referred to as the Ghent system). In Denmark, the Ghent system has a long history, with the trade unions managing unemployment insurance (UI) benefits since the 1930s. These benefits are based on individual contributions through employment; in the event of unemployment, claimants receive their benefit from the UI office, which tends to be run by the relevant sector trade union. Most wage earners in the Nordic Ghent countries are therefore dual members of both a trade union and a union-controlled Union Insurance Fund (UIF). However, research shows that workers often associate trade unions with UIF membership: surveys show that many indicate 'in order to become [a] member of a UIF' as an important reason for joining their trade union.

UIFs have been the subject to a number of reforms including terms of compensation rate, duration, eligibility and the level of state financing and the relationship between unemployment insurance benefits and alternative social assistance. In theory, such changes can make a UIF less attractive and consequently erode its role as a recruiting mechanism for its associated trade unions. In the 2000s reforms were introduced to restrict access to UIFs; the work requirement was doubled from 26 to 52 weeks of employment over the last three years (from 2012). This also cut benefit duration from four to two years. The reform added to the existing decline in union membership by introducing free choice and competition between organisations. Shortly after 2000 the government loosened the link between trade unions and UIFs by establishing cross-occupational funds which were operated by trade unions that were not affiliated to the Danish TUC (Landsorganisation, LO). Since 2000, the alternative 'yellow' unions went from 3.6% of all union members in 2000 to 14% in 2015 – or from 68,000 members to 253,000 members. Unemployed people claiming UI would be eligible to access activation programmes (wage subsidy and educational schemes) just as those claiming social assistance administered by the local authorities (municipalities, see later in this chapter, and Lind and Knudsen, 2018).

Activation programmes and marginalised groups

Work-first policies have always been present within Danish employment policy. Since 1990, this has been more explicit and has 'a more integral part of Danish labour market and social policy' focused around making work pay similar to the mantra of successive UK governments (Rosdahl and Weise, 2001: 160, 175). The municipalities (local authorities) have a central role in administering activation schemes for claimants on social assistance (SA), including disabled people, which are means-tested, and signpost claimants into work or those subsidised employment schemes. They operate under the overall supervision of the Regional Labour Market Councils, made up of social partners. Their role is to provide guidance and frameworks for planning the labour market within the regions. Formerly the councils operated at the local authority level, but this was changed during the late 2000s as part of an overall administrative rationalisation of local governance. Reform of the SA system in 2013 was especially targeted at young people, with creative incentives to take on education (or work). Instead of SA, they can receive educational help (uddannelseshjælp), which is a benefit lower than social assistance, at the same level as the state education grant, but they are required to participate in education. If they are not assessed as being able to take part in education, they will receive an 'activity benefit', which is contingent on their participation in various activities aimed at improving their chances of moving into employment or education (Refslund et al, 2017).

In the 2000s, the Danish Liberal–Conservative government introduced a series of measures that tightened conditionality for disabled people and people on long-term sickness benefits. The first measures were tougher work assessment tests and the creation of a special activation programme, Flex Jobs, involving subsidised employment. Flex jobs is integral to an occupational health intervention model for employed and unemployed people whose working capacity is reduced by at least by 50%. Within eight weeks of sick leave the local authority verifies eligibility to sickness benefits and sets in motion appropriate measures and instruments that will facilitate a speedy return to work. These include counselling, work capacity assessment, vocational rehabilitation, job training and phased return to work. Intervention measures are undertaken in liaison with relevant agencies and trade unions. If ordinary work is not possible, then a subsidised Flex Job under special conditions is offered to benefit recipients who have been assessed as having at least 50% reduced capacity to work (Etherington and Ingold, 2015).

The Flex Job itself involves specific work tasks, in-work support and reduced working hours. Those eligible for Flex Jobs but who are waiting to join the scheme receive an unemployment allowance which is equivalent to UI, averaging around 80 to 90% of the highest rate of daily social benefits. In 2011, 70,000 people were employed in Flex Jobs, half in the public sector and half in the private sector. Local authorities also operate a sheltered employment scheme for people with more severe disabilities, but Flex Jobs continues to be the main activation programme for disabled people, combined with other support services such as personal assistance, career counselling and access to training (Etherington and Ingold, 2015).

Gender equality and the Labour market

In the context of the dominant Danish dual-earner model, women who stay at home are few. The Nordic countries are the only states to provide a 'work-welfare' choice for women, in that female work as an end in itself is relatively desirable, as family benefits are high and are always paid to the mother. The universal breadwinner model aims to achieve gender equity by promoting female employment and in this model both men and women are viewed as breadwinners (Rostgaard, 2014).

Investment in childcare provision is a central feature of this. Day care provision for children is integral to the welfare system; a significant number of children start before they turn one (17%) while 90% of one- and two-year-olds attend childcare centres. This is heavily subsidised by the state, and parental contributions must not exceed 25% of running costs. Parents can pay between €226 and €365 a month (Rostgaard, 2014). Parental leave comprises a total of 32 weeks, leaving it up to the parents how they want to share leave (apart from the early weeks of paternity leave). The total leave allowance is 52 weeks; mothers have 18 weeks of maternity leave, of which four are before a baby's due date and fathers have two weeks of paternity leave. There is a right to childcare once the child is 26 weeks old, even though parental leave may continue until the child is 46 weeks old. Finally, the public sector is hugely important not only in terms of social support for families but also as a source of women's employment. A high proportion of women are organised, and members of trade unions and their wages and working conditions are covered by CAs (Mailand and Thor Larsen, 2017). However, this is an important aspect of the gendered nature of the labour market where there is a high degree of occupational segregation (Ingold and Etherington, 2013).

Preserving the social safety net

Table 7.1 shows some basic indications of welfare and social support in Denmark compared with countries with similar economies. The table shows conclusively the impact of redistributive welfare spending on the labour market and the degree to which the social safety net in Denmark has been to a large extent been maintained. The first relates to spending on and provision of childcare as reflected in the proportion of children between 0 and 5 years in formal childcare. There is a massive gap between Denmark (along with other Scandinavian countries) and the UK. Denmark's investment in childcare is one of the highest in the EU and was maintained after the economic crisis broke out. In addition, the proportion of households experiencing great/moderate difficulties in affording childcare is also significantly lower in Denmark than in the UK. The corollary to this is that the proportion of households in Denmark who gave financial reasons as a factor in not using childcare for pre-school-age was just 0.7% compared with 25.9% in the UK (European Commission, 2018: 18).

A trend in the growth of working poor is the increasing proportion of women in employment accessing low paid and/or part time jobs. As Table 7.1 shows, this is significantly higher in the UK than in

Table 7.1: Social expenditure indicators: childcare in-work poverty and benefit replacement rates, selected European countries (%), 2014–2016

	Proportion of children 0–5 in formal childcare	Proportion having great/ moderate difficulty in affording childcare	Proportion of individuals working poor	Replacement rates of benefits (average for a couple with one earner, two children)
UK	28	16.7	23.0	32
Denmark	70	3.8	8.3	47
Sweden	51	6.2	16.7	45
Finland	32	4.3	14.9	n.a.
Germany	32	3.9	24.9	42
Netherlands	52	10.9	18.7	29
Belgium	43	14.3	12.8	64
France	48	12.9	15.9	45

Sources: Childcare – European Commission (2018, adapted from Table 4, p 18); working poor – Filandri and Struffolino (2018, adapted from Table 2, pp 144–5); replacement rates – Spicker (2017, adapted from Table 4.1, p 62)

Denmark (Filandri and Struffolino, 2018). The replacement rates of benefits (benefit levels compared with average previous wages earned) is significantly higher in Denmark. The percentage of GDP spent on unemployment reflects this and is higher in Denmark (2.5%) compared with 0.2% in the UK (Esser et al, 2013).

Responding to austerity in Denmark? Social dialogue, collective bargaining and 'inclusive growth'

Neoliberalism and the rise in precarious work

To sum up, the overall changes in the Danish labour market model and policies have brought about what Lind and Knudsen (2018: 597) describe as a shift from a 'welfare ideology to a market ideology'. These include:

- The decentralisation of pay determination has changed the balance of power within the bargaining model in favour of employers, without having changed fundamentally the bipartite character of the model. This, however, has led to increasing wage inequalities.
- The rise of other types of trade unions without a collectivist tradition weakens the social solidarity element of IR traditions.

- Changes to the UI system have entailed cuts in unemployment benefits and the liberalisation of the rules concerning unemployment funds also have a special effect: undermining the close relationship between membership of an unemployment fund and a trade union, which historically has been extremely important for union organisation. This said, it can still be argued that the UI system still plays a strong and active role in the links between the trade unions and marginalised workers.

As in other countries, austerity in the form of tightening of benefit conditionality and the increase in precarious work can be seen as a growing challenge or threat to the Danish model. Changes to benefits have involved restricting access by increasing eligibility through employment status and hours of work, increasing diversity of types of benefits including a lower-level benefit that is designed for new entrants to the benefits system (and which is mainly designed for immigrants), and a more work-first approach to activation where claimants in the SA system were often pressurised to move into available employment (Andersen et al, 2017).

This trend has been driven by labour market changes and the increase in the 'marginal' workforce. Atypical workers defined as part-time workers, fixed-term workers, agency workers, self-employed without employees and any combination of these comprise 35% of the workforce (Andersen, 2018: 20). The expansion of employment in the service sector: industrial cleaning, restaurants and retail has been accompanied by the increase in number of workers vulnerable to precarious employment (low pay, low hours of work allocation). This has given rise to fragmentation and difficulties in organising with many workers – mainly young people and immigrants do not traditionally have contact with trade unions. These sectors are covered by CAs but there are high variations and significant challenges in terms of negotiating minimum wages. A study by Ilsøe et al (2017) considers that despite these challenges the CA system seems to guarantee an adequate wage floor compared with equivalent countries. However, like the UK, a key issue is hours of work. More than two-thirds of the workforce are part-time with a working week of less than 30 hours, and a large proportion of workers hold multiple jobs. So while CAs can determine pay and other renumerations they do not, as a rule, include guaranteed minimum hours.

> Unlike industrial cleaning, the sectoral agreements within retail, hotels and restaurants fail to secure a threshold for

> minimum weekly working hours and furthermore they differentiate wages according to age with the agreed hourly wages for young people being nearly half of their older co-workers. This appears to contribute to increased segmentation and polarisation within Danish private services. Employers seem to exploit the various loopholes in the IR system to curb costs and secure flexibility by offering contracts of limited hours and replace older workers for cheap younger labour – employment practices seen elsewhere in Europe. (Ilsøe et al, 2017: 889)

While the relatively high number of part-time workers in the service sectors is striking, there is also a large number of workers working fewer than 16 hours, which characterises them as being vulnerable to in-work poverty. They find that the hourly wage is relatively and comparatively generous but there is an hours–at–work deficit which plunges them into the 'working poor' category. Add to this the low levels of union densities within those sectors and it is possible to conclude that the crisis, combined with austerity, has led to a rise in social and labour market inequalities in some of the major employment sectors in Denmark. Another trend is a rise in agency work, which has been controversial among the trade union movement because of their understanding that the labour market is so 'flexible' they do not see the need for employers to use agencies. Employers justify their use in terms of the need to increase flexibility in the labour market.

Addressing precarious and insecure work

As part of an EU-wide study, drawing on Denmark as a case study, Søren Kay Andersen explores 'how and to what extent the social partners – i.e. employers' organizations and trade unions – are actively engaging in new strategies and practices of inclusive growth through collective bargaining in the developing post-crisis period' (Andersen, 2018: 3). The Danish LO (TUC) has adopted some broad principles such as everybody who wants to work should have a job (right to work), this should be paid at a living wage and the CAs are based on a solidarity principle that the stronger unions should help those weaker sections of the labour market. An example of this is that the stronger trade unions and sectors are in manufacturing and there is a tacit acknowledgement that wage agreements made will lead to similar agreements in other sectors. Furthermore, minimum wages are linked to benefits and are set above maximum benefit levels. Thus:

> ... all the larger LO trade unions recognise that the interlinking of the sector agreements ensures that all groups on the private labour market will get by and large identical improvements in wages and conditions when collective agreements are renewed ... Crucial in this context is that the enhanced terms and condition that the workers in manufacturing gain in the first agreement concluded, sets the pattern for what workers in construction, retail, cleaning, hotel and restaurants, etc. will get. Thus, they emphasise that bargaining coordination supports an 'inclusive growth policy' ... (Andersen, 2018: 23)

As outlined earlier in this Chapter, there are numerous challenges to the system, particularly the maintenance of a social solidarity approach to CA in the face of increasing fragmentation of the labour market. The system is, however, still intact and there some examples where the infrastructure has enabled trade unions to innovate in relation to engaging with and organising marginalised workers (platform, migrants and agencies).

The CA system and trade union organisation have led to the development of innovative practices to combat labour market marginalisation. Three examples illustrate this: responses to temporary agency work; recruiting migrant workers; and negotiating the platform economy. The key area of debate is how workers are categorised whether they are self-employed or employees of those companies who organise their work. The use of temporary agency workers' (TAWs) has been on the increase in Denmark, although not at the same scale as in the UK, and is generally associated with increased risks of low wages, high job/employment insecurity, weak representation and limited access to social benefits, career advancement and further training schemes. The Danish trade unions initially campaigned against the use of temporary agency work, arguing that it eroded conditions and that the Danish labour market was 'flexible' enough. This attitude has changed with the development of strategies to unionise and negotiate CAs. In some sectors, TAWs are covered by CAs signed by social partners representing the temporary workers' agency and the TAWs within a specific occupation, while those in other sectors are covered by the CAs of the user company. In other sectors, a different approach is used, where the TAWs' wages and working hours follow the collective agreement of the user company, while other working conditions such as pensions and further training are regulated by the collective agreement of the Temporary Workers' Agency. These approaches have inevitably led to some conflicts:

> A more persistent controversy concerns the representation of agency workers. As they are employed by the agency, they are in principle covered by the representative bodies and eventual shop stewards within the agency. However, they are covered by the collective agreements in the company that hired them and where they work. This has led to diverse practices where shop stewards and management in some manufacturing companies have agreed upon including the agency workers, while others stick to the rules underlining that agency workers should not be part of the user company's representative bodies. (Andersen, 2018: 21)

A joint task force among the social partners has been established in order to establish CAs for those working for temporary workers' agencies. Many aspects of temporary agency work are dealt with at a local and company level. Some temporary workers' agencies also collaborate closely with the user companies, local jobcentres, unions and their representatives to coordinate user companies' demands for temporary agency workers' services vis-a-vis recruitment of potential TAWs among the pool of unemployed people registered with the local unions and jobcentres (Rasmussen et al, 2016: 92). There is evidence that the trade unions are pursuing the issue more at the company level and negotiating within agreements whereby TAWs are made permanent (Pernille Larsen and Refslund, 2016).

The increase in numbers of migrant workers has led trade unions to adopt strategies of engagement and organisation. A starting point was understanding that migrant workers have varied backgrounds and situations – some are more transient, others have more stable residence experiences and are relatively easier to organise. Danish researchers have drawn on two case studies as examples of union and social partner strategies. One, in the fishing industry in North Jutland, involved unions running a shaming campaign of the local employer through the media in terms of the exploitative conditions, with shop stewards building trust among workers (who were often suspicious of trade unions from their experience in their homeland), which finally ensured that the workers received equal wages and overtime rates. This was established through the trade union negotiating a CA in the factory – thus the role of CAs was crucial as a means of securing wage levels, overtime payment and holiday remuneration along the lines of the collective agreement. Afterwards, most of the migrant workers – Romanians (around 70%) – have joined the local union; they have also elected a local stop steward who is Romanian and has a close cooperation with the local union chairman and has received training from the union (Rasmussen et al, 2016: 85).

The second case study relates to the construction sector, in which the construction trade union had established a network of organisers to encourage migrant workers to join the trade union, employing organisers with different ethnic backgrounds so the union could approach the migrant workers in their native tongue. The unions also have a phone-based translator service (there is no locally-based translator), through which the local union representatives can start a dialogue with migrant workers. Another example from the construction sector is in Copenhagen, where the construction workers' union has organised a Polish club, where migrants with a Polish background can meet; there are also presentations about issues such as taxes, social security and more social events. In many respects, Danish trade unions have been faced with similar challenges to UK trade unions in terms of insiders and outsiders where they have to adopt 'non-traditional' strategies to recruit and retain members.

One of the interesting developments is the response by trade unions and social partners to the growth of the 'platform' or 'collaborative' economy. This is where employment and service delivery are primarily organised digitally, via the internet, the Uber taxi service being a well-known example. This has naturally led to concern over not only the status of workers but how and to what extent the trade unions can organise them.

> In spring 2018 Hilfr.dk, a Danish platform for cleaning in private homes, signed a collective agreement with 3F, the United Federation of Danish Workers. The agreement gives room for the individual worker to decide whether he or she will appear as 'employee' or 'self-employed'. Further, the agreement guarantees people who work on the platform sick pay, holiday allowance and a contribution to their pension. So far, it is a pilot agreement running for 12 months, however, the parties aim for a permanent sector agreement, which eventually should include the dominant employers' organization, the Confederation of Danish Industries, DI, who has been assessor in the formation of the pilot agreement. (Andersen, 2018: 21)

This is seen as the world's first collective agreement for workers in the platform economy. A recent study (Pernille Larsen and Weber Madsen, 2018; Ilsøe and Larsen, 2020) underlines how complex the platform economy has become in terms of management by the government and social partners. The key area of concern for the trade unions is to establish employment rights for workers, but it is also important that income and hours worked should be counted as contributions in terms of eligibility for unemployment benefits. The Tripartite Agreement on unemployment benefit in 2018 recognised this in relation to 'combi workers' – those who are partly salaried and self-employed. The major trade unions have convened an expert panel to assess responses to the platform economy including cooperation with a private pension company who could offer a scheme with favourable terms for platform workers. However, the issue is complicated in terms of how tax is calculated in relation to income generated. An added complication is how far there is interest among the sectors around agreements, given the fact that many workers view the income earned as supplementary to other income sources – which can mean that there may not be an incentive to join a trade union or see the advantage of a collective agreement. This said, the main concern of the trade unions is that some platforms' wages are undercutting those in standard CAs.

Linking employment to welfare through job rotation

Although there has been a trend towards work-first policies, at the same time the trade unions and labour market partners (including the Local Government Association) have been revisiting job rotation as a way of addressing increasing labour market marginalisation (Eurofound, 2018). Job rotation is a labour market instrument involving recruiting unemployed people to undertake work-based and vocational training. The unemployed act as substitutes for employees who can be released to undertake vocational or other forms of training. An integral feature of the model is that the unemployed receive pre-employment counselling and training as well as in-work mentoring and support throughout the programme. The model allows organisations to retain staffing levels while upskilling their workforce, and at the same time providing high quality employment and training for unemployed people.

The idea of job rotation (JR) originated in Denmark by the trade unions in the early 1990s at a time when high structural unemployment led to a call for more action and policies around the distribution of work and to assist unemployed people. JR was mainstreamed throughout the EU, funded and heavily promoted by the Commission. An important feature of the JR approach is the involvement of the social partners (trade unions, community sector, employers and labour market authorities) in the planning and implementation process. Almost 90,000 employees have received training and 20,000 unemployed people have trained as substitutes and re-entered employment (Kruhøffer, 2007; Etherington, 2008).

Stabilising the public sector?

The public sector is not only a major employer but has traditionally been the bedrock of the welfare state (Etherington, 1998). Between 28% and 31% of all employees work in public services. It is also a source of atypical employment with 38% of jobs part-time (Mailand and Thor Larsen, 2017). Of key importance is how the 2008–09 crisis and the imposition of austerity impacted on the welfare state and its capacity to deliver and resolve the problems associated with increasing poverty and insecure work. The first major response to the crisis was by the then Liberal–Conservative government, which introduced a programme of new public management in order to make the sector more efficient. In 2011, the centre-left coalition implemented a stimulus package of €1.6 billion in the public sector for 'new initiatives' and 'targeted improvements in the public sector' while at the same time controlling overall spending (Mailand and Thor Larsen, 2017: 11).

The governments have not imposed wage freezes in the same way as in the UK, but wage growth has been curtailed and additional measures such as outsourcing and controlling recruitment have been implemented. These measures have had significant negative impacts on the economy and the key challenge is maintaining the flexicurity model in the face of increasing restrictions and conditions on UI and SA. However, the combination of policy changes and the economic crisis has put the model under stress compared to its earlier heyday during the long upswing of from 1993 to 2008. The balance between flexibility and security has without doubt to some extent drifted away from the equilibrium that until recently gave the Danish model widespread support from most political parties and social partners. Fiscal policies have the effect of dampening the economy but there are 'automatic stabilisers' which bring help to raise employment levels in the economy through targeted tax increases and investment in the labour market through training programmes. This said, employment levels have fluctuated since 2008 and dropped from 454,000 in 2010 to 416,000 in local government in 2016 (Mailand and Thor Larsen, 2017).

In their study of social dialogue in selected sectors (elder care, health [hospitals] and education), Mailand and Thor Larsen argue that considerable changes have taken place which can be seen as pressures on the public sector: increasing work intensification, reduction in work quality, efficiency and cost-cutting strategies becoming more dominant, and a pay squeeze, meaning that wages are declining. When compared with the UK there has been nothing like both the ideological and sustained attack and erosion in Denmark. Indeed, the proportion of employees covered by CAs is around 98%, despite the fluctuations in employment since the crisis. A central factor that has ensured the public sector has comparatively been preserved − even though in a modified way − is the strength of social dialogue:

> The reforms, the Great Recession and other drivers have impacted on the public sector, but fundamentally IR institutions are the same and the social partners show a high level of stability in the 15 year period. Although employment has been reduced in the most recent years, the job level in 2017 is the same as in 2008. (Mailand and Thor Larsen 2017: 68)

Mailand and Thor Larsen's study can be interpreted as providing evidence on the importance of the Danish system of social dialogue and collective bargaining as mitigating the impacts of austerity policies on the public (and private sectors).

Critical reflections (and lessons) of the Danish model

Industrial relations

Some argue that the traditional welfare model has reached its limits although a number of researchers seem to agree that, while under intense pressure, and perhaps in crisis, there is no indication that the 'model' will be swept away by the more aggressive neoliberal offensive that has occurred in the UK (compare Lind and Knudsen, 2018 with Bredgaard and Kongshøj Madsen, 2018). As suggested earlier, there have always been tensions within the welfare-through-work model because of conflicting interests between labour and capital over the reproduction and regulation of labour power. Shifts within the state political strategy towards a more neoliberal workfare agenda − as the social democratic government moved to the right throughout the 1990s − meant that the ground initially gained by the labour movement from the 1994 reforms became gradually eroded. The 2000s comprised a more decisive shift in class relations as collective bargaining was weakened through a more decentralised system of collective bargaining and the loosening of ties between trade unions and the UI system. The main thrust of labour regulation post-2010 has been to create a flexible system of allocating and 'upskilling' labour reserves in the context of a more intensely competitive (global) economy. As highlighted earlier, there is evidence that employers are exploiting these 'cracks' or weaknesses in the IR model particularly in those sectors dominated by low-paid and insecure employment (Ilsøe et al, 2017).

Work-first policies

The other key challenge is presented by the shift to a more work-first regime. Denmark has installed a complex system of work-related conditionality on accessing SA and UI so that more and more people are under pressure to take up job offers. This raises a number of issues around how disadvantaged groups are going to move away from the cycle of work and welfare. Within the sphere of activation programmes, there is engagement of just a few employers, in the main incentivised by the wage subsidy schemes. There is evidence that these act as an incentive for the recruitment of the unemployed, but among certain types of employers who employ predominantly unskilled workers. Employers comprise the public sector and some private firms. Wage subsidies can also tend to act as a means of 'parking' the unemployed as 'firms where the economic situation had worsened within the last years were more likely to participate in the wage subsidy scheme. The empirical evidence thus indicates that firms may use subsidized labour as a means of coping with economic hardship leading to distortion of competition and crowding out' (Bredgaard and Halkjaer, 2016: 57). The shift during the last 15 years in the delivery of activation programmes towards local government (municipalities) has led to a significantly increased and expanded role for local government in the delivery of employment services via jobcentres for people claiming SA and disability benefits. On the one hand, the jobcentres can call on other social and health support for vulnerable groups; on the other, the pressure to move people into employment quickly has been accompanied by even further conditionality and the increase use of sanctions on claimants – also including sanctions imposed by central government on municipalities in terms of financial reimbursement. This means that the local authorities have fewer resources for managing the activation system (Andersen et al, 2017).

Class, race and gender

There have been major shifts in policy that have implications for gender and ethnicity. In 2005 the shift towards tighter conditionality was reinforced in a package of measures focused on the integration of immigrants, including *300 timers reglen* (the 300 hours rule), which replaced the spouse supplement. For married couples claiming SA, both spouses needed to have accrued 300 hours (subsequently, 450 hours) of paid work in the last two years to continue receiving benefit. Underpinning the 300 hours rule was the idea that married women should be enabled to gain equality through the labour market. The context was the comparatively lower (50%) employment rates for immigrant women, compared with 80% labour force participation for all women (Ingold and Etherington, 2013). The policy was not framed as a way of addressing labour market disadvantage but as an economic incentive to work, but it was obviously targeted at immigrant families. This policy was seen by sections of the left as punitive and it was eventually abolished after considerable protest. However, if anything, the hostile environment towards immigrants, and particularly Muslims, has been ratcheted up with the introduction of the ghetto policy (the 'Ghetto Deal') focusing on areas of cities where high proportions of immigrant communities live, with special measures in place to tackle crime, and ensure that children especially are 'integrated' into Danish society through mandatory day care (Bendixen, 2018).

The shift to the right and more neoliberal policies have had implications for gender equality in Denmark. The construction of notions of gender equality grew out of 'combined effects of a strong feminist mobilization and favourable political opportunity structures (which) enabled female policymakers to use the state as an arena for political activism for advancing gender equality and for adopting women–friendly policies' (Borchorst and Siim, 2007: 221). There is an argument that processes of class and ethnicity have to be put into the equation when assessing gender relations. Borchorst and Siim sum up:

> From an analytical perspective, new challenges related to globalization and multiculturalism have changed the social conditions for woman-friendliness and state feminism. The Scandinavian population has become more diverse in terms of religion, culture and language. This development has raised critical questions about the ability of the Nordic welfare model to include immigrants in the labour market and about the normative foundation of the dominant

Nordic model of gender equality and woman-friendliness.
(Borchorst and Siim, 2007: 221)

Women's opportunities have been advanced under highly-developed social reproduction policies, but gender segregation and the gender pay gap present a major challenge to equal opportunities. Furthermore, special measures for immigrants (lower-level benefits) have implications for gender equality as policies tend to reinforce social and gender divisions in the labour market. New forms of inequality among women are an obstacle for achieving gender equality from the perspective of ethnic and religious minorities. Furthermore, patriarchal attitudes dominate the employment environment leading to unequal involvement of men and women in childcare because men still face different kinds of expectations at work in comparison to women in the Nordic countries. For instance, it might be easier for a mother to take a day off in order to care for a sick child at home. In order to realise dual caring, men's possibilities in shouldering care responsibilities would need to be addressed (Tanhua, 2017: 8).

Conclusion: the Danish way – a path to an inclusive labour market?

Social dialogue and collective bargaining can be seen as integral to the social safety net and there is a 'growing body of evidence that points to the diverse channels and constellations of actors in contributing to the raising and extending employment standards' (Grimshaw et al, 2016: 294) and which offers important lessons for the UK. In the UK, in contrast, the machinery of the welfare state tends to be viewed as a drain on national resources, and a brake on international competitiveness. This thinking, sustained throughout the 1990s, and dominating New Labour thinking on welfare state reform has been a central and pivotal argument behind the Osborne and post-Osborne austerity policies.

Moreover, this chapter has sought to highlight the way that trade unions play a prominent role in providing counselling and welfare advice to their unemployed members, through the UIF. In many cases, both the Employment Service and local authorities, when overwhelmed by pressure on their counselling services, have sought trade union services to undertake counselling. Thus, the implementation of a key aspect of the reforms, and the maintenance of commitments to counselling and career plans, has been achieved through trade union assistance. Trade unions, through securing relevant 'rates for the job', and in their general role of maintaining employee rights for the job, provide important safeguards for people entering work-based training programmes. Trade unions also ensure the validity of returning-to-work guarantees for those participating in the educational programmes. In turn, JR relies heavily on trade union and Workers' Educational Association involvement. This is because the whole package of training involves work-based negotiation, in which trade unions play a leading role, in terms of identifying those in employment wishing to undertake further education and training. As well as providing relevant vocational training programmes, the Workers' Educational Association, which is sponsored by and closely linked to trade unions, also plays a role in seeking out companies to participate in the JR initiative.

The significance of JR described earlier, and the future roles it may play, relate to the way it is situated within these ongoing political struggles around the maintenance of trade union influence on social dialogue and different areas of employment and social policy in Denmark. Even in the context of austerity and work-first politics, other discourses are still evident, centring the links between JR and issues of social solidarity – for example, building connections between the employed and unemployed as a vehicle for shaping a relevant and comprehensive adult vocational education system; the possibilities for influencing the politics of social inclusion within labour market policy; and a mechanism for improving the delivery of public services by upgrading low-skilled workers. In this way JR encapsulates many progressive aspects of the Danish welfare model – it remains an important instrument of struggle; for shifting the agendas within the workplace and enhancing union representation in relation to training, it is seen as an important feature of local government initiatives in relation to addressing the needs of marginalised groups in the labour market (Etherington and Jones, 2004a, 2004b; Eurofound, 2018).

In addition to this, an important question for future critical policy and political analysis is whether initiatives such as JR will evolve as an adaptation of workfare, and a continuation of the 'new paternalism' found in North America, or whether they will be deployed as pilots for more inclusive and radical labour market instruments, perhaps indicative of social solidarity, that could provide a space within which to challenge contemporary neoliberal orthodoxy. The next and final chapter will explore some of these themes with respect to possibilities and potentials for an inclusive labour market in the UK.

8

Conclusions: progressive alternatives to austerity

The UK government still upholds the idea that self-regulating markets represent the ideal economic model, despite two years of expansionary fiscal contraction mounting criticism not only from heterodox and feminist economists but also from the IMF, evidence that shows all the hallmarks of a depression with either very low or zero growth, a clear lack of effective demand, and, in complete contrast to their intentions and predictions, increases in government borrowing owing to falling tax revenues. ... Explaining the rigid adherence to these policies and why the ideas of feminist and heterodox economists are overlooked is clearly important. (Perrons, 2012)

So public ownership of the big five is essential. Even if the government bought all the shares at market price it would cost only a one-off 3% of GDP (not that full compensation to shareholders is merited). That could easily be financed by the issuance of government bonds and serviced easily with the revenues and profits from the big five. The top executives of these banks would then be paid civil service salaries and have no shares – bank workers and trade unionists would sit on the boards to ensure accountability. Public ownership does not mean more bureaucracy – on the contrary, it means more democracy. (Roberts, 2018: 3)

Introduction

The cause of the economic crisis is rooted in the tendencies towards over-accumulation and falling rate of profit. The state plays an active role in these processes in two important ways: first, through the deregulation and liberalisation of the financial system leading to financialisation of the economic system, which exacerbates the structural problems of the economy. Second, the slashing of public spending and imposing massive cuts to the welfare state have created problems in relation to increasing poverty and posing problems for the reproduction of labour.

Chapter 5 illustrates the broad and diverse nature of strategies and counter discourses to austerity and labour discipline both inside and outside the workplace. In Chapter 7, an analysis of Denmark and the Danish system of welfare and employment relations provides an example of the type of 'progressive policies' that the Corbyn-led Labour Party was aiming towards. Even under pressures of globalisation and neoliberal politics the Danish system has retained many features of its social democratic redistributive system, with a central role for local government in social and employment policies. Of particular relevance to the central theme of the book is the way the welfare system is shaped by industrial relations, collective bargaining and the key role trade unions play in this. There are some lessons which can be drawn from Denmark. In this concluding chapter, I will draw the threads of this discussion on Denmark by outlining possible and potential alternatives to austerity and neoliberalism.

Brexit and austerity as a key factor in the post-election outcome

The reasons for the electoral defeat of the Corbyn-led Labour Party in December are complex but, in my view, austerity and geography played a key role. In Chapter 3, I argue that policies post-Thatcher 'embedded' or normalised neoliberalism within political discourse. As Mark L. Thomas comments:

> One crucial effect of Labour's long march to the right in the 1980s, reaching its apogee in Tony Blair, was that it enabled the construction of a very narrow political consensus at the top of British society. This centered around the combination of that globalization required the market to have ever greater sway at home and an insistence of the pivotal role of Britain's long-term alliance with US imperialism abroad. Both were underpinned by an appeal to the 'national interest' and an insistence that class was irrelevant to British society. Such a consensus between the dominant 'opinion formers' in the media, much of intellectual life across the plethora of think tanks and research bodies that surround parliamentary parties and business. It helped create a 'common sense' worldview that would then be projected as the settled view of whole society with any challenges to it marginalized

and presented as extreme, outdated and utopian. (Thomas, 2016: 40)

The referendum campaign was effectively highjacked by the UK Independence Party (UKIP) and the Tory right with its appeal to nationalism and xenophobia among the working class (Gough, 2017). Leaving the EU became an issue of immigration overshadowing any debate about its role in pursuing austerity. Much of the media focus since the election result in December 2019 has been on the 'left behind' regions. As highlighted in the Greater Manchester and Sheffield examples, these areas have borne the brunt of austerity, a feature of economic and social policies since the early 1980s. For example, a Joseph Rowntree Foundation study I was involved with looking at policies for deprived areas under the previous Labour government (2005–07) found that funding cuts, privatisation and contracting out of employment services were the dominant policy models in deprived regions, which meant that regeneration initiatives lacked the commensurate resources to affect real change (North et al, 2007). The so called 'left behind' regions have been subject to similar policies implemented by the Thatcher government. However, since the 2008 crisis austerity policies carried out by the coalition and subsequent Conservative governments have had more devastating impacts on the UK and especially in the former industrial areas of the North and Midlands. Deindustrialisation also means de-unionisation – the loss of thousands of trade union jobs and trade union infrastructure which acted as an important voice and social glue within deprived areas. To sum up, deindustrialised areas and working class communities became disenfranchised and vulnerable to poverty leading to frustration and anger.

But as shown in Telford and Wistow's study of Brexit voters in Teesside, those who voted for Brexit also were highly critical of the 'establishment' and political classes:

> … It was striking that discussions about Brexit triggered more than anything else a deep and pervasive sense of loss and resignation linked to the inability or unwillingness of politicians to respond to the problems associated with living in an area characterised by long-term industrial decline. (Telford and Wistow, 2019: 13)

New Labour in fact abandoned of its core electorate even before Blair came to power with its remodelling of the party in a way that focused away from representation of disenfranchised communities and its ambivalence and sometimes hostility towards trade unions. This has been one major factor for the Brexit vote and a major shift in voting to other parties among working class communities. During the period 1997–2010 Labour lost an estimated 4 million votes (Byrne and Ruane, 2017). Since 2010 before the election of Jeremy Corbyn, the leadership of the Labour Party under Ed Miliband accepted the austerity argument. The 'Blairite' wing of the Labour Party, whose adherence to the politics of neoliberalism, played a key role in its attempt to undermine the 'progressive' agenda that was in the 2019 manifesto.

This may be the reason why the welfare reform agenda and the discredited, contested and unpopular Universal Credit (UC) did not become an election issue for the Conservative government. 'Getting Brexit Done' spoke louder than the criticisms of welfare reform. However, the attack by the Labour right on Corbyn seemed to speak even louder. In the absence of a coherent alternative to austerity for nearly 40 years, and more important a previous lack of Labour Party active engagement with its core electorate, voting for a change became a vote to leave the EU, and for some as an expression of protest (Telford and Wistow, 2019).

However, there is an argument that for the first time since the 1970s the accepted mantra of austerity and free market economics was effectively challenged by the Corbyn-led Labour Party. The proposals by the Corbyn–McDonnell leadership (Labour Party, 2019) were similar to the Danish model as outlined in the previous chapter in relation to a more redistributive welfare model and a more central role for coordinated collective bargaining. The spending plans were in fact similar to those of equivalent economies such as Denmark, Germany and France (Giles, 2019). From the left of the party, the proposals were not viewed as overly radical, were seen as classic 'Keynesian' and social democratic, and did not challenge the 'underlying structure of class power' (Callinicos, 2019). Nevertheless, the rejection of austerity and the pursuance of a more socially just economic model has its appeal as reflected in the fact that despite the leadership challenges, Corbyn was elected twice as leader. The Labour Party also became the fastest growing 'anti-austerity' party in Europe in terms of membership and Labour's vote share in the 2019 general election was higher than in 2006, 2010 and 2015 (Seymour, 2016).

The election of Kier Starmer as Leader of the Labour Party in April 2020 represents a more right-wing political shift in the leadership of the Party. His election victory was followed by a 'clear out' from Labour's front bench of those who are strong Corbyn supporters and loyal to Jeremy Corbyn. In an interview in the Financial Times, Starmer blamed Corbyn and the election manifesto for the electoral defeat. In the same article, Steve Howell, Corbyn's former Deputy Director of Strategy, when asked to comment considered that Starmer made his own contribution by openly supporting a remain position stating that 'it was clever of him to put himself at the helm of the Remainer campaign, it was good for his leadership ambitions, but it was disastrous electorally' (Pickard, 2020). The big question is if and how far the Starmer led Labour Party are going to challenge the Conservative Government's disastrous welfare reform and employment policies.

However, the 'Corbyn project' has created a political space for resisting austerity and, as outlined in Chapter 4, has brought about mobilisation on an unprecedented scale, especially against the welfare cuts leading to most of the trade unions and Labour leadership committed to the scrapping of UC. Reconnecting with the disenfranchised and marginalised is a major task for the Labour Party and trade unions. The struggle against austerity and neoliberalism, poverty and inequality will be at the forefront of the resistance to a 'no deal' Brexit as the Conservative government moves towards a more regressive economic and social model. Clawing back the lost votes was always going to be a big task. But the alternatives to austerity still have a mass appeal and interest (Smith, 2019).

The COVID-19 crisis: a further attack on the social safety net and insecurity

As analysed in Chapter 3, the undermining of the safety net after 30 years of austerity has led to a significant proportion of the population – around 14 million people in poverty. The scale of the economic and social crisis *before* the COVID-19 crisis cannot be over emphasised. The Johnson–led Conservative government has implemented a number of measures to mitigate the impacts of the COVID-19 shutdown. In summary (at the time of writing at the end of April 2020), these involve the *Job Retention Scheme*, which is designed to prevent redundancies for businesses affected by coronavirus. It will reimburse 80% of furloughed workers' wage costs, up to a cap of £2,500 per month. *Statutory Sick Pay (SSP)* entitlement has now been widened to make SSP payable from day one and is available not only to those who are at home self-isolating with symptoms of coronavirus but also to self-isolators who live in the household of a person with symptoms of coronavirus. The

Self-Employed Income Support Scheme will support people who had a self-assessment tax return for 2018/19, who make the majority of their income from self-employment, and whose profits are below £50,000, based on an average of their last three years of income (or the maximum number of years available). Self-employed people will be paid 80% of their incomes up to a maximum of £2,500 a month, and unlike those who are employed will be able to continue some economic activity. Many people who are not eligible for the schemes and/or made unemployed will be directed to apply for *UC*. This involves an increase in the UC standard allowance and the Working Tax Credit basic element will increase by £20 a week (equivalent to £1,040 a year) above the planned annual uprating. Eligibility for UC has been widened, with self-employed people no longer needing to meet a minimum income floor in order to qualify for the benefit. As well as this, housing benefit has been increased. The local housing allowance has been increased so that it covers up to 30% of the market rent in the local authority, restoring the position prior to the Welfare Reform Act in 2012, which dramatically cut housing benefit alongside many other forms of support. Around £3 billion has been allocated to local authorities for spending on social support (see TUC, 2020).

The Conservative government's 'rescue package' has received criticisms from the Institute of Fiscal Studies (IFS, 2020), Resolution Foundation (2020) and Child Poverty Action Group (CPAG, 2020a, 2020b) and Women's Budget Group (WBG, 2020) (to name a few) because of the inadequacies of the initiatives to deal with the impact of the crisis. According to John Hendy (2020) of the Institute of Employment Rights (IER), the government's interventions in many ways replicate and reinforce the precarious nature of work, and underline the lack of employment rights within the workplace. There are three aspects to this. First, the Job Retention Scheme (JRS) mirrors the existing insecurities of those who deviate from the 'standard' employment relationship on which it is predicated and does not fit well with the circumstances of those workers, once described as 'atypical', who are not direct, permanent employees working on fixed hours and wages. Second, the JRS continues to fit badly with existing employment law provisions. As a result, it may fail to meet some of its intended aims: in particular, it produces no real incentive on the part of an employer to re-engage workers already dismissed. Third, employers have powers to decide who is to be 'furloughed', giving no role to workers or unions in the process, with detrimental consequences for collective solutions to the crisis. So 'the absence of any requirement of social dialogue in this extraordinary situation is a really striking deficit that says everything about the disrespect in which workers and trade unions are held' (Hendy, 2020: 11).

In his analysis of the actual and potential impacts of the schemes, Hendy (2020) estimates that nearly 11 million workers could face destitution primarily because of the existence of huge gaps in all the schemes. This relates to a number of areas. First, not all people are eligible for SSP, including people who earn less than the Lower Earnings Limit of £118, and those on insecure contracts such as agency workers and on zero-hours contracts (totalling around 9 million workers). The level of SSP is around only 18.7% of current average weekly earnings of £512 per week (excluding bonuses). Second, the JRS applies to workers paid through PAYE and therefore does not apply to all workers, particularly those who are unlikely to be furloughed (agency and zero-hours contracts). Those forced to stay out of work to care for people who would otherwise be provided for by nurseries, schools, day care centres and other public services could miss out on the JRS. While it is possible for these workers to be furloughed, it is unlikely they will be. Over 1.25 million self-employed people could go out of business because the Self-Employed Income Support Scheme will not pay out until June. Many self-employed people are on low incomes with many possessing insufficient savings; an estimated one in four self-employed people do not have a high enough income to support themselves until they can access the schemes (see IFS, 2020). Two-thirds of households cannot survive a pause in their pay. Before the crisis, only one in three households had the savings available to cope with an emergency, and household debt averaged at 98% of household income (rising even higher for lower earners).

The emergence of mass unemployment as a result of the crisis and the 'lockdown' has led to unprecedented numbers (1.5 million and growing) having to apply for UC. As the Resolution Foundation observes:

> People are losing their jobs now, either because firms are already going bust, or because they can't afford to wait for the retention scheme to start making payments. Such is the scale of the shutdown to parts of our economy that it seems likely that the eventual rise in unemployment will be at least as large as, and much swifter than, that seen during the financial crisis, despite the unprecedented schemes put in place to halt its increase. (Resolution Foundation, 2020: 2)

The CPAG has highlighted the fact that not all groups will be eligible to apply for UC and that there are substantial challenges in providing claimant support because either advice services are completely overwhelmed or services that provide digital support such as libraries are closed (CPAG, 2020a). At the time of writing there is no evidence that the Conservative government will abolish the five weeks wait for benefits or write off the advance loans, abolish the two child tax credit and the benefit cap – the latter two 'penalties' which, from the first day of implementation, have had major detrimental impacts on the incomes of families with children (CPAG, 2020b). Once people are able to access UC, the level of benefits are extremely low (here including 'legacy benefits' such as JSA and ESA) and totally inadequate to live on. The basic rate of UC is worth around one-sixth of average weekly pay (17%) (TUC, 2020).

To sum up, the lockdown has brought more to the surface many aspects of class and gendered nature of social inequality highlighted in this book. A major cause for concern is the undermining of the safety net. The Women's Budget Group has observed that there are over 3 million people in jobs at high risk of exposure to COVID-19 in the UK – 77% of them are women. Over 1 million of these workers are low paid – 98% of them are women. The majority of the frontline jobs in health, social care, food distribution are occupied by women, BAME workers and immigrants; those jobs are low paid, insecure, precarious and dangerous because of the lack of protection against the virus (WBG, 2020).

The COVID-19 crisis, along with the election of Kier Starmer and a Labour leadership whose politics contains the legacy of Blair and right-wing labourism, is likely to change the UK political landscape. The policies implemented by the Conservative government are replicating the austerity policies that preceded the crisis. Searching for alternatives becomes an even more urgent task for the trade unions, labour and social movements.

Challenging the austerity narrative

Austerity is based on highly suspect theoretical frameworks (see Chapters 1 and 2) but also, more importantly, how the media and public discourse have drowned out the opposition and critical voices. The argument that high rates of public debt negatively impact on growth and output has been the basis for austerity policies across Europe and beyond. Some economists, however, have found that austerity is associated with the deterioration of public debt as a percentage of GDP ratio and that, during recession, cutting public spending actually deflates the economy. Furthermore, austerity is seen in an ideological sense by some as a vehicle to promote other agendas such as attacking the notion of collective public services and has little to do with reducing the debt (Konzelmann et al, 2017; Seymour, 2014).

The London School of Economics (LSE) Growth Commission has highlighted the failure to invest both in the private and public sectors as a cause of low growth (LSE Growth Commission, 2013). The IMF, traditionally an organisation that has promoted a more market orientated economic policy, considers that there may have been too much emphasis on austerity, which is leading to increasing inequality (IMF, 2016). Furthermore, economists have questioned the government view that only the private sector produces wealth and the public sector is a 'drain' on resources (Konzelmann et al, 2019).

The obvious retort from the neoliberals is that the public sector is unaffordable, although since the COVID-19 crisis this has far less purchase among the general public. Suddenly the Conservative Party, which has done so much to undermine the National Health Service (NHS) and the welfare state, is applauding NHS workers. So, part of the critical austerity narrative is to talk about a financial model that will create sustainable public services and economic growth based on equality and social justice. It is beyond the scope of the book to go into this any detail except to state that the issue of tax justice has been the subject of debate for some time (Byrne and Ruane, 2017). Establishing a stronger regulatory framework and funded system of management and compliance through the HMRC is a crucial basis to establishing a fairer tax system. Such a system would be based on strategies such as increasing top-rate tax or corporation tax (for instance, to 30%), which would immediately bring in total £30 billion (NEF, 2018); a wealth tax could raise in total over £40 billion based on taxing assets worth more than £700,000 (Painter et al, 2018); and combating tax avoidance and evasion could bring in untold billions. In terms of regulation Byrne and Ruane (2017: 127) propose an anti-tax avoidance principle in legislation which brings in the notion of avoidance as a criminal offence.

The question of what sort of economic model could be an alternative to austerity and that could deliver quality growth and jobs is addressed by Michael Roberts. His analysis (Roberts, 2016) is that the crisis is located in the profitability crisis of capital rather than lack of demand and under investment. One important factor in the crisis is the role of the banks. There are others that are discussed by Roberts, but the banks illustrate both causal processes and potential solutions. For Marx (1973), the drive and engine of accumulation is through the role of credit which is supplied by the banks and financial institutions. The expansion of credit becomes out of proportion to value and profitability in capitalist production. The banks did not cause the recession and depression, but the decisions related to private capital accumulation (and households in relation to the housing market, which is funded out of surplus value) did. However, the banks have been central to exacerbating the crisis.

> Instead, the regulators have decided that, as long as the banks keep a bit more of their cash and capital on their books, they can carry on as before speculating in financial instruments of 'mass destruction' (as billionaire mogul Warren Buffet described them), still using the deposits of the banks' customers (i.e. our money). After all, banks are commercial operations and must provide returns for their shareholders ... And it's business as usual already (and will now be for another 5–13 years!). Already the amount of transactions in the credit derivatives market (the one which spread the financial losses throughout the sector) is back to the same levels as before the crisis. And the bonuses and perks of the bank directors and top traders are back at their previously grotesque levels. (Roberts, 2010: 3)

As the banks make money from money, as argued by Roberts, and a number are partially owned by governments, why shouldn't they be considered as a public service like any other institution of the welfare state? The crucial point is that 'nationalising' the banks under the control of communities and trade unions is central to democratising the economy.

There are of course other counter-narratives produced by the welfare rights, social movements and trade unions in relation to the damaging effects of austerity on disadvantaged groups and society, which was the focus of Chapter 4. Vicki Cooper and David Whyte have coined the phrase 'the violence of austerity', which describes how austerity and the withdrawal of state support for vulnerable groups constitutes a form of violence 'that can be understood as a means of force which is not simply acted upon, but organised and administered through *legitimate* means' (Cooper and Whyte, 2017: 23, emphasis in original). As argued in this book, if the economic and political model of austerity is to discipline and indeed oppress labour then the term violence is both relevant and appropriate in describing the nature of policies and government actions. Furthermore, it also underlines how policies are being promoted on the back of an ideology of blame and demonisation. Benefit claimants are lazy and feckless, and trade unions are irresponsible and 'hold the country to ransom'. Negative and aggressive stereotyping is shaping and indeed a part of the violence of austerity.

Strengthening employment *and* social security through collective bargaining

Chapter 7, on the Danish model of industrial relations and welfare, puts forward the argument that Denmark can offer a relevant case study for an 'inclusive labour market' as strong and developed industrial relations and social security have secured a comparatively more equal society than most other developed capitalist countries. Trade unions, the left and progressive movements, including the Corbyn-led Labour Party, were putting forward a radical agenda for trade unions and employment relations that has similarities to the Danish system.

As outlined in the previous chapter the Labour Party at its 2019 conference adopted a number of measures on industrial relations and employment rights proposed by the IER (Glenister and Jones, 2019). With new legally protected powers to speak out collectively against injustice, workers will be provided with a means to protect and improve their job security, pay and conditions, and to further their careers through increased training. Underlying this system will be the reinstatement of collective bargaining as the foundation of workplace relations, together with stronger employment rights such as a higher minimum wage and better protection against discrimination. The importance of these proposals cannot be overstated and will have major implications for how the welfare system will operate.

Strengthening the role of trade unions in terms of rights to recognition and representation will alter the balance of power in favour of labour and enable workers to be properly represented at work. Rights will be guaranteed from the first day of work and not conditional on hours worked. There is a strong correlation between weak bargaining and industrial systems and increasing wage inequality. Reducing wage inequality will have a progressive impact on the economy in terms of lifting low-paid workers out of in-work poverty, increasing tax revenues (reducing the need for in-work subsidies). Workplaces with a strong trade union presence also tend to have higher rates of training, health and safety and work security overall. There is a greater opportunity to negotiate work–life balance and family friendly practices in unionised workplaces (Glenister and Jones, 2019). Strengthening the industrial relations system in favour of labour and trade unions could open up the space for stronger links between the trade unions with social security claimants.

A system of coordinated collective bargaining will address precarious work and zero-hours contracts, which will have significant impacts on claimants as this is generally the type of entry-level work offered to people in the benefit system. The IER study of the social care sector (Hayes, 2017) shows that poor-quality care is highly correlated with the poor terms and conditions of care workers. Collective bargaining and strengthened employment rights for care workers will combat the problems of low pay which 'are inseparable from those of employment insecurity, high labour turnover and growing risks to workers' physical and mental health. By putting sectoral collective bargaining into practice, the social care industry would break its deadlock over poor terms and conditions of work' (Hayes, 2017: 13).

They also have implications for the proposals by the Women's Budget Group (WBG, 2016) in relation to expanding the care economy. The WBG argues that most analysis on growth is gender-blind even though women have been severely disadvantaged by wider economic changes. Everyone gains from having a better-educated, healthier and better cared-for population and society, and the economy will continue to benefit from today's spending on health education and childcare well into the future. This form of expenditure investment is termed social infrastructure. Public investment in social infrastructure makes economic sense, as it not only generates employment but also contributes to gender equality and human development. Reducing the employment gap is not the only gender inequality that could be improved through investment in care. Wages and working conditions in the care industry would have to improve considerably if such an investment were to be successful, given existing retention and recruitment problems in the industry. As argued before, coordinated collective bargaining, and strengthening employment rights and union representation will be crucial for achieving these goals.

This section concludes with a note of caution. Strengthening employment and bargaining rights is a crucial step for an economy and society based on social justice. This will throw up challenges for trade unions in terms of adapting to the changing labour market and welfare policies. It will require further innovations in relation to their own cultures, structures and practices in terms of reaching out and engaging with communities beyond the workplace.

The link between social security, industrial relations and employment: the possibilities of job rotation

The other major Labour Party policy change is the scrapping of UC (Labour Party, 2019) which is more than likely due to campaigning by trade unions and grass roots organisations (see Chapter 4) and the adoption of this policy by the Unite trade union. The TUC Unemployed Workers' Centres formulated a *Welfare Charter* which has been adopted by most of the major trade unions and promoted by the Public and Commercialp Services (PCS) union, who launched a refreshed version in 2019 under the title *Social Security the Case for a Radical Change* (PCS, 2019). Some of the key areas covered by both the charter and the refreshed version have been a central element of the Danish labour market model of job rotation (see Chapter 7) which is focused on in more detail shortly. The PCS report includes a number of measures, including promoting a policy of full employment based on decent work providing regular, guaranteed hours that allows workers to meet any caring responsibilities; the implementation of a national living wage that people can live on; and enabling greater 'collective bargaining', which will facilitate and strengthen wage bargaining. The proposals also include the end to workfare schemes, particularly where claimants are required to work for benefits under compulsion and threat of benefit sanctions.

Representation for the unemployed is seen as a priority, not just as a way of assisting the reduction in sanctions (which should be abolished anyway); claimants can receive advice in relation to participation in their claimant agreement and improve communications between claimants and jobcentre advisors. This also includes the appointment of an Ombudsman for claimants to arbitrate on unresolved complaints. The proposal is important because it could involve a greater involvement of trade unions in representing claimants – whether they are in work or unemployed. One of the key institutions that provides a link between the trade unions and unemployed in Denmark (and other Nordic countries) is the Unemployment Insurance Fund. Although this institution cannot be replicated in the UK, there may be other ways of introducing a more formalised structure that links trade unions to claimants and precarious workers. Unsurprisingly, the policies include proposals to abolish (or redesign) Work Capability Assessments, to be replaced by a new system integrating health assessments with employment support that also involves employers (Etherington and Daguerre, 2015) with an increased focus on how workplaces can be adapted or adjusted to meet the needs of disabled people. State provision of high-quality information, advice and guidance on employment, training and careers is also proposed so that everyone can freely access the whole range of options offered by further and higher education, vocational training and apprenticeships.

I would argue that some of these proposals are put into practice in Denmark. In our comparative study of Denmark and the UK, Martin Jones and I identified ways in which community, trade unions and professional workers involved with employment and welfare programmes in Denmark are opening up a space to define an 'inclusive labour market' discourse and politics (or set of discourses) in which redistribution, empowerment and equality are dominant terms of reference (Etherington and Jones 2004a; see Ingold and Etherington, 2013). One example of such an inclusive labour market policy which has been given some attention is job rotation (JR), described briefly in Chapter 7.

An integral feature of the JR model is that unemployed people receive pre-employment counselling and training as well as in-work mentoring and support throughout the programme. The model allows organisations to retain staffing levels while upskilling their workforce, and at the same time provide high-quality employment and training for unemployed people. Unemployed substitutes would receive a wage at the collectively agreed rate. Significantly, JR has linked welfare-to-work and lifelong learning policies invoking the need for organisations to provide the necessary adjustments through human resources and organisational policies in terms of assimilating newcomers to the workplace. The other key feature of the Danish reforms and the introduction of JR is the strengthening of the regional labour market institutions and corporatist modes of governance with equal representation for the trade unions, local government and employers on the Regional Labour Market Councils. It is through this type of integrated approach that JR has been coined a 'welfare through work' model in that employment programmes are linked to workplace strategies around recruitment and vocational education and training. The essence of JR is that it raises interesting discussions around how people can be retained in employment, skills attainment and utilisation, and the appropriate strategies that are required to achieve this (Etherington and Jones, 2004a).

The trade unions who were well-positioned within the policy arena gained considerable control and influence in representing unemployed interests in terms of work-based training as well as shaping the vocational training programmes that were delivered to existing employees (Etherington and Jones, 2004a, 2004b). The dynamic for expanding the use of JR in Denmark was the introduction of various leave schemes, including education leave, under the 1994 reforms. Participation in the schemes was funded by the state via educational budgets and unemployment benefits but this was accorded as a right. The leave schemes were intended to raise the qualification profile of low-skilled unemployed and employed people. It is important to emphasise that the JR model is underpinned by the inclusion of education and training as part of 'activation' programmes – something which has arisen from pressures from the social partners and the trade unions representing unskilled workers.

Changing the narrative of work, non-work and conditionality

How should we approach and value non-paid work activities for people who find that they are unable or unwilling to be involved with paid work? There are numerous reasons why people are not in the labour market – health conditions and caring responsibilities are major factors. It is not just notions of paid work that need to be critically examined but whether people should have a 'right not to work' as put forward by Chris Grover (2015). This may be the corollary of the abolition or curtailing conditionality in social policies that is implied in the findings of the Welfare Conditionality Project (2018a). Grover's argument relates to a discussion on disabled people and he argues that the majority of disabled people would like to work, but there are those who do not want to work or are unable to do so. Within a conditionality system, those not wanting to work are

> othered as being particularly problematic and burdensome. If, however if there was a right not to work the othering of workless disabled people would no longer be an issue. Such an approach would be consistent with the disabled people's movement's desire that disabled people should have control over, and choice in their lives. (Grover, 2015: 251)

This argument is as much about abolishing policies and disciplining mechanisms which at the end of the day oppress and control disadvantaged groups and, even worse, reinforce their exclusion.

Grover's argument can be extended to analysing all groups in society. For example, this is central in the critique of lone-parent policies and the 'male breadwinner' assumptions of UC (contrasting with the individualised approach to benefits as operated in Denmark) (see Chapter 5). There is an increasing focus on the centrality of paid work as the key duty of all responsible citizens, including those with responsibilities for the care of children. Although the contribution made by parents as carers had been recognised as socially useful in the past, this position has declined, and unconditional entitlement to welfare has come to be regarded as a contributing factor in the entrenchment of welfare dependency. The idea that an engagement with paid work is compatible with responsibility for the care of children reveals some key assumptions about the nature of work and the status we attach to it. According to policy frameworks, a responsible engagement with work occurs when an individual takes paid labour and the activity is defined as work via the mechanism of wage work. The normalisation of maternal employment has influenced the process by which lone parents have come to be regarded as potential employees, rather than as actively engaged in caring duty. The care of children, on the other hand, is not valued, being framed only as a 'barrier' to paid work (Davies, 2012). While work-first policies operate in Denmark, lone parents are not subject to the same conditionality as in the UK, and publicly-funded affordable childcare is still a key element of welfare policies within a more gender-friendly welfare state (Ingold and Etherington, 2013).

This argument is extended to include 'work–life balance' assumptions in public policy, and why initiatives to reconcile work and caring often fail – but also why women are disproportionately disadvantaged in the labour market and vulnerable to austerity (Rubery, 2015b):

> Gendered identities, family relationships and informal family care are often seen as 'private' as in beyond the scope of intervention from governments or workplaces, but gendered identities, family relationships and informal family care arrangements are shaped, in part, through government assumptions and work place interventions ... Thus a failure to interrogate gendered assumptions of 'public' and 'private' within work-life balance discourses and initiatives further produces assumptions that gendered behaviours and responses from mothers and fathers are 'natural' *rather than* socially constructed and constrained. (Ben-Galim and Gambles, 2008: 194)

The devaluation of care work has been largely shaped by the ideologies of work-first policies which emphasise paid work as the answer to social exclusion. But these policies are highly gendered and therefore discriminatory. But, in the same fashion, work itself is socially constructed, illustrated by Diane Perrons (2012) when she points out that women are concentrated in those sectors and industries that carry out 'reproductive functions' such as catering, caring and cleaning. The outcome is that an 'executive from a failed United Kingdom bank was retained to advise on its restructuring at a monthly salary equivalent to three-and-a-half times the annual salary of a childcare worker with twenty years' experience provides a telling illustration of comparative values' (Perrons, 2012: 73–4).

Social security or universal income? More than a safety net

In this book I have argued that welfare conditionality is a way of disciplining labour and keeping benefits at a low rate is an important part of this (Chapters 3 and 4). The discussion about Denmark (Chapter 7) highlights that one of the key aspects of the welfare system is a relatively generous benefit system where social security is seen as a safety net in order to prevent poverty. Fixing social security is highly controversial: part of the austerity narrative is that the welfare system is 'unaffordable' and serves to support the 'undeserving poor'. As UC is rolled out and the campaigns challenging this are taking more of a hold in the public consciousness there is space to develop alternatives that can gain public support.

One way of assessing how benefits meet basic needs is to identify the minimum income that individuals and households require to acquire a 'socially acceptable' standard of living. The Minimum Income Standard (MIS) project run by the Joseph Rowntree Foundation (JRF) is calculated based on different baskets of goods and services required by different types of households. Research for the JRF has produced data on this using a focus group comprising people with a mixture of socioeconomic backgrounds. A minimum is defined as 'more than just food, clothes and shelter. It is about having what you need to participate in society' (Hirsch, 2019). In Hirsch's research assessing trends over the decade 2008–2018, when MIS budgets are compared with disposable income for people on minimum benefits or working on the minimum wage over the decade, it is clear that, in general, income has risen more slowly than minimum budgets, causing an increasing shortfall for such households. Hirsch continually emphasises that the key problems for families is rising costs and the failure of wages (and household incomes) to keep up with them:

> It is thus essential that alongside the ambition to abolish low pay, other determinants of low disposable income are

addressed. A full agenda for doing so needs to address a range of factors, including opportunities to access stable work and affordable housing. This report has identified two factors that urgently need to be addressed ... A starting point is to uprate benefits at least by inflation after the freeze in their level ends next year. A next step would be to improve their real value, with the long-term aim that at least families working full time on the NLW [national living wage] would reach MIS (which they almost did on the NMW [national minimum wage] in 2010) ... [and with respect to child care] ... While long-term solutions may need to involve a more coordinated approach to providing accessible childcare at affordable prices, a more straightforward first step would be to ensure that UC supports childcare at the prices actually being charged. (Hirsch, 2019: 19)

The issue of low benefits and wages and high rates of poverty has led to calls for the introduction of a Universal Basic Income (UBI). UBI is a sum of money paid to every individual regardless their income or employment status. A UBI differs from contributory or means-tested models of social security because people receive the same amount, regardless of whether they are in or out of work, or how much they earn. Some of the facets and arguments for a UBI are:

- *the pursuit of social justice:* particularly reducing poverty, tackling inequality and ensuring everybody has a basic level of income security;
- *improvement of the social security system:* reducing bureaucracy and removing 'conditionality' attached to social security;
- *support for creative, civic and family life:* rewarding currently unpaid forms of work such as family care and providing everybody with the means to pursue creative and voluntary activities. This is an interesting and important advantage as it addresses concerns around the paid work discourse on welfare and the importance of valuing unpaid work; and
- *more freedom for the market:* the reduction of state intrusion, the size of the welfare state, and potentially an overall reduction in government spending (this argument tends to come from the political right). (Harrop and Tait, 2017: 7)

The argument against UBI is that it can be viewed as a way of subsidising low-paid work and help to normalise precarity. UBI confirms the importance of generous, non-stigmatising income support, but it largely depends on how much money is paid, under what conditions and with what consequences for the welfare system as a whole. There are more effective and sustainable ways of meeting people's needs and fighting inequalities than just giving cash to everyone. These are the findings of a study by the New Economics Foundation (NEF) for the Public Services International and TUC (Coote and Yazici, 2019). While there are several UBI schemes operating across the globe, the evidence base is weak in terms of their success in meeting the objectives of combating poverty. This largely because many of them are small-scale, experimental and short term, and have not been rolled out at a national level for any period of time.

Coote and Yazici (2019) identify other key problems that a UBI can present. A UBI scheme can act as a substitute for collective bargaining on minimum wages and wages generally, and indirectly can weaken the industrial relations system which trade unions and the labour movement are campaigning to strengthen. This has been an argument put forward by the Danish trade unions, who have resisted any proposals to implement a legal framework for minimum wages. Considering the current climate of low wage growth following the 2008 crash this is an important criticism. The other key perceived weakness of the UBI model is that it ignores the complexity of the system of welfare and role of public services.

> It is necessary and possible to raise funds to bring greater security, opportunity and power to all people, but the money needed to pay for an adequate UBI scheme would better spent on reforming social protection systems, and building more and better quality public services. Many (although not all) proponents of UBI see it as a means to fix problems that unions care about. Thus the UBI debate creates important opportunities for unions to advocate for quality public services, progressive labour and welfare reform. (Coote and Yazici, 2019: 39)

I am sympathetic with these arguments, based on the underlying weakness of the UK industrial relations and welfare system which I have described in this book. Strengthening employment rights combined with 'welfare rights' is important to address labour market and welfare inequality.

Concluding reflections: investing in democratic accountable public services as a way forward

The solution to the crisis and austerity is not just about holding the banks to account, although this is important, but there is a need for greater public control of the economy. Strengthening employment rights and investing in public services is key to this. An important alternative to austerity is to expand the public sector through local government and democratise the development of local and city region strategies. Gough et al (2006: 234) argue that a socialist strategy for the state is to open it up to influence and control by working class communities and organisations. Expanding the role of public services through local government, which is accountable to electorates, will be an important step in that direction.

An important way forward in a strategy of universal basic services is therefore to invest in local government that can deliver a range of initiatives which support social reproduction, gender equality and support disadvantaged groups into employment and training. One important feature of the Danish welfare model is the major role of local government in the devolution and implementation of both welfare and employment policies. This 'municipalisation' of employment policy has involved the establishment of local employment committees (*Lokal Beskaeftelses Rad*, LBR), whose role is to advise and monitor jobcentre performance, establish local priorities and pilot or develop projects in accordance with these priorities. The central objective of the committee, which comprises representatives from all social partners, is to use its capacities and resources to assist those most disadvantaged in the labour market. A key element of the reforms was the increasing inclusion of disability rights organisations and the allocation of specialist disability advisers within jobcentres (Etherington and Ingold, 2015).

Further reforms have rationalised the structure with the creation of regional councils, based on the geographical boundaries of the Danish county councils (comprising the local authorities and county council) but the operation principles have been retained. As local authorities are responsible for social services, health, childcare, administering benefits they offer the possibilities for policy integration operating around principles of democratic accountability – to both the electorate and social partners. The Danish model regulates and *guarantees* systems of representation to involve the relevant interests strategically within policy arenas. Local government, far from being marginalised in labour market policy making, plays an *active* role. Danish labour market partnerships, despite their problems, are transparent and simple. By contrast, the increasingly complex and fragmented nature of UK partnerships does not guarantee the political space to challenge polarisation and counterbalance the more powerful groups such as local business interests (Etherington and Jones, 2004b; Etherington and Ingold, 2015).

Furthermore, employment is one area in which the public sector and local authorities can have a significant direct impact and influence. This is because the public sector is often the biggest employer in local areas, particularly deprived areas, and furthermore by leading through example the public sector can have an impact on the employment practices of private employers and the voluntary and community sectors. Local authorities have real potential to provide the communities they serve with secure employment opportunities and real routes for progression for those who would otherwise be in casual jobs. Furthermore, local authorities have a duty to promote equality and can provide opportunities for those who are discriminated against in the labour market. In this way local authorities, not unelected elitist partnerships run in the interests of business, can be the key institutions which 'manage' local labour markets and economies. City region and local governance structures can comprise local employment partnerships which have a broad representation of the social partners – trade unions, voluntary sector, local authorities and private sector – in a similar way as occurs in Denmark. They would be involved with 'real' devolution in which the relationship between the local and centre is one of equality and where devolved interventions are not shaped by central diktats but reflect locally-determined needs.

Notes

Chapter 4

[1] www.unionlearn.org.uk/news/west-midlands-signs-tuc-apprenticeship-charter
[2] https://unitetheunion.org/campaigns/stop-universal-credit/
[3] This is now the policy of the main Unite trade union.
[4] https://unitetheunion.org/news-events/news/2018/november/universal-credit-pushing-people-into-debt-and-housing-problems-reveals-survey/

Chapter 6

[1] Information obtained from Disability Sheffield, May 2018.

References

Alston, P. (2018) *Statement on Visit to the United Kingdom, by Professor Philip Alston, United Nations Special Rapporteur on Extreme Poverty and Human Rights*, www.ohchr.org/Documents/Issues/Poverty/EOM_GB_16Nov2018.pdf

Andersen, K. (2018) *Inclusive Growth through Collective Bargaining in Denmark*, Leuven: Research Institute for Work KU, https://hiva.kuleuven.be/nl/onderzoek/thema/arbeidenor/p/Docs/cawie3docs/cr/cawie3_cr_dk

Andersen, N., Caswell, D. and Larsen, F. (2017) *Innovation of Employment Services for Vulnerable Groups: The Case of Denmark*, Aalborg: Aalborg University, http://vbn.aau.dk/files/290192902/a_new_apporach_to_helping_the_hard_to_place_unemployed_2017.pdf

Bales, K., Bogg, A. and Novitz, T. (2017) *'Choice' and 'Voice' in Modern Working Practices: An Evidence Informed Response to the Taylor Review*, Policy Report 14, Bristol: University of Bristol.

Beatty, C. and Fothergill, S. (2014) *The Impact of Welfare Reform on Sheffield*, www4.shu.ac.uk/research/cresr/sites/shu.ac.uk/files/impact-welfare-reform-sheffield.pdf

Beatty, C. and Fothergill, S. (2016) *The Uneven Impact of Welfare Reform: The Financial Losses to Places and People*, Sheffield: CRESR Sheffield Hallam University, www4.shu.ac.uk/research/cresr/sites/shu.ac.uk/files/welfare-reform-2016_1.pdf

Beatty, C. and Fothergill, S. (2017) *Jobs, Welfare and Austerity: How the Destruction of Industrial Britain Casts a Shadow over Present Day Public Finances*, Sheffield: CRESR, Sheffield Hallam University.

Beel, D., Jones, M. and Jones, I.R. (2016) Regulation, governance and agglomeration: making links in city-region research, *Regional Studies, Regional Science*, 3: 509–30.

Beel, D., Jones, M. and Jones, I.R. (2017) Connected growth: developing a framework to drive inclusive growth across a city-region, *Local Economy*, 32: 565–75.

Beel, D., Jones, M. and Jones, I.R. (2018) Elite city-deals for economic growth? Problematizing the complexities of devolution, city-region building, and the (re)positioning of civil society, *Space and Polity*, https://doi.org/10.1080/13562576.2018.1532788

Bendixen, M. (2018) Denmark's 'anti-ghetto' laws are a betrayal of our tolerant values, *Guardian*, 10 July, www.theguardian.com/commentisfree/2018/jul/10/denmark-ghetto-laws-niqab-circumcision-islamophobic

Ben-Galim, D. and Gambles, R. (2008) The 'public' and 'private' of work-family reconciliation: unsettling gendered notions and assumptions, in M. Seeleib-Kaiser (ed) *Welfare State Transformations Comparative Perspectives*, Basingstoke: Macmillan, pp 182–94.

Berry, C. (2020) Don't be fooled: Britain's Coronavirus Crisis bail out will make the rich richer still, *Guardian*, 13 April.

Bhattacharya, T. (2017) How not to skip class: social reproduction of labour and the working class, in T. Bhattacharya (ed) *Social Reproduction Theory: Remapping Class Recentering Oppression*, London: Pluto Press.

Blackford, C. (1993) The best of both worlds? Women's employment in post war Britain, in J. Fryth (ed) *Labour's High Noon*, London: Lawrence and Wishart.

Blyth, M. (2016) *Austerity: The History of a Dangerous Idea*, Oxford: Oxford University Press.

Bohle, D., Burroni, L. and Marginson, P. (2012) *WP6 Governance of Uncertainty and Sustainability: Challenges at National, Sectoral, Territorial and Company Levels*, Final Report, University of Warwick, https://warwick.ac.uk/fac/soc/wbs/research/irru/publications/recresrep/wp6_final_report_final_31_08_21_l.pdf

Borchorst, A. and Siim, B. (2007) Gender equality woman-friendly policies and state feminism: theorizing Scandinavian gender equality, *Feminist Review*, 9(2): 207–24.

Bradley, H. (1999) *Gender and Power in the Workplace: Analysing the Impact of Economic Change*, London: Macmillan.

Brandl, B. and Traxler, F. (2004) Industrial relations system and social welfare expenditure: a cross national comparison, University of Vienna, https://ecpr.eu/Filestore/PaperProposal/219fcc13-0f3d-4cf6-ad31-86298957197d.pdf

Bredgaard, T. and Halkjaer, T. (2016) Employers and the implementation of active labour market policies, *Nordic Journal of Working Life Studies*, 6(1): 47–59.

Bredgaard, T. and Kongshøj Madsen, P. (2018) Farewell flexicurity? Danish flexicurity and the crisis, *Transfer*, 1–12, DOI: 10.1177/1024258918768613

Brenner, N., Peck, J. and Theodore, N. (2010) After neoliberalization, *Globalizations*, 7: 327–45.

Bricken, K. and Taylor, P. (2018) Fulfilling the 'British Way' beyond constrained choice – Amazon workers live experience of workfare, *Industrial Relations Journal*, 49(5–6): 438–58.

Brown, W. (2011) *Industrial Relations in Britain under New Labour, 1997–2010: A Postmortem*, https://doi.org/10.17863/CAM.982

Burnham, P. (2014) Depoliticisation, economic crisis and political management, *Policy & Politics*, 42: 189–206.

Butler, P. (2020) 'Judge me fairly': man who starved to death's plea to welfare officials, *Guardian*, 27 February.

Byrne, D. and Ruane, S. (2017) *Paying for the Welfare State in the 21st Century*, Bristol: Policy Press.

Callinicos, A. (2012) Contradictions of austerity, *Cambridge Journal of Economics*, 36: 65–77.

Callinicos, A. (2019) The wages of Brexit, *International Socialism*, 165, http://isj.org.uk/the-wages-of-brexit/

CAS (Citizens Advice Sheffield) (2018a) *Insecure Employment in Sheffield*, Sheffield: Citizens Advice Sheffield.

CAS (2018b) *Just Managing*, Sheffield: Citizens Advice Sheffield.

Caswell, D., Marston, G. and Larsen, J.E. (2010) 'Unemployed citizen or 'at risk' client? Classification systems and employment services in Denmark and Australia', *Critical Social Policy*, 30: 384–404.

Centre for Cities (2019) *Cities Outlook, A Decade of Austerity*, London: Centre for Cities.

CfRC (Centre for Responsible Credit) (2017) *Decline in Local Welfare Assistance Schemes in England: Why a New Approach is Needed*, London: CfRC, www.responsible-credit.org.uk/wp-content/uploads/2017/10/Decline-in-Local-Welfare-Schemes-final.pdf

Chakrabortty, A. (2019) It's labour you can turn on and off like a tap, *Guardian*, October, www.theguardian.com/film/2019/oct/10/ken-loach-sorry-we-missed-you-interview-poverty-homelessness-inequality-privatisation

Children's Society (2017) *The Parent Trap: Childcare Cuts under Universal Credit*, London: Children's Society.

Citizens Advice (2018) *Citizens Advice's Response to the Social Security Advisory Committee Consultation*, www.citizensadvice.org.uk/Global/CitizensAdvice/welfare%20publications/SSAC%20-%20Citizens%20Advice%20full%20response%20-%20revised%20.pdf

Clarke, S. (2017) *Forging Ahead or Falling Behind? Devolution and the Future of Living Standards in the Sheffield City Region*, Resolution Foundation, www.resolutionfoundation.org/app/uploads/2017/01/Sheffield2.pdf

Clarke, J. and Langan, M. (1993) The British welfare state foundation and modernisation, in A. Cochrane and J. Clarke (eds) *Comparing Welfare States*, London: Sage.

Clery, E., Dewar, L. and Bivand, P. (2020) *Untapped Talent Single Parents and In-work Progression – The National Picture*, London: Gingerbread.

Clegg, D., Graziano, P. and van Wijnbergen, C. (2010) *Between Sectionalism and Revitalization: Trade Unions and Activation Policies in Europe*, Edinburgh Reconciling Work and Welfare, REC-WP 07/2010, www.era.lib.ed.ac.uk/handle/1842/3498

Clough, B. (2017) *The Influence of Peak-Level Social Partnership and Vocational Education and Training Policy: The Rhetoric and the Reality*, CERIC Working Paper No.3, Leeds: University of Leeds.

Coats, D. (2012) *From the Poor Law to Welfare to Work: What Have we Learned from a Century of Anti Poverty Policies?* London: Smith Institute.

Cobham, D., Adam, C. and Mayhew, K. (2013) The economic record of the 1997–2010 Labour government: an assessment, *Oxford Review of Economic Policy*, 29(1): 1–24.

Cochrane, A. (1993) *Whatever Happened to Local Government?* Milton Keynes: Open University.

Cochrane, A. (2012) Spatial divisions and regional assemblages, in D. Featherstone and J. Painter (eds) *Spatial Politics: Essays for Doreen Massey*, RGS-lBG Book Series, Chichester: Wiley-Blackwell, pp 87–98.

Cochrane, A. and Etherington, D. (2007) Managing local labour markets and making up new spaces of welfare, *Environment and Planning A*, 39: 2958–74.

Coderre-LaPalme, G. and Greer, I. (2018) Dependence on a hostile state: UK trade unions before and after Brexit, in S. Lehndorff, H., Dribbusch, and T. Schulten (eds) *European Trade Unions in a Time of Crises*, Brussels: European Trade Union Institute, pp 259–84.

Cooper, V. and Whyte, D. (2017) Introduction, in V. Cooper and D. Whyte (eds) *The Violence of Austerity*, London: Pluto Press, pp 1–34.

Coote, A. and Yazici, E. (2019) *Universal Basic Income: A Report for Unions*, Ferney-Voltaire Cedex, France: Public Services International.

Corlett, A. (2016) *Paved with Gold? Low Pay and the National Living Wage in Britain's Cities*, London: Resolution Foundation.

CPAG (Child Poverty Action Group) (2017) *The Austerity Generation: The Impact of a Decade of Cuts on Family Income and Child Poverty*, London: CPAG.

CPAG (2018a) *Rough Justice: Problems with Monthly Assessment of Pay and Circumstances in Universal Credit, and What can be Done About Them*, London: CPAG.

CPAG (2018b) *Early Warning System: Universal Credit Top Ten Issues*, London: CPAG, https://cpag.org.uk/policy-and-campaigns/report/top-universal-credit-issues

CPAG (2020a) *Mind the Gap, Reporting on Families' Incomes During the Coronavirus*, 16 April, London: CPAG.

CPAG (2020b) *Mind the Gap, Reporting on Families' Incomes During the Coronavirus*, 23 April, London: CPAG.

Crouch, C. (1999) Employment, industrial relations and social policy: new life in an old connection, *Social Policy and Administration*, 33(4): 437–57.

Crouch, C. (2014) Introduction: labour markets and social policy after the crisis, *Transfer*, 20(1): 7–22.

Crouch, C. (2018) Membership density and trade union power, *Transfer*, 23(1): 47–61.

Cumbers, A., Helms, G. and Swanson, K. (2010) Class agency and resistance in the older industrial city, *Antipode*, 42: 46–73.

Daguerre, A. and Etherington, D. (2014) *Workfare in 21st Britain: The Erosion of Social Rights to Social Assistance*, London: Middlesex University, http://workfare.org.uk/images/uploads/docs/Workfare_in_21st_century_Britain-Final.pdf

Damgaard, B. and Torfing, J. (2010) Network governance of active employment policy: the Danish experience, *Journal of European Social Policy*, 20(3): 248–62.

D'Arcy, C., Gardiner, L. and Rahman, H. (2019) *Low Pay in Greater Manchester: A Report for the Greater Manchester Independent Review*, London: Resolution Foundation.

Darling, J. (2016) Privatising asylum: neoliberalisation, depoliticisation and the governance of forced migration, *Transactions of the Institute of British Geographers*, 41: 230–43.

Davies, S. (2008) Contracting out employment services to the third and private sectors: a critique, *Critical Social Policy*, 28(2): 136–64.

Davies, L. (2012) Lone parents: unemployed or otherwise engaged? *People Place and Policy*, 6(1): 16–28.

Davies, J. (2017) *Governing In and Against Austerity: International Lessons From Eight European Cities*, Leicester: De Montford University.

De Brunhoff, A. (1979) *State, Capital and Economic Policy*, London: Pluto.

Department of Communities and Local Government (DCLG) (nd) *Devolution: A Mayor for Greater Manchester: What Does it Mean?*, www.lepnetwork.net/media/1481/plain_english_guides_to_devolution_greater_manchester.pdf

Dewar, L. and Clery, E. (2019a) *Held Back: Single Parents and In Work Progression in London*, London: Gingerbread.

Dewar, L. and Clery, E. (2019b) *Making Apprenticeships and Traineeships Work for Single Parents*, London: Gingerbread and Trust for London.

Disability Benefits Consortium (2018) SSAC consultation on Universal Credit (draft) (transitional provisions) (managed migration) amendment regulations 2018: response by the Disability Benefits Consortium (DBC), https://disabilitybenefitsconsortium.wordpress.com/author/dbconsortium/

Disability Rights UK (2014) Disability Rights UK's response to the fifth annual review of the Work Capability Assessment led by Dr Paul Litchfield, www.disabilityrightsuk.org/news/2014/june/consultation-5th-wca-review

Disability Rights UK (2019) 9 out of 10 Work and Health Programme participants do not have a job outcome, www.disabilityrightsuk.org/news/2019/may/9-out-10-work-and-health-programme-participants-do-not-have-job-outcome

Disability Sheffield (2015) *Disability Sheffield Consultation Response to the Extra Costs Commission*, Sheffield: Disability Sheffield.

Donald, B., Glasmeier, A., Gray, A., and Lobao, L. (2014) Austerity in the city: economic crises and urban service decline, *Cambridge Journal of Regions, Economy and Society*, 7: 3–15.

DPAC (Disabled People Against the Cuts) and Inclusion London (2017) Follow up submission: response to the UNCRPD Inquiry report and UK Government response, www.inclusionlondon.org.uk/campaigns-and-policy/act-now/follow-submission-response-uncrpd-inquiry-report-uk-government-response/

Dromey, J. (2018) *Power to the People: How Stronger Unions can Deliver Economic Justice*, London: IPPR.

Dromey, J. and McNeil, C. (2017) *Skills 2030: Why the Skills System is Failing to Build an Economy that Works for Everyone*, London: IPPR.

Dukelow, F. and Kennett, P. (2018) Discipline, debt and coercive commodification: post crisis neoliberalism and the welfare state in Ireland, the UK and the USA, *Critical Social Policy*, 38(3): 482–504.

DWP (Department for Work and Pensions) (2018) *Universal Credit Full Service Survey*, London: DWP.

Ebbinghaus, B. (1998) European labour relations and welfare-state regimes: a comparative analysis of their 'elective affinities', background paper for Cluster 3: The Welfare State and Industrial Relations Systems Conference on Varieties of Welfare Capitalism in Europe, North America and Japan, Max Planck Institute for the Study of Societies, Cologne, 11–13 June.

EHRC (Equality and Human Rights Commission) (2018) *The Cumulative Impact of Tax and Welfare Reforms*, London: EHRC.

End Child Poverty and the Church of England (2018) *Unhappy birthday: the two child limit at one year old*, www.endchildpoverty. org.uk/wp-content/uploads/2018/04/Unhappy-birthday-report-on-two-child-limit-final.pdf

ERSA (Employment Related Services Association) (2014) *ERSA response to the Fifth Independent Review into Work Capability Assessment*, http://ersa.org.uk/documents/ersa-response-fifth-independent-review-work-capability-assessment

Esping-Andersen, G. (1990) *The Three Worlds of Welfare Capitalism*, Cambridge: Polity Press.

Esping-Andersen, G. (1992) The emerging realignments between labour movements and welfare states, in M. Regini (ed) *The Future of Labour Movements*, London: Sage.

Esser, I., Ferrarini, T., Nelson, K., Palme, J. and Sjoberg, O. (2013) *Unemployment Benefits in EU Member States*, Brussels: Employment Social Affairs and Inclusion.

Etherington, D. (1998) From welfare to work in Denmark: an alternative to free market policies? *Policy and Politics*, 26(2): 147–61.

Etherington, D. (2008) *Incapacity Benefit Claimants and Job Rotation: New Opportunities for Labour Market Inclusion*, London: British Academy.

Etherington, D. (2018) Ideology or evidence base? The role of Work Capability Assessments for people with disabilities in UK welfare to work programmes, in B. Greve (ed) *Handbook of Social Policy Evaluation*, Cheltenham: Edward Elgar, pp 364–82.

Etherington, D. and Daguerre, A. (2015) *Welfare Reform, Work First Policies and Benefit Conditionality: Reinforcing Poverty and Social Exclusion*, Middlesex University, www.mdx.ac.uk/our-research/centres/ceedr/employment-skills-and-quality-of-work/welfare-reform

Etherington, D. and Hampton, C. (2018) *Submission to the Social Security Advisory Committee on Proposals to Move Existing Claimants on Income Related Benefits on to Universal Credit: Report of Findings of Survey and Research in Chesterfield, Derbyshire*, Chesterfield: Derbyshire Unemployed Workers Centre, www.advicederbyshire.org/duwc/documents/SSAC%20Submission%20DUWC_Mdx%20August%20 2018.pdf

Etherington, D. and Ingold, J. (2012) Welfare to work and the inclusive labour market: a comparative study of activation policies for disability and long term sickness benefit claimants in the UK and Denmark, *Journal of European Social Policy*, 30(1): 22–44.

Etherington, D. and Ingold, J. (2015) Social dialogue, partnership and the Danish model of activation of disabled people: challenges and possibilities in the face of austerity, in C. Grover and L. Piggott (eds) *Disabled People, Work and Welfare*, Bristol: Policy Press.

Etherington, D. and Jones, M. (2004a) Beyond contradictions of the workfare state?: Denmark, welfare-*through*-work, and the promises of job-rotation, *Environment and Planning C: Government and Policy*, 22: 129–48.

Etherington, D. and Jones, M. (2004b) What ever happened to local government? Local labour market policy in the UK and Denmark, *Policy and Politics*, 32(2): 137–50.

Etherington, D. and Jones, M. (2009) City regions and new geographies of uneven development and inequality, *Regional Studies*, 43(2): 247–65.

Etherington, D. and Jones, M. (2016a) The city-region chimera: the political economy of metagovernance failure in Britain, *Cambridge Journal of Regions, Economy and Society*, 9: 371–89.

Etherington, D. and Jones, M. (2016b) *Devolution and Disadvantage in the Sheffield City Region: an assessment of employment, skills and welfare policies*, Sheffield University/Middlesex University, www.sheffield.ac.uk/polopoly_fs/1.643923!/file/Devolution_and_disadvantage.pdf

Etherington, D. and Jones, M. (2017) *Devolution Austerity and Inclusive Growth in Greater Manchester*, Middlesex University/Staffordshire University, www.mdx.ac.uk/__data/assets/pdf_file/0030/368373/Greater-Manchester-Report.pdf?bustCache=92145287

Etherington, D. and Jones, M. (2018) Restating the post-political: depoliticisation, social inequalities, and city-region growth, *Environment and Planning A*, 50: 51–72.

Etherington, D., Jefferey, R., Thomas, P., Brooks, J., Beel, D., and Jones, M. (2018) *Forging an Inclusive Labour Market – Empowering Workers and Communities: An Interim Report on Low Pay and Precarious Work in Sheffield*, Sheffield: Sheffield Hallam University, http://shura.shu.ac.uk/21918/3/Jeffery%20Forging%20an%20inclusive%20labour%20market.pdf

Eurofound (2018) Job rotation, www.eurofound.europa.eu/observatories/emcc/erm/support-instrument/job-rotation

European Commission (2018) *Barcelona Objectives on the Development of Childcare Facilities for Young People*, Brussels: European Commission.

European Work and Employment Research Centre (EWRC) (2017) *Just Work in Greater Manchester*, www.research.mbs.ac.uk/ewerc/Portals/0/Documents/just-work-report-2.pdf

Ewing, K.D., Hendy, J. and Jones, C. (eds) (2018) *Rolling out the Manifesto for Labour Law*, Liverpool: Institute of Employment Rights.

Farnsworth, K. (2006) Capital to the rescue? New Labour's business solutions to old welfare problems, *Critical Social Policy*, 26(4): 817–42.

Farnsworth, K. and Irving, Z. (2018) Austerity: Neoliberal dreams come true? *Critical Social Policy*, 18(3): 461–81.

Fazi, T. (2016) How austerity has crippled the European economy – in numbers, *Social Europe*, www.socialeurope.eu/austerity-crippled-european-economy-numbers

Filandri, M. and Struffolino, E. (2018) Individual and household in work poverty in Europe: understanding the role of labor market characteristics, *European Societies*, 21(1): 130–57, DOI: 10.1080/14616696.2018.1536800

Fine, B. (2003) Contesting labour markets, in A. Seed-Fihlo (ed) *Anti-Capitalism: A Marxist Introduction*, London: Pluto Press.

Finn, D. (2015) *Welfare to Work Devolution in England*, York, Joseph Rowntree Foundation.

Folkman, P., Froud, J., Johal, S., Tomaney, J. and Williams, K. (2016) *Manchester Transformed: Why we Need a Reset of City Region Policy*, Centre for Research on Social Cultural Change, University of Manchester/Open University, http://hummedia.manchester.ac.uk/institutes/cresc/research/ManchesterTransformed.pdf

Fuller, C. (2018) Entrepreneurial urbanism, austerity and economic governance, *Cambridge Journal of Regions, Economy and Society*, 11: 565–85.

Giles, C. (2019) Labour seeks huge jump in borrowing, tax and spending, *Financial Times*, 21 November, www.ft.com/content/7364ee82-0c6e-11ea-bb52-34c8d9dc6d84

Gingerbread (2018) *Where next on Universal Credit?* www.gingerbread.org.uk/wp-content/uploads/2018/05/Where-next-on-Universal-Credit.pdf

Ginsburg, N. (1979) *Class Capital and Social Policy*, London: Methuen.

Glenister, S. and Jones, C. (2019) *A Guide to a Progressive Industrial Relations Bill*, Liverpool: Institute of Employment Rights.

GMCA (Greater Manchester Combined Authority) (2013) *Manchester Public Services Reform First Phase Implementation Plan*, Manchester: GMCA, www.manchester.gov.uk/download/downloads/id/21368/local_implementation_plan.pdf

GMCA (2018) *Welfare Reform and Universal Credit in Greater Manchester*, Manchester: GMCA.

GMCA and New Economy (2015) *Welfare Reform in Greater Manchester Impact on People, Services, Housing, and the Economy*, Manchester: GMCA/New Economy.

GMCDP (Greater Manchester Coalition of Disabled People) (2018) *Disabled People's Manifesto*, Manchester: Greater Manchester Coalition for Disabled People.

Gough, J. (2014) The difference between local and national capitalism, and why local capitalisms differ from one another: A Marxist approach, *Capital and Class*, 38(1): 197–210.

Gough, J. (2017) Brexit, xenophobia and left strategy now, *Capital and Class*, 41(2): 366–72.

Gough, J., Eisenschitz, A. and McCulloch, A. (2006) *Spaces of Social Exclusion*, London: Routledge.

Gracio, M. and Giugni, M. (2016) *Do Issues Matter? Anti-Austerity Protests, Composition, Values and Action Repertoires Compared*, Sheffield: Sheffield University, https://pdfs.semanticscholar.org/f1c5/9225e61 44629b05ad4ec14799479f8ac44d2.pdf

Grady, J. (2017) The state, employment and regulation: making work not pay? *Employee Relations*, 39(3): 274–90.

Gray, M. and Barford, A. (2018) The depth of the cuts: the uneven geography of local government austerity, *Cambridge Journal of Regions and Society*, 11: 541–63.

Greater Manchester Law Centre (2017) *ESA Claims: A Study by Paul Cosier*, Manchester: Great Manchester Law Centre.

Greater Manchester Law Centre (2018) Cross city groups hold day of action against Universal Credit evictions, 18 April, www.gmlaw.org. uk/2018/04/18/universal-credit-evictions/

Greater Manchester New Economy (2016) *Low Pay and Productivity in Greater Manchester*, Manchester: Greater Manchester New Economy.

Greer, I. (2016) Welfare reform, precarity and the recommodification of labour, *Work Employment and Society*, 30(1): 162–73.

Grimshaw, D., Johnson, M., Kaizer, A. and Rubery, G. (2016) *Reducing Precarious Work Through Social Dialogue; The Case of the UK*, University of Manchester: Work and Employment Research Centre, www.research.mbs.ac.uk/ewerc/Our-research/Current-projects/ Reducing-Precarious-Work-in-Europe-through-Social

Grover, C. (2009) Privatizing employment services in Britain, *Critical Social Policy*, 29(3): 487–509.

Grover, C. (2012) Personalised conditionality: observations on active proletarianisation in late modern Britain, *Capital and Class*, 36(2): 283–301.

Grover, C. (2015) A right not to work and disabled people, in C. Grover and L. Piggott (eds) *Disabled People Work and Welfare: Is Employment Really the Answer?* Bristol: Policy Press, pp 239–56.

Grover, C. and Piggott, L. (2015) Disabled people, work and welfare, in C. Grover and L. Piggott (eds) *Disabled People, Work and Welfare: Is Employment Really the Answer?* Bristol: Policy Press, pp 1–26.

Grover, C. and Stewart, P. (1999) Market workfare: social security, social regulation and competitiveness in the 1990s, *Journal of Social Policy*, 28(1): 73–96.

Gumbrell-McCormick, R. and Hyman, R. (2018) *Trade Unions in Western Europe: Hard Times, Hard Choices*, Oxford: Oxford University Press.

Harrop, A. and Tait, C. (2017) *Universal Basic Income and the Future of Work*, Fabian Society, https://citizensincome.org/book-reviews/harrop-and-tait-universal-basic-income-and-the-future-of-work/

Hastings, A., Bailey, N., Bramley, G. and Gannon, M. (2017) Austerity urbanism in England: The 'regressive redistribution' of local government services and the impact on the poor and marginalised, *Environment and Planning A*, 49: 2007–24.

Haughton, G., Deas, I., Hincks, S. and Ward, K. (2016) Mythic Manchester: Devo Manc, the Northern Powerhouse and rebalancing the English economy, *Cambridge Journal of Regions, Economy and Society*, 9: 355–70.

Hayes, L. (2017) *8 Good Reasons Why Adult Social Care Needs Sectoral Collective Bargaining*, Liverpool: Institute of Employment Rights.

Hayes, L. and Novitz, T. (2014) *Trade Unions and Economic Inequality*, London: CLASS/Institute of Employment Rights.

Healy, G. and Bergfeld, M. (2013) *The Organisational Challenges Presented by the Increasing Casualisation of Women's Work*, London: TUC.

Helm, T. (2013) Labour will be tougher than the Tories on benefits, promises new welfare chief, *Guardian*, 12 October, www.theguardian.com/politics/2013/oct/12/labour-benefits-tories-labour-rachel-reeves-welfare

Hendy, J. (2020) *The Gaps in the Government's Coronavirus Income Protection Plans*, Liverpool: Institute of Employment Rights.

Heyes, J. (2013) Flexicurity in crisis: European labour market policies in a time of austerity, *European Journal of Industrial Relations*, 19(1): 71–86.

Himmelweit, S. (2016) *Changing Norms of Social Reproduction in the Age of Austerity*, www.iippe.org//wp-content/uploads/2017/01/suegender.pdf

Hincks, S., Deas, I. and Haughton, G. (2017) Real geographies, real economies and soft spatial imaginaries: creating a more than Manchester region, *International Journal of Urban and Regional Research*, 41: 642–57.

Hirsch, D. (2019) *Minimum Income Standards 2019*, York: Joseph Rowntree Foundation.

Hirsch, D. and Miller, J. (2004) *Labour's Welfare Reform: Progress to Date*, York: Joseph Rowntree Foundation.

Holgate, J. (2018) Trade unions in the community: Building broad spaces of solidarity, *Economic and Industrial Democracy*, https://doi. org/10.1177/0143831X18763871

House of Commons Library (2017) *Jobcentres and the Department for Work and Pensions Estates*, CDP-2017-0152, 19 July, London: House of Commons Library.

House of Commons Library (2018) *Further Education: Post 16 Area Reviews*, London: House of Commons Library.

Howard, M. and Skipp, A. (2019) *Unequal, Trapped and Controlled: Women's Experience of Financial Abuse and Potential Implications for Universal Credit*, London: TUC.

Hudson, R. (2011) From knowledge based economy ... to knowledge based economy? Reflections on changes in the economy and development policies in the North East of England, *Regional Studies*, 45: 997–1012.

Hunt, M. (2012) *Greater Manchester: Social, Economic and Sustainability Context*, Retrofit 2050 Working Paper, Cardiff: Welsh School of Architecture, Cardiff University.

Hyman, R. (1989) *The Political Economy of Industrial Relations*, London: Macmillan.

Hyman, R. (2018) What future for industrial relations in Europe? *Employee Relations*, 40(4): 569–79, https://doi.org/10.1108/ER-02-2018-0056

Hyman, R. and Gumbrell-McCormick, R. (2017) Resisting labour market insecurity: old and new actors, rivals or allies? *Journal of Industrial Relations*, 59(4): 538–61.

Ilsøe, A. and Larsen, T.P. (2020) *Digital platforms at work. Champagne or Cocktail of Risks?* Copenhagen: University of Copenhagen.

Ilsøe, A., Pernille Larsen, T. and Felbo-Kolding, J. (2017) Living hours under pressure: flexibility loopholes in the Danish IR-model, *Employee Relations*, 39(6): 888–902, https:// doi.org/10.1108/ER-03-2017-0049

Ingold, J. and Etherington, D. (2013) Work, welfare and gender inequalities: an analysis of activation strategies for partnered women in the UK, Australia and Denmark, *Work Employment and Society*, 27(4): 621–38.

Institute of Employment Rights (IER) (2018) *Manifesto for Labour Law*, Liverpool: IER.

Institute for Fiscal Studies (2018) *The Fair Funding Review: Is a Fair Assessment of Council Spending Needs Feasible?* London: IFS.

Institute for Fiscal Studies (2020) *Income Protection for the Self-Employed and Employees During the Coronavirus Crisis*, London: IFS.

International Monetary Fund (IMF) (2016) Neoliberalism oversold? *Finance and Development*, June, www.imf.org/external/pubs/ft/fandd/2016/06/ostry.htm

IPPR (Institute for Public Policy Research) (2016) *Devo-health: What and Why?* London: IPPR.

IPPR (2017) *Skills 2030: Why the Skills System is Failing to Build an Economy for Everyone*, London: IPPR.

IPPR (2018) *Prosperity and Justice: The Plan for the New Economy*, London: IPPR.

Ishkanian, A. (2019) *Social Movements, Brexit and Social Policy*, LSE Research online, http://eprints.lse.ac.uk/88297/

Jessop, B. (2016) *The State: Past, Present, Future*, Cambridge: Polity Press.

Johnson, M., Lucio, M.M., Cartwright, J., Mustchin, S. and Grimshaw, D. (2017) *Just Work in Greater Manchester*, University of Manchester/Alliance Business School.

Johnston, A., Kornelakis, A. and Rodriguez d'Acri, C. (2011) Social partners and the welfare state: Recalibration, privatization or collectivization of social risks? *European Journal of Industrial Relations*, 17(4): 349–64.

Jones, K-M. (2019) Is Universal Credit working for working people? USDAW's members experience, CPAG, https://cpag.org.uk/news-blogs/news-listings/universal-credit-working-working-people-–-usdaw-members'-experiences

Jones, M. (1999) *New Institutional Spaces: Training and Enterprise Councils and the Remaking of Economic Governance*, London: Routledge.

Jones, M. (2019) *Cities and Regions in Crisis: The Political Economy of Sub National Economic Development*, Cheltenham: Edward Elgar.

Jonna, R.J. and Foster, J.B. (2016) Marx's theory of working class precariousness its relevance today, *Monthly Review*, 67(11), https://monthlyreview.org/2016/04/01/marxs-theory-of-working-class-precariousness/

Joseph Rowntree Foundation (2020) *Poverty in the UK 2019/2020*, York: Joseph Rowntree Foundation.

Kalleberg, A. (2018) *Precarious Lives: Job Insecurity and Well Being in Rich Democracies*, Cambridge: Polity Press.

Keep, E. (2014) *What Does Skills Policy Look Like Now That the Money has Run Out?* London: Association of Colleges.

Kelly, J. (1998) *Rethinking Industrial Relations: Mobilization, Collectivism and Long Waves*, London: Routledge.

Kennett, P. and Dukelow, F. (2018) Introduction to themed section: Neoliberalism's afterlives: states of neoliberalisms, power and resistence in post crisis societies, *Critical Social Policy*, 38(3): 453–60.

Keune, M. (2018) *Industrial Relations and the Quantity and Quality of Jobs in the Public Sector in Europe: The Crisis and Beyond*, BARSOP Overview Report Part I, Amsterdam: University of Amsterdam.

Konzelmann, S.J. (2014) The political economics of austerity, *Cambridge Journal of Economics*, 38: 701–41.

Konzelmann, S., Gray, M. and Donald, B. (2017) Introduction to the *Cambridge Journal of Economics*, *Cambridge Journal of Regions, Economy and Society* and *Contributions to Political Economy* virtual special issue on assessing austerity, https://static.primary.prod.gcms.the-infra.com/static/site/cje/document/Introduction-to-Austerity-virtual-issue.pdf?node=1ac8f46a7d82786951e2&version=41398:2d660ed5 2686c96cd812

Konzelmann, S., Himmelweit, S., Smith, J. and Weeks, J. (eds) (2019) *Rethinking Britain, Policy Ideas for the Many*, Bristol: Policy Press.

Kruhøffer, J. (2007) *Job Rotation in Europe as the Feasibility Environment for the Jobrotation e-Service*, Berlin: AOF.

Labour Party (2019) *It's Time for a Real Change: Labour Party Manifesto 2019*, London: Labour Party.

Laskos, C. and Tsakalotos, G. (2013) *Crucible of Resistance: Greece the Eurozone and the World Economic Crisis*, London: Pluto.

Lavalette, M. and Mooney, G. (2000) Introduction: class struggle and social policy, in M. Lavelette and G. Mooney (eds) *Class Struggle and Social Welfare*, London: Routledge, pp 1–12.

Lehndorff, L., Dribbusch, H. and Schulten, T. (2018) European trade unions in a time of crises – an overview, in S. Lehndorff, H. Dribbusch, and T. Schulten (eds) *European Trade Unions in a Time of Crises*, Brussels: European Trade Union Institute, pp 7–38.

Levitas, R. (1998) *The Inclusive Society? Social Exclusion and New Labour*, Basingstoke: Macmillan.

Lind, J. and Knudsen, H. (2018) Denmark: the long lasting class compromise, *Employee Relations*, 40(4): 580–99.

Lowndes, V. and Gardner, A. (2016) Local governance under the Conservatives: super-austerity, devolution, and the smarter state, *Local Government Studies*, 42: 357–75.

LSE (London School of Economics) Growth Commission (2013) *Investing for Prosperity Skills Infrastructure and Innovation*, www.lse.ac.uk/researchAndExpertise/units/growthCommission/documents/pdf/LSEGC-Report.pdf

MacLeavy, J. (2011) A 'new politics' of austerity, workfare and gender: The UK coalition government's welfare reform proposals, *Cambridge Journal of Regional Economy and Society*, 4: 355–67.

MacLeod, G. and Jones, M. (2018) Explaining 'Brexit capital': uneven development and the austerity state, *Space and Polity*, 22: 111–36.

Mailand, M. and Thor Larsen, P. (2017) *Bargaining and Social Dialogue in the Public Sector (BARSOP)*, Copenhagen: University of Copenhagen FAOS.

Manchester City Council (2016) *Cumulative Impact of Welfare Reforms*, Manchester: Manchester City Council.

Manchester City Council (2017) *Roll out of Universal Credit*. Manchester: Manchester City Council, Resources and Governance Scrutiny Committee, 9 November.

Manchester City Council (2018) *Working Well and Work and Health Update*, Manchester City Council Economic Scrutiny Committee, 5 September, https://democracy.manchester.gov.uk/documents/s1027/Working%20Well%20and%20Work%20Heath%20update.pdf

Manchester City Council (2019) *The Impact of Welfare Reform and Universal Credit on the Manchester Economy*, Manchester: Economy Scrutiny Committee, Manchester City Council, 6 March, https://democracy.manchester.gov.uk/documents/s4998/The%20Impact%20of%20Welfare%20Reform%20and%20Universal%20Credit%20on%20the%20Manchester%20Economy.pdf

Marois, T. (2016) Banking on alternatives to neoliberal development, in L. Pradella and T. Marois (eds) *Polarising Development: Alternatives to Neoliberalism and the Crisis*, London: Pluto, pp 27–38.

Martin, R. (1986) Thatcherism and Britain's industrial landscape, in R. Martin and B. Rowthorne (eds) *The Geography of De-Industrialisation*, London: Methuen, pp 238–90.

Marx, K. (1973) *Capital Volume 1*, London, Harmondsworth: Penguin.

Massey, D. (1979) In what sense a regional problem? *Regional Studies*, 13: 233–43.

Massey, D. (1984) *Spatial Divisions of Labour: Social Structures and the Geography of Production*, Basingstoke: Macmillan.

Massey, D. (1988) Uneven development: social change and spatial divisions of labour, in D. Massey and J. Allen (eds) *Uneven Re-Development Cities and Regions in Transition*, London: Hodder and Stoughton, pp 250–76.

McCafferty, T. and Mooney, G. (2007) Working 'for' welfare in the grip of the 'iron' Chancellor: modernisation and resistance in the Department for Work and Pensions, in G. Mooney and A. Law (eds) *New Labour Hard Labour? Restructuring and Resistance Inside the Welfare Industry*, London: Policy Press, pp 209–32.

McNeil, C. (2016) *The Politics of Disadvantage: New Labour, Social Exclusion and Post-Crash Britain*, London: IPPR.

Meegan, R. (2017) Doreen Massey (1944-2016) A Geographer who really mattered, *Regional Studies*, 51(9): 1285–1296, DOI: 10.1080/00343404.2017.1329434

Meegan, R., Kennett, P., Jones, G. and Croft, J. (2014) Global economic crisis, austerity and neoliberal urban governance in England, *Cambridge Journal of Regions Economy and Society*, 7: 137–53.

Mellor, M. (2016) *Debt or Democracy: Public Money for Sustainability and Social Justice*, London: Pluto Press.

Mercille, J. and Murphy, E. (2015) *Deepening Neoliberalism, Austerity and Crisis in Europe, Treasure Ireland*, London: Palgrave.

Miller, J. and Bennett, F. (2017) Universal Credit: assumptions, contradictions and virtual reality, *Social Policy and Society*, 16(2): 169–82.

Mullaly, C. (2018) A woman's place is in her trade union, TUC blog, www.tuc.org.uk/blogs/woman%E2%80%99s-place-her-trade-union

NAO (National Audit Office) (2013) *Funding and Structures of Local Economic Growth*, London: National Audit Office.

NAO (2016) *Local Welfare Provision*, London: NAO.

NAO (2018) *Financial Sustainability of Local Authorities*, London: NAO.

Navitel, C., Sunley, P. and Martin, R. (2002) Localising welfare to work? Territorial flexibility and the New Deal for young people, *Environment and Planning C Government and Policy*, 20: 911–32.

NEF (New Economics Foundation) (2017) *Understanding Devolution: A Critical Appraisal of the Greater Manchester Devolution Deal*, London: NEF.

NEF (2018) *Austerity by Stealth*, https://neweconomics.org/uploads/files/NEF-AUSTERITY-BY-STEALTH_2018.pdf

Nelson, K. (2017) Devolution in Greater Manchester: Explanations, Responses, Concerns, Public Services International Research Unit (PSIRU) Seminar: Future of Local Government, 24 January.

Newman, J. (2007) The 'double dynamics' of activation: institutions, citizens and the making of welfare governance, *International Journal of Sociology and Social Policy*, 27(9/10): 304–75.

Newman, J. (2014) Landscapes of antagonism: local governance, neoliberalism and austerity, *Urban Studies*, 51: 3290–305.

Norfield, T. (2016) *The City: London and the Global Power of Finance*, London: Verso.

North, D., Syrett, S. and Etherington, D. (2007) *Devolution and Regional Governance: Tackling the Economic Needs of Deprived Localities*, York: Joseph Rowntree Foundation.

North, D., Syrett, D. and Etherington, D. (2009) Tackling concentrated worklessness: integrating governance and policy across and within spatial scales, *Environment and Planning C: Government and Policy*, 27(6): 1022-1039.

North West TUC (2018) *A City Region Employment Charter*, Liverpool: North West TUC.

O'Grady, F. (2018) This deal will threaten UK Worker rights: open letter to Members of Parliament, TUC, www.tuc.org.uk/openletter

O'Hara, M. (2015) *Austerity Bites: A Journey of the Sharp End of Cuts in the UK*, Bristol: Policy Press.

Painter, A., Thorold, J. and Cook, J. (2018) *Pathways to Universal Basic Income: The Case for a Universal Basic Opportunity Fund*, London: Royal Society of Arts (RSA).

Patrick, R. (2016) *For Whose Benefit? The Everyday Realities of Welfare Reform*, Bristol: Policy Press.

Payne, J. (2018) *In the DNA or missing gene? Devolution, local skills strategies and the challenge of inclusive growth in England*, SKOPE Research Paper No. 126, Oxford: University of Oxford.

Payne, J. and Keep, E. (2011) *One Step Forward and Two Steps Backwards: Skills Policy in England under the Coalition*, SKOPE Research Paper, No. 102, Oxford: University of Oxford.

PCS (Public and Commercial Services Union) (2017a) *PCS Briefing: Universal Credit December 2017*, London: PCS.

PCS (2017b) *PCS DWP Sheffield Branch Response to the Proposed Closure of Eastern Avenue Jobcentre*, Sheffield: PCS.

PCS (2019) *Social Security: The Case for Radical Change*, London: PCS https://www.pcs.org.uk/campaigns/social-security/pcs-welfare-pamphlet

Peck, J. (2002) Political economies of scale: fast policy, interscalar relations and neoliberal workfare, *Economic Geography*, 78(3): 331–60.

Peck, J. and Theodore, N. (2000) Work first: welfare-to-work and the regulation of contingent labour markets, *Cambridge Journal of Economics*, 24: 119–38.

Peck, J. and Theodore, N. (2007) Variegated capitalism, *Progress in Human Geography*, 31: 731–72.

Peck, J. and Theodore, N. (2019) Still neoliberalism? *South Atlantic Quarterly*, 118(2): 245–65.

Pernille Larsen, T. and Refslund, B. (2016) *Reducing Precarious Work: Protective Gaps and the Role of Social Dialogue in Denmark*, Copenhagen: University of Copenhagen, FAOS.

Pernille Larsen, T. and Weber Madsen, L. (2018) *Industrial Relations and Social Dialogue in the Age of the Collaborative Economy (IRSDACE)*, FAOS Research Paper 163, Copenhagen: University of Copenhagen, FAOS.

Perrons, D. (2012) Gender inequality and the crisis, in G. Johnsson and K. Steffansson (eds) *Retrenchment or Renewal? Welfare States in Times of Economic Crisis*, Helsinki: Nordwel.

Pickard, J. (2020) Starmer blames Corbyn for Labour's election defeat, *Financial Times*, 7 May.

Pike, A., Lee, N., MacKinnon, D., Kempton, L. and Iddawela, Y. (2017a) *Job Creation for Inclusive Growth in Cities*, York: Joseph Rowntree Foundation.

Pike, A., MacKinnon, D., Coombes, M., Champion, T., Bradley, D., Cumbers, A., Robinson, L. and Wymer, C. (2017b) *Uneven Growth: Tackling City Decline*, York: Joseph Rowntree Foundation.

Pike, A., Coombes, A., O'Brien, P. and Tomaney, J. (2018) Austerity states, institutional dismantling and the governance of sub-national economic development: the demise of the regional development agencies in England, *Territory, Politics, Governance*, 6: 118–44.

Pring, J. (2017) Welfare reform and the attack on disabled people, in V. Cooper, and D. Whyte (eds) *The Violence of Austerity*, London: Pluto, pp 51–8.

Rabindrakumar, S. (2017) *Paying the Price, Still Just Managing?* London: Gingerbread, www.gingerbread.org.uk/wp-content/uploads/2017/09/Paying-the-price-still-just-about-managing.pdf

Rabindrakumar, S. (2018) *One in Four: A Profile of Single Parents in the UK*, London: Gingerbread.

Raffass, T. (2017) Demanding activation, *Journal of Social Policy*, 46(2): 349–65.

Rafferty, A. and Jelley, R. (2018) *Ways to Promote a Responsible Business Agenda in UK Cities: Greater Manchester*, Manchester: University of Manchester IGAU.

Rasmussen, S., Refslund, B., Sørensen, O. and Larsen, T.P. (2016) *Reducing Precarious Work Through Social Dialogue: The Case of Denmark*, Copenhagen: University of Copenhagen FAOS.

Ray, K., Hoggert, L., Vegeris, S. and Taylor, R. (2010) *Better Off Working? Work Poverty and Benefit Cycling*, York: Joseph Rowntree Foundation.

Refslund, B., Rasmussen, S. and Sørensen, O.H. (2017), Security and labour market flexibility: an alternative view from Denmark, in A. Piasna and M. Myant (ed) *Myths of Employment Deregulation: How it Neither Creates Jobs nor Reduces Labour Market Segmentation*, Brussels: European Trade Union Institute, pp 207–24.

Resolution Foundation (2020) *No Work, No Pay: Supporting the Unemployed Through Coronavirus*, London: Resolution Foundation.

Roberts, M. (2010) Banking as a public service, Michael Roberts Blog, 15 September, https://thenextrecession.wordpress.com/2010/09/15/banking-as-a-public-service/

Roberts, M. (2016) *The Long Depression: How it Happened, Why it Happened, and What Happens Next*, Chicago, IL: Haymarket.

Roberts, M. (2018) More momentum on the banks, Michael Roberts Blog, 25 September, https://thenextrecession.wordpress.com/2018/09/25/more-momentum-on-the-banks/

Roberts, M. (2019) Finance, fiddling, fetish and fiction, Michael Roberts Blog, 12 August, https://thenextrecession.wordpress.com/2019/08/12/finance-fiddling-fetish-and-fiction/

Rosdahl, A. and Weise, H. (2001) When all must be active – workfare in Denmark, in I. Lødemel and H. Trickey (eds) *'An Offer You Can't Refuse': Workfare in International Perspective*, Bristol: Policy Press.

Rostgaard, T. (2014) *Family Policies in Scandinavia*, Stockholm: Frederich Ebert Stiftund.

Rowan, K. and Roper, C. (2013) For the people, of the people, by the people, in D. Whittle (ed) *The Future for Union Community Organising*, London: Unions 21.

Rubery, J. (2015a) Change at work: feminisation, flexibilisation, fragmentation and financialisation, *Employee Relations*, 37(6): 633–44.

Rubery, J. (2015b) Austerity and the future of gender equality in Europe, *Industrial and Labor Relations Review*, 68(4): 715–41.

Rubery, J., Grimshaw, D., Keizer, A. and Johnson, M. (2018) Challenges and contradictions in the 'normalising' of precarious work', *Work, Employment and Society*, 32: 509–27.

Sainato, M. (2020) 'I'm not a robot': Amazon workers condemn unsafe, gruelling conditions at warehouse, *Guardian*, 5 February, www.theguardian.com/technology/2020/feb/05/amazon-workers-protest-unsafe-grueling-conditions-warehouse

Sayce, L. (2018) *Switching Focus: Whose Responsibility to Improve People's Employment and Pay*, London: Disability Rights UK.

Sayer, A. (2016) *Why We Can't Afford the Rich*, Bristol: Policy Press.

Seymour, R. (2014) *Against Austerity: How We Can Fix the Crisis They Made*, London: Pluto.

Seymour, R. (2016) *The Strange Birth of Radical Politics*, London: Verso.

Sheffield Carers Centre (2019) Carers Centre Big Survey: the results! *Connect: The Newsletter of Sheffield Carers Centre*, Winter, https://sheffieldcarers.org.uk/wp-content/uploads/2019/02/Sheffield-Carers-Centre-Newsletter-024-Winter-2019-3.pdf

Sheffield City Council (2019a) *Budget Report*, 2019/2020, http://democracy.sheffield.gov.uk/documents/s33893/Revenue%20Budget%20Report%202019-20.pdf

Sheffield City Council (2019b) *The End of Austerity? The Impact of Nine Year Austerity Programme on our City*, http://democracy.sheffield.gov.uk/documents/b21495/Impact%20of%20Austerity%20on%20Sheffield%20Wednesday%2009-Jan-2019%2014.00%20Council.pdf?T=9

Sheffield City Region Local Enterprise Partnership (2014) *Sheffield City Region Growth Plan*, Sheffield: Sheffield LEP.

Sheffield NHS Commissioning Group (2019) *Universal Credit Briefing Note*, Sheffield: Sheffield NHS Clinical Commissioning Group, www.sheffieldccg.nhs.uk/Downloads/C%20UPDATE%20ON%20UNIVERSAL%20CREDIT.pdf

Shildrick, T. (2018) *Poverty Propaganda: Exploring the Myths*, Bristol: Policy Press.

Shukaitis, S. (2013) Recomposing precarity: notes on the laboured politics of class composition, *Ephemera*, 13: 641–58.

Simms, M., Holgate, J. and Heery, E. (2013) *Union Voices: Tactics and Tensions in UK Organising*, Ithaca, NY: Cornell University Press.

Smith Institute (2017) *Devo–Work: Trade Unions, Metro Mayors and Combined Authorities*, London: Smith Institute.

Smith, J. (2019) Introduction, in S. Konzelmann, S. Himmelweit, J. Smith and J. Weeks (eds) *Rethinking Britain: Policy Ideas for the Many*, Bristol: Policy Press, pp 1–6.

Smith, P. and Morton, G. (2006) Nine years of New Labour: neoliberalism and workers' rights, *British Journal of Industrial Relations*, 44(3): 401–20.

Spicker, P. (2017) *What's Wrong with Social Security Benefits?* Bristol: Policy Press.

SSAC (Social Security Advisory Committee) (2017) *In Work Progression and Universal Credit, A Study by the Social Security Advisory Committee (SSAC)*, Occasional Paper No 19, London: SSAC.

SSAC (2018) *The Draft Universal Credit (Managed Migration) Regulations 2018*, www.gov.uk/government/publications/draft-universal-credit-managed-migration-regulations-2018-ssac-report-and-government-statement

Stephensen, L. (2012) Able to fight: how disabled people are taking on the Tories, Red Pepper, 29 August, www.redpepper.org.uk/able-to-fight/

Strauss, K. (2017) Towards a geography of precarity?, *Progress in Human Geography*, https://doi.org/10.1177/0309132517717786

Stuart, M., Cutter, J., Cook, H., Valizade, D. and Garcia, R. (2016) *Evaluation of the Union Learning Fund Rounds 15-16 and Support Role of Unionlearn*, Leeds: University of Leeds.

Swyngedouw, E. (2005) Governance innovation and the citizen: The Janus face of governance-beyond-the-state, *Urban Studies*, 42(11): 1991–2006.

Tanhua, I. (2017) *Gender Equality and Nordic Welfare Societies*, NORDEN, https://stm.fi/documents/1271139/8492720/Report+Gender+equality+and+Nordic+welfare+societies.pdf/

Taylor, G. and Mathers, A. (2008) *Organising Unions, Organising Communities? Trades Union Councils & Community Union Politics in England and Wales*, Working Paper 10, Centre for Employment Studies Research, Bristol: University of West of England.

Taylor, M., Marsh, G., Nicol, D. and Broadbent, P. (2017) *Good Work: The Taylor Review of Modern Working Practices*, London: Royal Society of Arts.

Taylor-Gooby, P. (2017) Re-doubling the crises of the welfare state: the impact of Brexit on UK welfare politics, *Journal of Social Policy*, 46(4): 815–35.

Telford, L. and Wistow, J. (2019) Brexit and the working class in Teesside: moving beyond reductionism, *Capital and Class*, https://doi.org/10.1177/0309816819873310

The Children's Society (2017) *The Parent Trap: Childcare Cuts under Universal Credit*, London: Children's Society.

Thomas, M.L. (2016) A house divided Jeremy Corbyn and the Labour Party, *International Socialism*, 149: 39–70.

Trampusch, C. (2006) Industrial relations and welfare states. The different dynamics of retrenchment in the Netherlands and Germany, *Journal of European Social Policy*, 16(2): 121–33.

Trussell Trust (2019) *#5 Weeks is Too Long, Why We Need to End the Wait for Universal Credit*, London: Trussell Trust, www.trusselltrust.org/wp-content/uploads/sites/2/2019/09/PolicyReport_Final_ForWeb.pdf

TUC (2008) *Opposing Workfare and Privatization*, www.tuc.org.uk/research-analysis/reports/opposing-workfare-and-privatisation

TUC (2010) *Swords of Justice and Civic Pillars: The Case for Greater Engagement Between British Trade Unions and Community Organisations*, London: TUC.

TUC (2011a) *Women and the Cuts*, London: TUC/Fawcett Society/Women's Budget Group.

TUC (2011b) *Trade Unions and Disabled People Fighting Austerity*, London: TUC.

TUC (2014) *TUC Submission to the City Growth Commission*, London: TUC.

TUC (2015a) *Disability Employment: A Social Model Study of the Experiences of Disabled People in Great Britain, with a Focus on Mental Illness*, London: TUC.

TUC (2015b) *Reasonable Adjustments Disability Passports*, London: TUC.

TUC (2018a) *In Work Progression: TUC Submission to the Work and Pensions Inquiry on Universal Credit*, London: TUC.

TUC (2018b) TUC Response to Social Security Advisory Committee's consultation on Government proposal for managed migration on to Universal Credit, www.tuc.org.uk/sites/default/files/SSAC%20consultation%20response%20on%20UC%20migration%20FINAL%20in%20PDF.pdf

TUC (2018c) *Disability Employment and Pay Gaps*, London: TUC.

TUC (2019) *In Work Progression: TUC Submission to the Work and Pension Committee Inquiry into Universal Credit*, London: TUC.

TUC (2020) *Fixing the Safety Net: Next Steps in the Economic Response to the Coronavirus*, London: TUC.

TUC and GMB (2019) *Reasonable Adjustments and Disability Passports*, London: TUC.

TUC and Unionlearn (2019) *Celebrating 20 years of the Unionlearn Fund*, London: TUC and Unionlearn.

Tuckman, A. (2018) *Kettling the Unions: A Guide to the 2016 Trade Unions Act*, Nottingham: Spokesman Books.

Umney, C.R. (2018) *Class Matters: Inequality and Exploitation in 21st Century Britain*, London, Pluto.

Umney, C.R., Greer, I., Onaran, O. and Symon, G. (2017) The state and class discipline: European labour market policy after the financial crisis, *Capital and Class*, 42(2): 333–51.

Unison (2016) *Public Consultation on the Devolved Powers in Greater Manchester*, Unison North West response, May, Manchester: Unison.

Unison (2018) *Unison Evidence to the Low Pay Commission on Minimum Wage Rates*, London: Unison, www.unison.org.uk/content/uploads/2018/06/UNISON-evidence-to-Low-Pay-Commission-2018.pdf

Unison (2019a) *Unison's Response to the SSACs Consultation on the Draft Universal Credit Managed Migration Regulations*, London: Unison.

Unison (2019b) Chancellor should ditch the two child tax credit limit to Universal Credit and tax credits says Unison, press release, 12 March, www.unison.org.uk/news/press-release/2019/03/chancellor-ditch-two-child-limit-universal-credit-tax-credits-says-unison/

Unite Community (2019) *Universal Credit Not Fit For Purpose: Unite Universal Credit Survey Report*, London: Unite Community, https://unitetheunion.org/media/2631/8869_universal-credit-report_a4_finaldigital.pdf

University of Manchester IGAU (Inclusive Growth Analysis Unit) (2018) *GMCA Good Employment Charter Consultation Response*, Manchester: University of Manchester IGAU.

WBG (Women's Budget Group) (2016) *Investing in the Care Economy to Boost Employment and Gender Equality*, https://wbg.org.uk/wp-content/uploads/2016/11/De_Henau_Perrons_WBG_CareEconomy_ITUC_briefing_final.pdf

WBG (2017) *Universal Credit: A Briefing from the Women's Budget Group*, https://wbg.org.uk/analysis/universal-credit-briefing-uk-womens-budget-group/

WBG (2018) *The Impact of Austerity on Women in the UK*, www.ohchr.org/Documents/Issues/Development/IEDebt/WomenAusterity/WBG.pdf

WBG (2020) It is women, especially low-paid, BAME and migrant women putting their lives on the line to deliver vital care, https://wbg.org.uk/blog/it-is-women-especially-low-paid-bame-migrant-women-putting-their-lives-on-the-line-to-deliver-vital-care/

Webster, D. (2018) *Evidence to the United Nations Special Rapporteur on Extreme Poverty and Human Rights*, Glasgow: University of Glasgow.

Welfare Conditionality Project (2018a) *Final Findings Report: Welfare Conditionality Project 2013–2018*, York: University of York.

Welfare Conditionality Project (2018b) Visit by the United Nations Special Rapporteur on extreme poverty and human rights to the United Kingdom of GB and Northern Ireland from 5th to 16th November 2018: Written Evidence, York: University of York.

Whitham, G. (2018) *The Decline of Crisis Support in England*, Manchester: Greater Manchester Poverty Action.

Whitworth, A. and Carter, E. (2014) Welfare-to-work reform, power and inequality: from governance to governmentalities, *Journal of Contemporary European Studies*, 22: 104–17.

Wiggan, J. (2012) Telling stories of 21st century welfare: The UK coalition government and the neo-liberal discourse of worklessness and dependency, *Critical Social Policy*, 32(3): 383–405.

Wiggan, J. (2015) Reading active labour market policy politically: an autonomist analysis of Britain's work programme and mandatory work activity, *Critical Social Policy*, 35: 369–92.

Williams, F. (1994) Social relations and welfare and the Post-Fordism debate, in R. Burrows, and B. Loader (eds) *Towards a Post Fordist Welfare State*, London: Routledge.

Wills, J. (2008) Making class politics possible: organising contract cleaners in London, *International Journal of Urban and Regional Research*, 32(2): 305–23.

Wintour, P. (2015) Welfare Bill: Labour in disarray as 48 MPs defy the whip to vote no, *Guardian*, 21 July, www.theguardian.com/politics/2015/jul/21/labour-disarray-welfare-48-mps-defy-whips

WPC (Work and Pensions Committee) (2014) *Employment and Support Allowance and Work Capability Assessment: First Report of Session 2014–15*, HC 302, London: TSO.

WPC (2018a) *Universal Credit: Support for Disabled People: Twenty First Report of Session 2017–2019*, HC 1770.

WPC (2018b) *Sanctions: Nineteenth Report of Session, 2017–2019*, HC 955.

WPC (2018c) *Universal Credit: Childcare*, HC 1771.

Yates, E. (2017) Reproducing low wage labour: capital accumulation, labour markets and young workers, *Industrial Relations Journal*, 48(5–6): 463–81.

Index

Note: Page numbers for tables appear in italics.